SPIRIT HIGH AND PASSION PURE

.

Spirit High
and Passion Pure

· · · · · · · · · · · · · · · · · · ·

A Journey Through European Football

Charlie Connelly

MAINSTREAM
PUBLISHING

EDINBURGH AND LONDON

First published in Great Britain in 2000 by
MAINSTREAM PUBLISHING COMPANY (EDINBURGH) LTD
7 Albany Street
Edinburgh EH1 3UG

ISBN 1 84018 157 5

A catalogue record for this book is available from the British Library

Typeset in Opti Civet and Stempel Garamond

Printed and bound in Great Britain by
Butler and Tanner Ltd, Frome and London

CONTENTS

This book is dedicated to
Phil White
4 MARCH 1948 – 29 APRIL 2000
UNCLE AND CHARLTON ATHLETIC SUPPORTER

'For love is of The Valley, come thou down
And find him; by the happy threshold . . .'
ALFRED LORD TENNYSON

ACKNOWLEDGEMENTS

A book of this scale cannot be undertaken without the help of a great number of people.

Special thanks go to Sarah Williams for providing the outstanding photographs contained here. Her cheery, supportive companionship on these journeys was invaluable and I am immensely grateful to her for her friendship, tolerance and conversation, from pink-sky dawns at Bratislava Castle to chasing the midnight sun around the Faroe Islands.

To my long-suffering but eternally cheerful partner Katie, thanks for everything. The value of your understanding, love and support is incalculable. May we forever sit side-by-side in the Covered End of life.

Heartfelt thanks go to Dominic O'Reilly, the last and best sports editor of *The European*, for his advice and encouragement. The inspiration for this book came from reading stories broken originally by Dominic and I am indebted to him for his enthusiasm and friendship.

Working on a budget tighter than that of Crystal Palace FC, I am indebted to the following people and organisations for providing me with travel, accommodation or just helpful free stuff in response to my (at first polite, later pleading) requests: Urd, John and Birita at the Faroe Islands Tourist Office, Ethel Power and Barbara Kiernan in the Ryanair press office, Maria Maestre at the Spanish Tourist Office and Martha at the Bilbao Tourist Office, Trevor Williams and family, Heri Niclaesen at Atlantic Airways, Barbara Gigler at the Austrian Tourist Board, Elisabeth Haddow, Melanie Grubb and Monika Warburton at Austrian Airlines, Karen Houlahan at the Derry Visitor and Convention Bureau, Kate Talbot and Braathens and Helga Marie Johnsen at Destinasjon Tromsø.

I am also hugely grateful to the following people for their help, assistance, encouragement and, in some cases, hard cash in the research and travel that has resulted in this book: Lars Aarhus,

Michael Adler, Wolfgang Aicher, Marc Andries, Tim Bennett, Joe Boyle, An Van Den Broeck, Caroline Budge, Bill Campbell, Tommy Carlin, Gabriel Chiminato, Eddie Clark, Amanda Collins, Mick Collins, the Connelly family, Niall Conway, Philip Cornwall, Donald Cowey, Madelaine Davidson, David Dick, Barry Didcock, Robert Diermair, Michael Duggan and all at the Coach & Horses, Jean-Louis Dupont, James Eastham, Rick Everitt, John Eysturoy, Paul Giblin, Tim Glynne-Jones, Michael Grant, Wyn Grant, Sid Griffin and family, Nuala Griffiths, Michael Hann, John Hanson, Dan Hart and Vicki Solly, Stijn Henrickx, Pete Howls, Tina Hudson, Richard Hunt, Emil Jacobsen, Urd Johanesson, Julian Johnsson, Werner Koisser, Heidi Kragesteen, Tomáš Král and Gabi, Paul Krier, Martin Kuric, Dr František Laurinec, Andy Lopata, Don Macglew, Ian Macrae, Eddie Mahon, Danjál Petur Mariusárson, Matthias Marschik, John McCafferty, Pat McGarvey, Gunnar Mohr, Richard Mueller, Hugh Murnaghan, Kristjan á Neystabø, Birita Nolsø, Lapo Novellini, Juraj Oblozinský, Tim O'Brien, Murat Odabasi, Mark Perryman, Kevin Portch, Avi Reuveni, Jim Roddy, Ann Rooney, the Sands family, Revd Nigel Sands, the Shackletons of Moers, Allan Simonsen, Erdinc Sivritepe, Dolya Slavco, Magnus á Stongum, Jerry Stovall, Tracey Stuart, Karl Suykerbuyk, Matt Tench, Craig Turp, Michael Vana, Patrizia Della Vedova at Windcloak, Hugh Vivian, Mark Wijnants, Louis Wilson and Jane Wright.

Thanks to Charlton Athletic for providing a welcome distraction during weekends at home by winning the Nationwide League.

And big thank-yous to everyone who has helped me pull off the extraordinary scam of travelling through Europe watching football matches and being able to call it work.

PROLOGUE

ENGLAND v. POLAND, MARCH 1999

'You are Jewish. The Second World War was your fault.'

It's a warm spring day in the White Eagle Club in Balham High Road, south London, and the conversation has lurched suddenly and disturbingly from the fact that Polish football doesn't have a lot of money, to blaming an entire culture for a war in which they were the prime victims.

'I'm not Jewish,' I reply.

'The Second World War was your fault,' repeats the white-haired man with the heavily lined features, breathing high-octane fumes over me, and lurching towards the exit. He pauses briefly to accuse another man, randomly selected at the bar, of being a freemason. And he misses Paul Scholes's third goal against his home nation at Wembley, for at the very moment the ginger one's thumping header hits the back of the net the paranoid Pole from Peckham is lumbering up Balham High Road in pursuit of Stalin and Attila the Hun.

The White Eagle Club. An impressive building joined to a spiritualist church (lantern-jawed erstwhile England coaches welcome), it is the cultural nerve-centre for the 3,000-odd expatriate Poles who live in south London – or Polonia, as the Polish diaspora is popularly known. Around 10 million Poles live outside their homeland: a popular joke there is that the second-largest Polish city after Warsaw, is Chicago.

The dark, cool, flock-wallpapered bar is packed with expats staring at a tiny television set in the corner. All the seats are long taken and it's standing room only. Around 200 people are gathered here, of all ages and both genders. It is a subdued group. Poland's long, unbeaten run has fooled no one and the spectators are well aware that this is not the strongest Polish team to have represented their nation. But in this tiny corner of Poland, to the people watching the match in near silence, the result is not their prime concern.

Patriotism can grow stronger the further you are from home. This is the London-based Poles' opportunity to show their adopted country how fiercely proud they are of their heritage and to express their national identity. It gives a rare opportunity for these people, from all walks of life, each with their own different stories of emigration to tell, to be a nation once again.

All they have at the moment is a large room decorated with prints of peasants in national dress and half a dozen varieties of Polish vodkas behind the bar. Centuries of invasion and oppression demand a battling performance on national television today. There is a wide range of people here, united by something that goes beyond flags and national costumes. They are banking on eleven men in white shirts to do them proud in the nation they now, for whatever reason, call home.

The result is hardly a surprise, but the crowd is unhappy with the lack of passion and fire shown by their side – characteristics demonstrated by their ancestors throughout history, from battling against the Russians in the eighteenth century, to the rise of Solidarity in 1980. The biggest cheer of the afternoon, bigger even than for Poland's goal, greets the yellow card awarded to a Polish defender for a ferocious tackle – a rare moment of aggression.

The eleven men in white at Wembley let them down. By the time the whistle blows and the defeated Polish players trudge from the Wembley turf, the dingy room is half-empty. One of the shutters clatters down over the bar. The poker-faced, cauliflower-haired old woman who has been spectacularly overcharging me for drinks all afternoon has given way to a younger man with a moustache, who removes slightly more reasonable sums from my palm in return for bottles of chilled Polish beer. Sweeping out from behind the bar to collect up the empties, he arrives at my table. 'Sweden v. Luxembourg is on now,' he tells me, waggling three empty pint glasses at the television screen. It's as if he's trying to convince me that what we'd witnessed was just a meaningless football match, not the pricking of an expatriate community's pride.

A steady trickle of Poles emerges blinking into the bright spring sunshine and melts into the crowd of south London shoppers.

1.

EUROPE: WAR MINUS THE SHOOTING?

Speaking on Radio Free Europe's Bulgarian service late in 1999, the historian and journalist Timothy Garton Ash, probably the leading authority on contemporary European history, was asked how he defined the borders of Europe.

'Europe doesn't end,' he said, 'it fades away. It fades away across the Eurasian continent somewhere between Moscow and Vladivostock and it fades away into Turkey.'

Fortunately, those of us concerned with European football have no such problems of definition. Europe for us ends where the Caspian Sea laps against the eastern coast of Azerbaijan, with a tiny pocket nudging the Mediterranean in Israel. UEFA has decided what constitutes our Europe, a 51-nation empire stretching from the southern tip of Spain to the frozen north of Norway, and from south-eastern Turkey to Iceland.

Europe is home to a range of climates and people. What we refer to as 'European' is a mixture of different national styles and cultures. As long ago as 1770, Rousseau commented that 'there are no longer Frenchmen, Germans, Spaniards or even English, but only Europeans'. Thankfully he was wrong, and the nature and strength of 'Europeanness' is in its diversity, its capacity to bring together a number of different cultures.

Hence the term 'European football' could refer to the dour tactics that have characterised the recent campaigns of the Norwegian national team; the calm, assured passing game of the Portuguese; the effortless skill of the Italians or the refined artistry of the Dutch. For European football is not a single, definable entity. Rather, it is a vehicle for a range of nations to assert their nationalities on a flat plateau. A plateau where 11 Liechtensteiners, from the tiny principality of just 30,000 folk, can take on a Russian XI representing 150 million people, on roughly equal terms.

European football possesses a diversity unique to itself. No other continent boasts such a range of nations, climates and cultures. In the course of writing this book I have watched football matches on a windy hillside in the north Atlantic; amongst the tightly packed gravestones resulting from southern Europe's bloodiest land war; in a city that has produced some of the greatest cultural figures in the last 200 years; and amongst belching chimneys in the heart of Teutonic industry. Nowhere more clearly than on the football field are the diversity and unity of Europe asserted. Wherever you might travel in the continent – to the Russian steppes, the Portuguese coast, the west of Ireland, the Slovak countryside, wherever – one of the few sights you will find everywhere is a football pitch.

I grew up on the glory nights of European football in the 1970s when English clubs ruled the continent. Flickering pictures accompanied by a commentary crackling down a telephone line helped with a perception of the distances involved. Supporters would return from epic three-day coach journeys with tales of strange people, officious border guards and handfuls of pin badges. The subsequent ban on English clubs competing in Europe meant that we didn't know much about the game in Europe and we didn't need to. When we were beating everyone, it didn't matter because we were the best; and when we were banned, it didn't matter because it was all going on somewhere else. We knew that Real Madrid were a great team, that the Italians dived around and played boring football, that you could never write off the Germans . . . But that was about it.

Such was our parochial arrogance, born of the island mentality, and it dated back further than the '70s. British federations had loftily ignored the foundation of FIFA at the beginning of the twentieth century. The foundation of the European Cup was cemented in response to British press claims that Wolverhampton Wanderers were the champions of Europe because they had beaten Honved in a friendly at a foggy Molineux in 1954. Moscow Dynamo had briefly captured the imagination in 1945, but *we* had invented the game so we were the best at it. Simple.

In his timeless book *Soccer Revolution*, first published in 1955, the Austrian anglophile sportswriter Willy Meisl recalled a conversation he had at the 1950 World Cup. After England's embarrassing elimination from their first-ever tournament at the hands of a hungover collection of journeymen representing the United States, Meisl noted that all the British journalists but one flew home before the semi-finals. As pioneers of the game, the British had been living off their reputation for many years. Their reluctance to compete on the international stage had left them behind the rest in terms of tactics and technique. Now, with the opportunity to study arguably the world's four best teams in the semi-finals – Brazil, Uruguay, Sweden and Spain – the British press had high-tailed it from Rio on the first BOAC out of town. Meisl told the remaining journalists that the

British 'will not realise what has happened to their soccer until they have experienced a string of humiliating defeats, and home defeats at that'. He went on:

> The defeat in the World Cup might have a sobering effect, but it's doubtful. Brazil is a long way from the British Isles. Only seeing for themselves is, to them, believing, and they must see it not once but repeatedly. Remember that the British sports press doesn't tell them what is happening elsewhere, for the very good reason that the sporting journalists themselves are not aware of it.

Within three years Hungary had become the best team in the world. In 1953 the Hungarians came to London to face England, never beaten by continental opposition on their own ground – a proud record, but one aided enormously by the fact that England didn't play continental opposition at home very often. Hungary, as has been well documented, ran out 6–3 winners. It was supposed to be a much-needed lesson, one outlined by Meisl in Brazil.

Ferenc Puskas, writing in his autobiography *Captain of Hungary*, recalled:

> The factor which determined the result was the unpreparedness of the English defence for the method of attack adopted by our forwards. England just could not cope with the situations we developed, and what seemed to puzzle their defence the most was the fact that the attacks were often led from behind.

The following year England travelled to Budapest and this time were hammered 7–1. Of that game Meisl wrote, 'I can truthfully say that in this match of the century, Hungary had forgotten nothing and England hadn't learnt a thing.'

In their reluctance to pit themselves against nations outside the British Isles, England were out of touch. 'Their attacks are so obviously organised according to the textbook and it is easy for their opponents to recognise and take steps to counter their intentions,' said Puskas. Despite the heavy defeat at Wembley, England had not changed their tactics in the slightest for the return in Budapest.

Today, the influx of overseas talent into the British game has diluted that parochialism. The success of English clubs in the Champions League has also increased the coverage of the game in Europe to armchair fans. The mystery of the game across the water is disappearing.

For too long, European football to the British has meant little more than Real Madrid, Barcelona, Bayern Munich, Juventus and AC Milan. When Dynamo Kyiv gave Arsenal the runaround at Wembley in the 1998–99 Champions League, Ron Atkinson commented, 'Hey, I'll tell you what, for me these boys can play.' Most of Europe knew this already, but because Dynamo had had no reason to enter the British consciousness until that night, they were regarded a revelation. The following day the press crowed about what a great 'discovery' Andriy Shevchenko was, and how it wouldn't be long before one of Europe's top clubs tempted him away now that he had been 'unveiled'. The rest of Europe knew this already: Shevchenko had been a Ukrainian international for a number of years and the previous season had scored a first-half Champions League hat-trick in the Nou Camp against Barcelona.

When Chelsea played the Latvian champions (and effectively the Latvian national team) Skonto Riga, in the qualifying rounds of the Champions League in 1999, ITV's Barry Venison referred to them throughout as the 'Skontons', who sound more like a bunch of humanoid amphibians ripe for extermination by Dr Who. Presumably he'd never heard of Riga. He also expressed dismay that the Latvians – a tightly knit, well-organised side who have developed over a number of years in a similar manner to Dynamo Kyiv, and have won most of the Latvian league titles since Baltic independence – were not at least ten goals behind.

OK, Ron Atkinson and Barry Venison are soft targets. But given their lofty positions in the British branch of the European football media, you would hope that they'd heard of one of the continent's most lethal strikers and be able to identify which European capital city the opposition came from (especially with the 50:50 chance the two-word name offered them). And recognise that they're not actually a pub team, but a collection of experienced internationals.

The European game outside these islands has now made significant inroads into Britain, not least through the overseas players who have joined British clubs. Live Serie A action from Italy has been available on terrestrial television for the best part of a decade, whilst cable and satellite have long shown matches from Spain's Primera Liga and, less frequently, the German Bundesliga.

There has lately been a distinct widening of horizons in Britain, particularly since Euro 96. The realisation and admission that England's national team was little more than a mediocre football power in Europe, after Euro 2000, has brought refreshing humility and given hope that England may at last learn from their victors and return to the pinnacle they left so long ago.

Throughout the journeys I have made for this book I have been constantly amazed by the in-depth knowledge supporters in continental Europe have of the British game. But this is not because they think the game here is any better than anywhere else. They display the same knowledge of all the major European leagues. For example, in the Faroe Islands I was chatting to the chairman of one of the Faroese provincial clubs in their spartan clubhouse. We were just discussing the problems he faces in attracting players to the club when suddenly he noticed the Charlton Athletic pin badge on my lapel. His eyes lit up.

'Aaah,' he said, 'Charlton Athletic?'

'Mmmm,' I affirmed with a bemused smile.

'Oh, I was so sorry when they were relegated. I remember well the match in the play-offs, with Sunderland.' He let out a long exhalation, spread his arms wide and said, 'One of the best matches I've ever seen. Clive Mendonca . . .' He let out a low whistle and drifted away, obviously reliving the Charlton striker's hat-trick in the 1998 First Division play-off final.

A couple of days later I was in the press room at the Faroese national stadium at Toftir, which doubles up as the venue for the players' post-match meal. The Faroes had just drawn 2–2 with Bosnia-Herzegovina in a Euro 2000 qualifier and I was waiting to grab a quick word with the former European Footballer of the Year, Allan Simonsen, the Faroese national coach. I felt a tap on my shoulder, turned round and saw one of the Faroese players whom I'd bumped into in a bar a couple of nights earlier. We exchanged greetings, he noticed my badge, nodded knowledgeably, waggled his finger between the badge and Simonsen and said, 'Charlton Athletic'. And with a conspiratorial nod he was away to join his team-mates for their post-match meal.

How many players and matches involving the continental equivalent of Charlton Athletic can we name? Hansa Rostock, maybe? Osasuna, anyone? Belenenses? FC Utrecht?

This could say more about television coverage in different nations than a wilful avoidance of an international perspective; but having spent most of my football-watching life on English grounds I found the wide-ranging depth of knowledge abroad astounding and, in a way, embarrassing.

The growth in stature of the European Championships has broadened perspectives, not least as a ready-made scouting mission for British clubs. And at least now British journalists don't board the first plane home after England's exit from major tournaments. Five years ago the only decent football book available about the international game was Simon Kuper's groundbreaking *Football Against The Enemy*. Now as I look at my shelf, I find British-produced books on French, Dutch and Japanese football to name but three.

The expansion of the Champions League and the never-ending growth in stature of the European Championships have given us unprecedented access to the game on the continent. Every game, every goal, every player can be watched – every shimmy, every dive repeated in slow motion to the faux-classical strains that accompany every European club or international tournament. It's all a long way from Wolves v. Honved under the gloomy candescence of Molineux's primitive floodlights, or the mystery of the 1945 Moscow Dynamo tourists (whose captain had to be shown the difference between heads and tails before the toss-up at the first match).

Much of the mystery has gone out of the European game at the highest level, but Europe is a big place. It still has relatively uncharted 'dark corners' about which we know little because their international impact has been minimal to date: clubs with exotic names like FC Jazz in Finland, the Azerbaijani champions Kapaz Ganja, Bylis Ballsh in Albania, or the snappily titled Ukrainian club Prykarpattya Ivano-Frankivsk.

It was dark corners such as these that I set out to explore, as well as the better-known nations. I wondered whether, beneath the cash-cow of the Champions League, the same spirit and passion rampages through the game in nations emerging, established, or fallen on hard times. Is the excitement aroused by the Torshavn derby on the Faroe Islands the same as that experienced at, say, Real Madrid v. Atlético Madrid? How far does having a national team competing on the international stage help the profile of smaller or emerging nations? Who would have heard of Moldova or the Faroes if it wasn't for football? Or, for a young nation like Slovakia – struggling to emerge from the shadow of its former federal partner, the Czech Republic – how important is it for the national team to be on television, the Slovak flag flying and the national anthem being belted out with gusto by a Bratislavan military band?

Europe is a fascinating and diverse place, a remarkable mixture of culture, history and politics for such a relatively small continent. Football is a vehicle for 'European-ness' and individual nationhood. England, for instance, has a long-held obsession – whose roots lie in warfare and conflict – with Germany. A simple way of 'resolving' a complex and many-headed conflict is on the football field: whoever scores the most goals is the winner. Easy. There are very few other areas where nationalism can be so easily defined, even if it is a latent '90-minute nationalism'. The elevated status accorded to England's narrow Euro 2000 victory over what was arguably the weakest team ever to leave German shores demonstrates that the result of an international football match can carry much more emphasis than perhaps it should.

The way that football inflames the passions makes this pinning of a nation's hopes perhaps inevitable. The Eurovision Song Contest is yet to be blighted by rampaging violence through the streets of its host city. Bucks Fizz's 1981 Eurovision victory has yet to achieve the popular cultural heights of Geoff Hurst's 1966 World Cup final hat-trick, even though they, too, had seen off a workmanlike, efficient German effort to win for Britain. And I bet Geoff Hurst couldn't do that miniskirt trick with the skill and aplomb of Mike Nolan and Bobby G.

For the English, matches with Germany are a chance to recreate and settle historical differences. Ditto, matches between the Dutch and Belgians. And when the Faroe Islands met their former mentors Denmark early in their international career, it was 11 Faroese against 11 Danes, the Danish and Faroese flags flying side by side, former colony and master meeting as theoretical equals for the first time. George Orwell said football was 'war minus the shooting'. The man may not have been a football fan, but he wasn't far wrong in the case of Europe.

In Yugoslavia, Red Star Belgrade's hooligan faction became the notorious Serbian Tigers ethnic cleansing unit during the conflicts of the early '90s, under the leadership of the head honcho from the terraces Zejlko Ražnátović – later to become better known as the terror specialist, Arkan. In Russian football today, coaches are shot, club president's wives are kidnapped and leading players have acid thrown in their faces in public parks. In Albania in 1999 a club president and referee were shot dead; and a 13lb bomb was discovered at an Albanian First Division match between Lushnja and Elbasan that was being watched by 12,000 people. Elsewhere in eastern Europe, the 2000 Croat Cup final between Hajduk Split and Dinamo Zagreb was abandoned four minutes from time because of crowd trouble that left more than a hundred people requiring hospital treatment.

Yet football can also act as a valuably positive tool. Witness the busload of Muslim children returning to the site of the infamous Srebrenica massacre to play football against the Serbian children who now live there. Or how Kosovo, Catalonia, the Basque Country and Palestine can play matches as a 'national' team giving an important focus for what are at present independent nations in language and theory alone.

The Belgian lawyer Jean-Louis Dupont rocked European football when he won the freedom-of-contract case for his client Jean-Marc Bosman to change the face of European football forever. As a result of the Bosman ruling, which introduced a new noun to football parlance whereby players can be transferred 'on a Bosman', Dupont has become Europe's most sought-after sports lawyer. As will be seen later, Dupont has assisted the Catalans and Basques in organising a case for having their own national football teams which could open a can of worms bigger than that marked 'Bosman'.

'Basically the philosophical bottom line is that in certain regions of the world the concept of nationality is becoming more and more distinct from the concept of the state,' Dupont told me from his office in Brussels. 'Examples of this are, say, Catalonia, Scotland and Flanders. At the same time "sport representivity" is now one of the criteria for the recognition of nationality. I'm not sure if this is really correct, but I was told that one of the republics of the former Yugoslavia applied to join FIFA before applying to the United Nations!

'So, the key question is that since some "nationalities" will never be likely to become a state in the traditional sense, should they be denied a sporting national identity when such an element is essential to their self-affirmation? Your guess is as good as mine . . .'

A professional football federation is being set up in Kosovo after the first league season was blighted by allegations of bribery and match-fixing. However, the Kosovans are keen to join the international throng and there is even talk of 'doing a Slovenia' and qualifying for the European Championships within a decade.

The Kosovans are wresting back their football infrastructure. In 1991 a rule had been introduced that Albanians in Yugoslav professional football teams had to swear a pledge of loyalty to the Serb government. Most refused to do so and were refused permission to play. The Kosovan Albanians set up their own makeshift league, but the police closed stadia and confiscated equipment, often when matches were in progress.

'After what has happened we cannot play football with the Serbs again,' said Mehmet Fetahu, coach of the Kosovo Priština club. 'They did all sorts of terrible things to us – Europe knows this and will help us.'

Matches played by Basque and Catalan representative teams have provided a valuable focus for members of those societies desirous of independence and nationality. As Jean-Louis Dupont rightly says, 'sport representivity' is an important rallying-point for communities deprived of nationhood in a way that music or cuisine can't provide. What stirs the patriotic fervour more: an old man belting out folk songs, a good hot traditional meal, or roaring on your representative football team, wearing your national colours and with your flag over their hearts, against historic rivals?

Football can provide a valuable focus for nationality, particularly in times of crisis. In history, struggling governments would embark on 'short, victorious wars' in order to boost national morale. These often backfired spectacularly, the 1905 Russo-Japanese war being possibly the best example, but today football can replace such drastic action. The game can also work the other way. Before Euro 2000, leading Dutch economists pleaded with their national side not to win the championship because the already-booming Dutch economy might not have been able to sustain the 'feelgood' spending that would inevitably have followed. The way the Dutch peppered everywhere but the goal in their semi-final penalty shoot-out suggests, perhaps, that their players missed out on the final of Euro 2000 in an act of greater patriotism.

Football is important in Europe for a number of reasons. The words 'tragedy' and 'disaster' trip too often from the tongue in football circles, yet if anyone knows the true meaning of disaster and tragedy it is the Turks. Around 17,000 people were killed, thousands more injured and whole communities razed to the ground by the earthquake which centred around the city of Izmit in the autumn of 1999. A few days later, another quake hit Adapazari; the following day Bolu shook in yet another shifting of tectonic plates and today the talk in Turkey is of when, not if, the next major quake will strike.

Against this background Turkey qualified via the play-offs for Euro 2000. At times like this football is trivial. Yet in a nation obsessed with the game, its re-emergence from the rubble provided a valuable rallying point, a return to some semblance of normality in a nation struggling to restore power, communications, utilities and morale to its beleaguered populace. The Turkish League programme recommenced after only a couple of weeks' lull. The national side went to Belfast and turned over Northern Ireland before moving on to Munich and comfortably holding Germany in front of a crowd largely made up of Turkish *Gastarbeite*. The national team's endeavours gave hope to an embattled people.

In the northwestern city of Izmit the stadium of the resident club, Kocaelispor, reopened three months after the disaster. Ironically, the ground had been closed all season for refurbishment and, remarkably, the quake left the half-finished arena relatively unscathed. Kocaelispor, who take their name from the heavily industrialised Kocaeli region of which Izmit is the regional capital, had been playing every match away from home.

As Kocaelispor is the only top-flight club affected by the quake, the Turkish lower divisions suffered most. Viewers of the television coverage of the immediate aftermath of the quake may recall seeing helicopters carrying the dead and injured coming in to land at a football stadium. That ground belongs to Sakaryaspor of the Turkish Second Division, whose stadium became an emergency helipad and makeshift hospital. The damage suffered by the ground meant that Sakaryaspor were given permission to opt out of the league programme for the season, as were Düzcespor and Gençlerbirigli. Only one week of the season had been played at the time of the quake, with Sakaryaspor losing by a single goal, and Düzcespor and Geçlerbirigli both drawing their opening matches. After their withdrawal, all these three clubs' cancelled fixtures were logged as 0–3 defeats, much to the consternation of their opening day opponents.

The Turkish Football Federation offered what support it could to its members. This included opening its Istanbul facilities to affected clubs. As most of these were hundreds of miles from the capital, few were able to take up the offer. The TFF has tried to arrange loan deals for the players suddenly left without a competitive club (and, by consequence, a wage packet), but the sheer numbers involved mean that many professionals are struggling to find employment in a country rocked economically by the disaster.

While no footballers were actually killed, a number of club officials, trainers and supporters perished in the August earthquake. Genuine tragedy afflicted Turkey's best-known player: Hakan Sukur was told that his parents had died in the quake, only to learn later that they had in fact survived, but shortly afterwards he discovered that his ex-wife and her mother had perished. Star footballers can often seem to inhabit a different world to the rest of us. But Hakan Sukur's experiences can only make one guess at the similar human tragedies that have befallen thousands upon thousands of ordinary Turks whose world fell literally about their ears in the early hours of a humid August night.

When Greece suffered its own serious earthquake a few weeks after the Turks, the traditionally bitter rivals found themselves with a shared tragic experience. One upshot was the mooted joint Greco-Turkish bid to host the 2008 European Championships.

However, for all its passion, spirit and unifying potential, back in the real world European football is still beholden to money. Whilst the Bosman ruling was an important victory for players as a workforce, its effects have included an explosion in the wages demanded by the agents of leading players. Jean-Louis Dupont is aware of this, and also aware of the sacrifice made by his client who suffered the break-up of his marriage, the end of his football career and (until recently) financial ruin.

'Bosman was a human-rights case,' says Dupont, 'but it is clear that part of the result is that the top clubs are stronger than ever. It is true that the players who benefited, and continue to benefit, from the judgement paid very little tribute to Jean-Marc. It is not a legal problem but a moral one and it seems that the players can very well live with it.

'At the moment, because of Bosman, the labour market is European but the football competition market is still national. It is good for Germany and Italy, but bad for Belgium and Denmark. For these "small" countries, regional leagues may be the solution, such as the Atlantic League – although at the moment it's an approximate draft, the idea is right.'

Barely two weeks into the new century the first new scheme for European football was already upon us. Speaking in the Netherlands, PSV Eindhoven president Harry van Raalj urged leading clubs from outside the 'big five' European nations of Italy, Germany, Spain, England and France to resign from their national leagues and set up a 16-club Atlantic League. As the Champions League gallops away from the chasing pack, the money is increasingly polarised at the pinnacle of the game. Whilst the former eastern bloc nations continue to struggle for money and sponsorship, they find that the closed shop developing amongst the rich clubs is depriving them of a chance to earn much-needed income from a decent European run or a money-spinning tie against one of the game's leading lights.

Now the poorer clubs scrap it out in the early rounds, spending money they don't have to travel to a club in a similar position, to play a two-legged tie from which they will earn little in addition to the opportunity of playing a similar club in the next round. The chances of landing a pairing with one of Europe's big clubs are slimmer than ever before and the game is becoming top heavy.

Hence Harry van Raalj's Atlantic League concept for clubs which are too big for the qualifying rounds but which have little likelihood of progressing to the latter stages of European competition. 'A true European league will never happen because the big five nations are happy with their TV money and everything else,' said van Raalj. 'So what we want to establish is a sixth league in Europe, made up of teams from Denmark, Holland, Portugal and elsewhere. It is the only way for small countries to keep up with the big teams in the Champions League: they are so far ahead because of the money streaming in from TV.'

While van Raalj has a valid point about the polarisation of the European game and the concentration of wealth in just a few countries, an Atlantic League could have calamitous effects on football in the countries from which his clubs would be drawn.

The implications for Scotland, for example, could be disastrous. Van Raalj is hoping that Rangers and Celtic will resign from the Scottish Premier League and throw in their lot with his scheme. For all the criticism of the way the Old Firm dominates the game north of the border, Scottish football without Rangers and Celtic is not a viable proposition. The game would inevitably wither and die. A championship tussle between St Johnstone and Kilmarnock is unlikely to have the television money pouring in.

Other clubs lined up for inclusion in the 16-club league include Bruges and Anderlecht from Belgium, Benfica and Porto from Portugal, van Raalj's own PSV Eindhoven as well as Ajax and Feyenoord from the Netherlands, Grasshoppers Zurich from Switzerland, Greece's Panathinaikos and AIK Stockholm from Sweden. Oh, and possibly clubs from Germany, but as long as they're not Bayern Munich or Borussia Dortmund.

PSV's manager Frank Arnesen backed his president's scheme: 'We are prepared to resign from the Dutch League but we must find out what other clubs want to do,' he said, sticking his neck out.

Whilst many similar schemes have been tabled in the past, none have come to their threatened fruition. A central and eastern European superleague was proposed a year or two ago in response to the westernisation of the Champions League, but the threat of losing Steaua Bucharest, Slovan Bratislava and Zimbru Chisinau from the qualifying rounds did not exactly have Silvio Berlusconi waking up in a cold sweat in the middle of the night. The idea soon disappeared.

An Atlantic League is unlikely to attract major sponsorship and without the biggest clubs the only television rights it is likely to secure are perhaps an hour's highlights on Eurosport. Who would find irresistible a televised mid-table clash between Rosenborg and Bruges? If these clubs still had the opportunity to compete at the highest level and had a fairer share of the huge pile of cash marked European football, maybe they could attract the players to make such ties more appealing to fans and television viewers.

Perhaps van Raalj is hoping merely to coerce UEFA into giving middling European clubs a better financial deal from European competition. After all, the Italian firm Media Partners have still not given up on its Superleague idea despite wringing concessions from UEFA over the terms of the Champions League. Just before Christmas 1999 Media Partners' supremo Rodolfo Hecht announced he had lodged a complaint with the European Union that UEFA were breaking EU law by preventing the founding of their Superleague earlier in the year. 'You can't tell people they can't play football,' he said, obviously not having attended a Chester City match recently where the supporters tell the players precisely that every week.

If Media Partners do gain a favourable ruling then perhaps the Atlantic League would be a viable proposition as a second tier. But if both schemes come off, it would surely be another step down the road to the death of grass-roots football. I asked Omar Smarson of the Football Association of Iceland what he felt about an Atlantic League, as his nation, surrounded by the Atlantic Ocean, had not been invited. What implications would the scheme hold for football outposts like Iceland? Would they be isolated further?

'The KSI [the Icelandic FA] has not been approached regarding a proposed Atlantic League,' he told me. 'In fact, this is the first I have heard about it. Icelandic clubs are ranked rather low on a European scale. I believe the best Icelandic teams would be an average team in the Scottish Premier, so Celtic and Rangers would by no means be playing stronger teams than they are playing today. The league in the Faroe Islands is a lot weaker than the Icelandic one, and Greenland – well, I don't even think there is an organised league there. There is not even a single grass pitch there!

'In my opinion the German league is one of the strongest in the world, so why change that? The only thing the Germans would be interested in is a European Superleague, which I personally hope will never happen.

'Also, there are different climate conditions. Iceland, Norway, Finland and Sweden all play a summer season because of the very cold winters. Denmark is the only Nordic country that plays a winter season. I would also mention travelling costs, different stadia and security standards. I could go on . . .

'I honestly don't see this becoming a reality.'

Meanwhile, the game in central and eastern Europe continues to flounder. Dynamo Kyiv are the only success story, but even they are frustrated by the lack of competition in the Ukrainian domestic league. Corruption and violence are rife and there is little money available. The western clubs grow richer and are now almost uncatchable by the clubs from former communist nations. The European game, at club level at least, is developing a two-tier structure between rich and poor – a dichotomy which is not for the ultimate good of the European game.

The fact that a club can now be champions of Europe without even being champions of their own country is the most blatant evidence that European competition has gone beyond competition and become little more than a whirligig of sponsorship, television and high finance. After all, the trophy lifted by Real Madrid in 2000 still bears the name European Champion Clubs' Cup, a title which eliminates immediately many of the clubs seeking to win it every year. It does seem unfair that the champions of Belarus or Bosnia – who have every right to be in a 'Champions League' – have no chance of meeting Real Madrid, whereas Chelsea – who last won a league title nearly half a century ago – have every chance.

What, then, is there for smaller clubs from smaller nations to look forward to, beyond the chance of regular elimination by clubs of similar ilk and the slim chance of a crack against a team of middling status? Fortunately, football has other motivations than money, as this volume seeks to show.

The book sets out with two objectives. One, to give a broader aspect to the game in Europe; the other, to find the place of the game in Europe, to set football in its context (be it a vehicle for nationalism, or the reflection of a locality falling on hard times). All through Europe I have met players, officials, journalists and fans who care deeply about the game in their country. Some of their opinions and issues matched, some didn't. This book seeks to find both common links and differences in the game and the continent. In this task some 23,000 miles have been covered: but at the end of each journey was the simple ritual whereby 11 lined up against 11 to contest possession of a football on a rectangular field, whilst people watched.

When I started out, I knew that the stadia, nations and, indeed, the weather would vary dramatically. But everywhere I went I hoped to find that the game was united by a spirit high and a passion pure.

2.

LUXEMBOURG: GOING DUCHY

When I drove to Luxembourg I missed it at first because there was a tree in the way.

OK, that's a cheap shot. In truth Luxembourg is a beautiful place, somewhere which struck me as possibly one of the most 'European' places in Europe. That is if your vision of Europe is the same as mine, involving forests, valleys, sloping cobbled streets and castles that look like they've come straight out of a fairy-tale.

Diminutive Luxembourg is a wonderful mixture of proud national identity and eclectic multiculturalism. This is particularly true of the capital, Luxembourg City, where I sit on a bright spring afternoon, supping a Bofferding beer and waiting to move on to the Stade Josy Barthel for the Euro 2000 qualifier between Luxembourg and Bulgaria. The Place D'Armes, where I have parked myself for a leisurely hour, is about as central as you can be in Luxembourg City. It's pedestrianised, cobbled and peaceful, surrounded on all sides by beautiful old steep-roofed buildings. A few people come and go quietly about their business. Luxembourg City must be the most tranquil capital in the world. Nobody's shouting, there's no music blaring, and when the clock at the end of the Place strikes six it's such a disruption to the peace that I nearly fall off my chair.

To reach this most idyllic of pre-match rituals, I've crossed the Pont Viaduc, an enormous bridge across the canyon carved out over millions of years by the River Petrusse which flows modestly far below.

With characteristic foresight, I've elected to stay in the worst part of town. But in Luxembourg that's no bad thing. It takes me a while to realise that I'm actually slap in the middle of the red-light district, although the only way you'd notice is by inadvertently catching sight of a few postcards in the doorway of an unobtrusive strip club. The pictures feature naked temptresses pouting at the camera, but their dignity is preserved by the coloured stickers covering the appropriate places. Very civilised, very Luxembourg.

Although the duchy has its own official language, blessed with its first dictionary as recently as the 1950s, most Luxembourgers speak both French and German. Therefore, when I unfurl the *Luxembourger Wort*, a stern-looking but accessible broadsheet, I am surprised to find that some articles are in French and the rest in German – a bilingual newspaper. Not being proficient in either tongue, any attempt on my part to translate the match preview is doomed to failure.

My French classes at school all seemed to involve tales of smugglers in the Basque region, whilst German for me meant Hans and Lieselotte going to a fancy-dress party where Hans takes an unfortunate tumble and breaks his leg. Therefore my chances of getting to the bottom of the Luxembourg team selection are practically nil unless they have suddenly selected the whiskery captain of a Basque fishing vessel who wants to talk contraband.

As a football nation, Luxembourg display a tenacity without which many other nations would have given up and gone home long ago. They have entered every World Cup since 1934 and every European Championship ever contested. They have finished bottom of their group every time except once, when Malta pipped them to the wooden spoon in their World Cup 1998 qualifying group.

After the break-up of Eastern Europe at the end of the '80s and in the early '90s, several new nations emerged blinking on to the European scene. Many of these have since become cannon-fodder for the bigger nations, not to mention a few mediocre ones too. These new nations could certainly turn to Luxembourg in order to find out how to cope with the perpetual crushing disappointment of defeat after defeat, as the football fans and players of the tiny duchy certainly know all about losing. Over the years it has become a bit of a speciality.

However, with the increase in smaller nations of Europe, Luxembourg have now found themselves to be a slightly bigger fish in a much larger pond. And if you thought Manchester United deserved credit for sticking with Alex Ferguson during his unsuccessful early years at Old Trafford, then how about the Fédération Luxembourgeoise de Football (FLF)? The current trainer waited a decade before Luxembourg won their first match under his tutelage. A *decade*.

Luxembourg's lowly position in the international rankings is hardly surprising. In terms of area and population, Luxembourg can be compared to Greater London, occupied by the population of, say, Croydon. Of Luxembourg's population (roughly 400,000) only 70 per cent are actually natives of Luxembourg – which merely serves to make the national coach's job even harder.

The history of the Duchy of Luxembourg can be traced back to a precise year. It was 963 when Count Siegfroid of Ardennes constructed a castle on the site of the modern Luxembourg City, where he and his wife then set about creating a number of future European nobles with vigorous enthusiasm. Between energetic reproduction sessions, the count found the time to ward off several armies who noted the valuable position of the castle at the junction of two important rivers. The Burgundians, Spanish, French, Austrians and Prussians all attacked in turn and the castle was besieged, wrecked and rebuilt on average once every twenty years over four centuries. Maybe that's where the football team gets its staying power from. Years of tug-of-war with Holland and Belgium ended with the 1867 Treaty of London, which conferred Grand Duchy status upon the principality and asserted its autonomy. The Luxembourgers promptly demolished the castle themselves to save anyone else the trouble.

Since then, after a brief period of German occupation in the '40s, Luxembourg has fiercely pronounced its independence, bordered as it is on two sides by giants Germany and France. The duchy was a founder member of the European Community in 1958 and now houses the European Court and the Secretariat to the European Parliament.

To football fans, however, Luxembourg was always the team you hammered home and away if you were lucky enough to be drawn in the same group. So how has Luxembourg coped with being the perennial losers of European football? Why do they keep coming back for more?

Despite having entered every World Cup since 1934 (their first game saw them ship nine goals against Germany, but that didn't seem to put them off), it wasn't until the '60s and the introduction of the European Championships that Luxembourg began to play international matches on a regular basis. The early part of that decade produced some of Luxembourg's greatest-ever results. In 1961, for example, they went into a World Cup qualifier with Portugal after 14 straight defeats dating back ten years. The previous decade had seen them find the net just four times, while their unfortunate goalkeepers had picked the ball out of the net on no less than 65 occasions.

Making his début for Portugal that day was a promising youngster from Mozambique called Eusebio. However, it was a 21-year-old Luxembourg locksmith named Andy Schmidt who stole the show, scoring a hat-trick in an astonishing, and highly unlikely, 4–2 win. Eusebio at least marked his début with a goal; but his team, who just four months earlier had held England to a 1–1 draw at Wembley, left the duchy amid scenes of wild celebrations among the home fans.

Well, as wild as they get in civilised Luxembourg – apparently a wineglass was broken.

It was in the European Championships of 1964 that Luxembourg really caught the attention of the rest of the continent. Drawn against Holland, who were fresh from 1–0 victories over France and Brazil, the Luxembourgers, convinced they were on a hiding to nothing, opted to play both legs away from home.

The first game in Amsterdam saw the Dutch field their strongest team. In previous matches with the duchy, their opponents had generally put out a B team, but these were the European Championships and there was to be no messing about. When Nuninga gave Holland a fifth-minute lead, most assumed it would be the first of many. Astonishingly, the Dutch found themselves increasingly pinned back by their opponents; and ten minutes from half-time May equalised for the principality. A frustrating second half saw the Dutch unable to break down the visitors' stout defence and the first leg ended in an unlikely draw.

The return in Rotterdam saw both sides hit the crossbar early in the game. After twenty minutes Luxembourg went a goal up, only for Kruiver to equalise. In the second half, Holland piled forward but were frequently denied by the inspirational Schmitt in goal. Late in the game Dimmer scored his and Luxembourg's second, Schmitt carried on the heroics (despite dislocating his shoulder) and the tiny principality had reached the quarter-finals.

Once again Luxembourg were expected to lose. Their opponents, Denmark, resolved not to take them lightly, but when Louis Pilot put the minnows ahead in the first minute it looked likely that another upset might be on the cards. In a topsy-turvy game, Madsen banged in a hat-trick for the Danes, but Klein scored twice for the duchy and the Danes faced a frightening trip to central Europe.

Trailing 2–1 with six minutes remaining of the second leg Luxembourg appeared to be out of the competition, but the former hat-trick hero Andy Schmidt popped up with an equaliser and the tie went to a replay in Amsterdam. This time, the Danes scraped through by a single goal to nil.

After that brief flurry of success, things returned to normal for Luxembourg. It was to be eight years before they won another competitive match. Then, after a 2–0 victory over Turkey in a 1972 World Cup qualifier, Luxembourg football commenced possibly the most unsuccessful run in the history of the international game. If you don't count friendly victories over Thailand and South Korea in 1980 (and who would?), Luxembourg went 22 years without a win. During that time they played 103 matches, losing 97. In a run like that, even a 1–1 draw with Iceland would have sparked celebrations not seen in the duchy since the Petrusse was a puddle.

In the meantime, Paul Philipp had progressed from player to national coach. A long playing career had taken Philipp into the professional game in Belgium with Standard Liege and Charleroi. In all he played 58 times for his country between 1968 and 1982. On retiring from playing, he returned to Luxembourg and coached Avenir Beggen to three championships in four seasons before being invited to take over the Luxembourg national side in July 1985. In the years since then, Philipp has become something of a deity to Luxembourg football fans.

Outside the Stade Josy Barthel, I bump into Paul Krier, selling the Luxembourg fanzine *Huel Se*. I buy one but it's in Luxembourgish, of which I know nothing except that the place names sound to my untutored ear like tin trays being dropped on the floor: Differdange, Mondercange and Dudelange. Luckily, Paul Krier speaks perfect English.

'Paul Philipp is a kind of messiah for Luxembourg football,' he tells me. 'He came from Belgium where he played for 13 years as a pro, and immediately showed the value of that experience as coach of Avenir Beggen. His professional outlook is probably what led to him being promoted to national team coach.

'His head was full of ideas and plans for the game in Luxembourg and I think today he has realised nearly all of them. He introduced the so-called "Luxembourg Model' plan for professional training methods for our amateur players who have to go to work during the day. As part of the plan, the FLF made contracts with the players and their employers to allow them a week off before international matches – the FLF compensates the companies for the lost time.

'So these days our players have the opportunity to train at least three or four times a year in a professional way. Soon the football centre at Mondercange will be completed as well and all these moves have had, and will have, a positive influence on our team.

'These plans, and their results, are why Paul Philipp is not just respected but celebrated by the supporters. Everyone knows that without him we probably wouldn't play at the level we do today.'

Despite dreadful results, the FLF and the Luxembourg supporters have stuck by Paul Philipp throughout his reign. Although the defeats kept on coming, they sensed that a change had to come. And when it did, boy would they celebrate.

As the winless run of matches approached three figures. Luxembourg's Euro 96 qualifying campaign began in characteristic style with heavy defeats to Holland (twice), Belarus and Israel. In February 1995 Luxembourg then made the trip to the Mediterranean to face Malta at Valletta's Ta Q'ali stadium. Two hundred supporters also made the trip, punch-drunk from 22 years of defeat after defeat.

The first half ended goalless, a rare occurrence in a match involving Luxembourg. But ten minutes into the second period, Roby Langers fed Manuel Cardoni – a dead-ringer for Michael Schumacher, incidentally – who slotted the ball past David Cluett in the Maltese goal to give Luxembourg the lead.

As the minutes ticked by, it began to dawn on the Luxembourgers that maybe, just maybe, they might be in with a chance of winning a match. The final minutes must have been more tense than a closely fought World Cup final; and in the last minute, just when victory had got up a heady gallop from over the horizon, the Croatian referee awarded Malta a penalty. The supporters were crushed. To have come so close, only to have a historic moment snatched from them by a last-minute spot-kick. Their last hopes rested on either goalkeeper Paul Koch making a save or the Maltese striker suddenly going down with a debilitating illness. Of the two options the former seemed most likely, but even then there still wasn't much hope.

The kick was taken and Koch went the right way. Time seemed to freeze the goalkeeper's plunging form as his arm reached out for the ball. His fist made contact: the ball spun away from him, but towards the post. It struck the upright . . . and bounced gently to safety.

There was barely time to restart the match before the final whistle brought to a close Europe's most prolonged victory drought. The fans swarmed on to the pitch. Paul Philipp, who had played in the last victory 22 years earlier, was overcome. Back home in Luxembourg, Paul Krier was in front of his television.

'I can remember it as if it was yesterday,' he says four years on, a smile spreading across his face. 'The Cardoni goal, the last-minute penalty save. The commentator was crying, you could hear it, he couldn't speak anymore. That day is the only time I've seen people rushing out of their houses or opening their windows and shouting with joy. I had tears in my eyes and realised that this team had just written itself into the history books. No one could really take it in; I was just repeating 'Twenty-two years' to myself, over and over again.

'When the team came home the airport was absolutely packed with supporters and well-wishers, it was all simply incredible. In the following months, Luxembourg supporters retained a real tangible pride in their team at every match.'

Four months later, after two defeats to Norway, Luxembourg entertained the Czech Republic at the Stade Josy Barthel. The Czechs had built an exciting team since splitting with Slovakia, and had beaten Holland 3–1 in their previous qualifier. The Luxembourgers found themselves up against the team that would go on to reach the final of Euro 96, losing out only to a 'golden goal' against Germany.

The match was heading for a highly creditable 0–0 draw when, with a minute to go, Langers turned creator again. This time it was Guy Hellers who finished the job off and Luxembourg had pulled off one of the great shocks of European football. Skuhravy, Berger, Nemecek and the rest trooped off dejectedly, but the crowd of 1,500 partied long into the night.

Luxembourg finished that campaign with ten points thanks to another win over the Maltese and a draw with Belarus – easily their biggest haul ever. Paul Philipp's strategy appeared to be paying off and he was rewarded with a six-year extension to his contract.

The France '98 qualifying campaign was a disappointment by comparison, with Luxembourg failing to register a single point from their eight matches against Bulgaria, Russia, Israel and Cyprus. The Euro 2000 campaign was faring little better when I showed up in the duchy. Luxembourg had opened their campaign with 3–0 defeats in Poland and at home to England, and a 2–0 reverse in Sweden. While they weren't disgraced in any of the games, it still took the run of consecutive defeats since the draw with Belarus well into double figures.

At the Stade Josy Barthel the fans are gathering outside the front entrance. Luxembourg has its own *ultra* movement, calling themselves the M-Block Fanatics. Named after the section of the Stade in which they stand, the M-Block banners became quite a talking point at the 1998 World Cup. Despite the absence of their heroes from the finals, the Luxembourg supporters still turned up with their flag proclaiming 'M-BLOCK FANATICS – 101% LUXEMBOURG'.

'After the successful Euro 96 campaign, some supporters tried to start up a supporters' club for the national team,' says Krier. 'There were differences among the younger and older supporters, so two separate clubs sprang up, the "Roude Leiw – Huel Se! [Red Lion, catch them!]" and the M-Block Fan Club started by the younger fans. Inspired by the Italian and French *ultra* groups, we organised some *tifos* [choreographies] and quickly earned a good reputation amongst some foreign *ultra* groups.'

Given the fierce pride Krier and his fellow fans have in their team, their country and their language, I wondered whether the Luxembourg team offers a rare opportunity to assert Luxembourgish national identity.

'Well, people look at you suspiciously if you talk about national identity in Luxembourg. All the people here are taught at school and reminded by politicians that we are Europeans first and Luxembourgers second. Some of these people automatically assume that you are hostile to foreigners as soon as you go to watch the national team, wear the national colours and sing the national anthem. I've always had the feeling that people in Luxembourg just swim with the prevailing tide. Too many people here don't have, or at least don't express, their personal ideas or opinions; they just go with the flow in whichever direction.

'The older people and a few younger ones believe that Luxembourg as a completely independent country is better than a lost identity in a united Europe. What no one seems to realise is that if the European Union ever becomes one state, we, Luxembourg, the smallest country, will certainly be the first to disappear – which will spell the end of our national team for a start. But many people here are more proud of being "perfect Europeans" than of supporting the national football team.

'This is one of the reasons I publish the fanzine in our mother tongue. We try to show people that we have a country-related fan scene that has little to do with "big" Europe. This certainly doesn't mean that we don't like people from other countries. Quite the opposite. Everywhere I've been in Europe I've been made welcome and hopefully everyone who's been here feels the same. Naturally, you'll always have a few idiots around, but that's something different.

'Another reason why our fanzine appears in Luxembourgish is that if we wrote in French or German we'd be accused of being *nearly* French or nearly German, which is something I hate. So how important is football to us? In terms of participation and the number of clubs it is certainly the most popular sport in Luxembourg, but I guess it's no more important to us than any other country in Europe.'

Standing outside the Stade Josy Barthel, you can tell the Bulgarians because they're all men, they're all wearing belted raincoats and they all look sulky. A moody-looking cameraman in a raincoat films a moody-looking man in a raincoat interviewing another moody-looking man in a raincoat in front of the main entrance. Inside the ground I take my seat in the press box and find myself surrounded by sulky-looking Bulgarian reporters. In raincoats.

Eventually the teams emerge on to the pitch. Leading out the Bulgarians is perennial sulky-boots Hristo Stoichkov. I note that even the Bulgarian national anthem is moody. The crowd numbers a little over 3,000; a couple of hundred noisy fans have made the trip from Bulgaria.

Finally I set eyes on the legendary Paul Philipp. Slightly overweight and moustachioed, he wears a shirt and tie that won't quite do up at the neck, like a small boy at a wedding. Once the game starts he immediately turns into Mr Angry, firing himself out of the dugout at the slightest provocation to harangue players, officials and – on one occasion, I swear – a passing aircraft. He spends the next 90 minutes permanently puce.

Far away to my left I recognise the M-Block Fanatics, standing on their seats behind banners that say 'ULTRAS LUXEMBOURG' and 'CURVA M'. After an early Bulgarian effort flies hopelessly wide, the very English strains of 'You're shit and you know you are' drift across the pitch. This is followed by an equally impeccably enunciated version of 'Everywhere we go . . .'

The match begins slowly, with Luxembourg creating the first opportunity. From a seemingly offside position, Marcel Christophe races through and raps the outside of the post with a stinging shot from 12 yards. Within a minute Hristo Stoichkov opens the scoring at the other end, lashing home a right-wing cross at the far post.

He may be an old misery, but there is no doubting the greatness of Bulgaria's most successful player. Throughout the 75 minutes that his tired old legs last in this game, most eyes are trained on him. He is also deceptively quick – not least when he dashes across the pitch to upend an unfortunate Luxembourger close to the touchline. He may look like he's not doing much, but he controls this game, making little decoy runs, always being available for wall-passes and popping up in the right place time and time again without appearing to break sweat.

Shortly after the goal, I turn to ask the sulky reporters in raincoats which player had provided the cross for Stoichkov's finish. They angrily gesture at the pitch, admonishing me for even daring to attempt to break their concentration.

Within seconds, a vision of womanhood appears to the right of the press box. I have to rub my eyes. On a cold March evening this woman, clopping delicately in improbably high stilettos down the steps of the VIP section, is wearing pink hot-pants and a skimpy white cap-sleeve T-shirt. Her hair is Diana Dors lampshade style, *circa* 1958, and her face is caked in make-up so thick it arrives a couple of minutes before she does.

As she is escorted to her seat by (guess what) a couple of sulky men in raincoats I realise that the fluffy bundle in her hands isn't a muffler after all but a lap-dog, complete with a little pink bow on top of its head. I've never seen anything like it. Presumably she's some kind of

Bulgarian film star, because suddenly the studious, moody gentlemen of the Bulgarian press – whose attention to the game wouldn't even waver long enough to mouth the name of one of their players to me – are scrambling over the seats, desks, each other, and most disconcertingly, me, to gain a better view of this Bulgarian belle. Notepads, dictaphones and pens go flying as the flurry of raincoats passes by me. At least two of them tread on my head.

They form an undignified scrum and snap away with instamatic cameras before returning to their seats grinning and gossiping like schoolchildren, holding their cameras like trophies – as if they can barely believe that the subject of their adoration could be captured on something as mortal as Kodak. I wipe a footprint off my notebook and lament the fact that they haven't missed a goal.

Shortly afterwards the goal that I'd prayed would come while the Bulgarian press were capturing on film the world's most inappropriately dressed woman is turned in from six yards by Ivano Yordanov. At 2–0 the match is effectively over as a contest, and the Bulgarians know it. The colourful contingent to my right dance and chant 'Hristo!' Sitting near me is a Bulgarian radio commentator who, as far as I can tell, only took two breaths throughout the entire first half. I notice that during his commentary he called all the Bulgarians by their last names, with the exception of the enigmatic number eight, who was referred to simply as Hristo. The only time his last name was used was after the opening goal, when he carefully enunciated 'Hri-sto Stoich-kov', which, it turns out, is pronounced 'Steetchkuff', not 'Stoychkov'.

Late in the second half Philipp, who looks permanently on the point of actually exploding, replaces the not inaccurately named Patrick Posing with Mikhail Zaritski, a Russian-born striker who attained citizenship after marrying a Luxembourgish woman. Within minutes Zaritski has cut inside from the right, beaten two players and rattled the crossbar with a tremendous shot. The rebound falls invitingly to Dan Theis, who lashes the ball high into the night sky.

Philipp wraps his arms around his head in anguish. Here is a man who doesn't know when he is beaten. Even after countless defeats, even though this match is palpably lost, Paul Philipp is haring up and down the line as if it's a delicately poised cup final. When he wants to make a late substitution, the UEFA official isn't quick enough to reach for the digital board. Philipp gets there first, screaming in the official's face. Unfortunately, he doesn't know how it works and after a couple of uncertain prods and a short, undignified tug-of-war bout, the official finally wrests it back and the substitution is made.

The M-Block keeps up a constant stream of encouragement. This is almost rewarded when, in the third minute of injury-time, Zaritski again hares through the Bulgarian defence and sees his shot brush the top of the crossbar.

The final whistle goes. It's three points for Bulgaria, and Luxembourg have still to find the net in the Euro 2000 qualifiers.

Paul Krier is sanguine about this latest setback: 'During the '80s morale and attendances were very low. Paul Philipp's first match in charge was also against Bulgaria and the crowd was less than a thousand. Tonight 3,000 were here. The players gave what they could, but for them the only motivation is playing for our small country all over Europe. Realistically, something like the ten-point Euro 96 qualifying campaign is the highest we can reach, although I think every supporter dreams of qualification for a major tournament.'

So for the M-Block Fanatics, the most they can hope for is the odd win over Malta. Yet still they turn out, still they follow Luxembourg all over Europe. After all, they are apparently Europeans first, Luxembourgers second.

Possibly the only time the words 'Luxembourg' and 'second' will appear together in any football-related sense.

3.

ITALY: IL GRANDE TORINO AND THE SUPERGA DISASTER

It's a misty May morning in Turin. My taxi leaves the centre of the city and races through the outskirts towards the hills. Eventually we begin the ascent of Turin's second-highest hill, Superga. As we wind our way up and around it, the bustling industrial city disappears from view below us, and in the fog I lose all sense of direction. Religious icons at the roadside appear from the gloom and disappear as we pass. Finally, out of the mist looms the outline of the enormous Basilica di Superga, a 300-year-old church whose situation offers breathtaking views of the city below on a clear day.

Built on the site of the vantage point from which Princes Vittorio Amedeo II and Eugenio of Savoy observed the Franco-Spanish siege of Turin in 1706, the basilica is an impressive building. The two princes built the church in thanks to the Virgin Mary for the liberation of Turin. This morning its dome is just visible, through the haze, above the huge triangular portico supported by six pillars atop a majestic flight of stone steps.

Walking past the impressive frontage, I crunch along the gravel path and at the rear of the building find what I have come to see. On the left of the rear wall as you look at the back of the church, slightly off centre, is a simple memorial garden. It is adorned with scarves and floral tributes, ranging from elaborate wreaths to plain bunches of wild flowers tied with string. The cards contain messages from all over Italy. A couple of candles burn in jamjars. Thirty-one names adorn the memorial, the majority of which are grouped together under the title IL CAMPIONI D'ITALIA – the Champions of Italy. One tribute finishes, simply, 'grazie campioni'.

Exactly 50 years earlier to the day on 4 May 1949, on the other side of the wall, priest Don Ricca was going about his normal duties inside the basilica. The weather was abysmal. It had been a strange springtime in Piedmont, and on that day the rain had fallen incessantly. Whole areas were flooded and the River Po had burst its banks in many places to the south. So appalling was the weather that, although it was just a little after five o'clock in the afternoon, the sky was as dark as night.

Gradually, above the noise of the tempest raging outside Don Ricca discerned a low roaring sound that seemed to be growing louder above the drumming of the rain on the roof. Suddenly a huge crash at the rear of the basilica caused the whole building to shake. It was followed by an explosion. The roar was heard in the city below and people looking in the direction of the noise saw a fireball light up the sky above Superga hillside.

Don Ricca gathered up his robes, ran out of the doorway at the front of the church and sprinted to the rear of the building. Within seconds he was soaked to the skin. Skidding around the corner he found, just as he had feared, the burning wreckage of an aircraft. Twisted bodies were scattered all around. It was immediately obvious, from the extent of the carnage and the silence from the wreckage, that there were no survivors. The rain dampened the flames and Don Ricca fell to his knees in the mud, praying loudly through the rain and his tears.

The Fiat G-212 aircraft that lay in pieces at the rear of the basilica had been carrying the Torino football team back from a testimonial match in Lisbon. Everyone on board – eighteen players, three members of the coaching staff, three directors, three journalists and four crew – was killed instantly. The cause of the crash has never been established. Given the abysmal weather conditions, the pilot had been given permission to divert to Milan. Instead he chose to proceed to Turin as planned, but the plane hit the ground flying in the wrong direction.

The team that perished in the mud and oil that day were within four matches of clinching their fifth consecutive Italian title. Such was Torino's dominance of the Italian game that in 1948 they had finished 16 points clear of Milan at the top of the table (this in the days of two points for a win), racking up a record 125 goals in the process. The previous season their winning margin had been ten points. They numbered ten Italian internationals in their squad, six of whom had represented Italy against Spain just five weeks before the tragedy. For a game against Hungary in 1947, ten of the Italian team came from Torino. Rarely has the world seen a team like it. They weren't nicknamed *Il Grande Torino* for nothing.

Half an hour was to pass before the emergency services were able to reach the scene. Don Ricca and Amilcare Rocco, a bricklayer who lived just below the basilica and whose garden now contained debris and bodies thrown there from the explosion, were beaten back by the flames. It didn't really matter. All the passengers and crew had been killed on impact.

The word spread quickly through Turin that the eerie glow up at the basilica was the wreckage of the Torino plane. Torino's secretary, Giusti, was among the first to arrive, followed shortly afterwards by Vittorio Pozzo, the famous Italian coach who had been instrumental in building this incredible team in the early '40s. To Pozzo fell the grim task of identifying the broken bodies in the mud. It was a difficult process, owing to the effects of the explosion. Pozzo recognised a ring here, a watch there.

Dino Ballarin, killed with his brother Aldo, still had his passport in his pocket. Ruggero Grava, a keen philatelist, had some Portuguese stamps about his person. Throughout the wreckage lay poignant debris – photographs of loved ones, a silk shirt still in its wrapping, broken bottles of perfume brought home as gifts that would never be given.

Down in the city, grief and panic filled the streets. Relatives of the dead hurried to the basilica. Sauro Toma, the only member of the first-team squad not to travel to Lisbon (because of a knee injury), returned to his home from an errand to find a crowd gathering outside his house. On hearing what had happened, Toma rushed to the scene. He was prevented from reaching the crash site by Giusti, who spared the distraught player the ordeal of seeing his friends and team-mates lying dead in and around the wreckage.

As the news reached the Italian parliament, all activities were suspended. In Rome people displayed photographs of the team garlanded with flowers, whilst in Naples and Florence they threw flowers into the river.

The team had been returning from Lisbon, where they had lost narrowly to Benfica in a testimonial match for the Portuguese team's captain, Francisco Ferreira. He was a long-time friend of the great Torino and Italy captain Valentino Mazzola: the two players had faced each other in Genoa in February that year when an Italian national team containing seven Torino players defeated Portugal 4–1 in front of 60,000 fans. At a Genoese restaurant after the game, Mazzola agreed to take his Torino side to Lisbon for Ferreira's celebration. By the time the match came around Mazzola had been suffering with the flu, but he insisted on travelling to honour his commitment to Ferreira.

Torino lost the match 4–3, possibly a tactful defeat given the occasion, and boarded their plane at ten o'clock the next morning. Torino had been one of the first clubs in Italy to use an aircraft for travelling to matches that would otherwise have involved lengthy road journeys. The players were reportedly apprehensive about this development at the time. After a short refuelling stop in Barcelona at lunchtime, the plane took off again, heading for Milan's Malpensa airport because of the inclement weather around Turin. However, shortly into the flight the captain asked to head straight for the players' home city and requested the Turin beacon to be switched on. At 4.55 p.m. he radioed that all was well and that he expected to arrive in Turin within 15 minutes. That was the last communication from the aircraft.

It is difficult to convey the extent of that team's achievements and what they meant to both the city of Turin and Italy as a whole. The roots of its success lie back in 1939, when Turin industrialist and former Toro player Ferruccio Novo took over the club. Novo had a vision of a great team playing in the 'WM' formation created by Herbert Chapman at Arsenal. By 1943 Novo had assembled the team that was to achieve so much. On 25 April that year, a goal by skipper Valentino Mazzola at Bari gave Torino the title by one point from Livorno. A month later they carried off the Coppa Italia with a 4–0 thumping of Mazzola's old team Venezia. Torino had signed both Mazzola and Ezio Loik – one of the most feared inside-forward pairings in football history – from Venezia the previous season. The lives of the two men were exact parallels. They were both born in Venice on the same day, made their débuts for both Venezia and Torino in the same matches, made their Italian national team débuts together, scored their first goals for the national team in the same match, and both died together in the wreckage of Superga.

The 1944–45 campaign was cancelled because of the war, but in 1946 the title returned to Torino's Campo Filadelfia stadium, sealed with a 9–1 thumping of Livorno on the last day of the season. In 1946–47 Toro stretched their winning margin to ten points, scoring a record 104 goals in the process. The following season, the last full season of Il Grande Torino, the Filadelfia club won the title by sixteen points – translated into three points for a win, the margin today would be 25. This time they rattled in 125 goals, including a 10–0 mauling of Alessandria.

Before leaving for Portugal the team had won one and drawn three of their previous four matches, leading Inter by five points at the top. On 30 April they had played their last match on Italian soil, a hard fought 0–0 draw with their title rivals from Milan, gaining a point which most commentators agreed had effectively sealed the destination of the title.

The list of records is incredible. As well as the enormous winning points margins, Toro's 10–0 win over Alessandria remains a Serie A record, whilst their 7–0 win at Roma in 1946 is the biggest-ever away win in the Italian top flight. In 1947–48 Torino dropped just one point at home; and over their five seasons together, that team scored over 400 goals. At the time of the crash, Torino had not been defeated at the Campo Filadelfia for over six years.

Statistics barely do the team justice, however. Their role went beyond figures. The effects of war and the fascist Mussolini regime ravaged Italy in the 1940s. When Mussolini was deposed in 1943, Germany invaded and Allied forces had gradually to fight their way up the country from the south. The nation was left in economic turmoil: her gross national product in 1945 was back to the level it had been in 1911, a drop in real terms of nearly 50 per cent on the last year before the war. Wages at the end of the war were a quarter of their pre-conflict levels. Morale reached an all-time low and major industries were on strike. There were chronic food shortages, as Italy became a battlefield for 18 long months.

As Il Grande Torino rose to dominance, so the Italian economy recovered. Turin itself was a major success story in the Italian post-war 'economic miracle' which saw industrial production grow by nearly 10 per cent every year. The nation voted overwhelmingly in favour of becoming a republic. And the Torino team, and the players from it that made up almost the entire Italian national side, were the most tangible representation of Italy's recovery, for their growth and development had mirrored that of the nation itself.

Not only, then, did Turin lose its greatest team at Superga: Italy also lost most of its national side and with it the fragile pride built up by the nation as it picked itself up from the war. The team that perished on that hilltop was more than 11 men on a football field. They had come to represent the hopes and dreams of a resurgent nation.

The players and officials lay in state at the Palazzo Madama. A week of national mourning was declared. All the coffins were draped with Italian flags, save those of Ernesto Egri Erbstein – the Jewish-Hungarian trainer who had survived the concentration camps during the war only to perish in the crash – and the English coach Leslie Lievesley, a former Crystal Palace and Torquay United player, whose coffin was decorated with the Union flag.

The funerals took place two days after the crash. Half a million people flocked into the centre of Turin to watch the slow procession of coffins pass through the Piazza San Carlo and along the Via Roma to the cathedral. After the service the players, officials, journalists and crew were buried at private family services.

As I walk back around the basilica to the front the sun begins to burn off the morning mist and the city opens up below. Turin is a non-stop bustle of activity. On the night I arrive, one of Italy's biggest pop stars is giving a free concert in the Piazza San Carlo – through which the funeral cortège had passed half a century earlier – outside my hotel window. Listening to the soft-rock caterwauling and wailing guitars, it's easy to work out why the concert was free. The next morning, with all evidence of the gig removed, the Turin Marathon thunders through, accompanied by motorcycle outriders beeping their horns, sponsors' floats and the buzz of ubiquitous scooters. Juventus have just lost at lowly Salernitana and the newspapers are full of speculation about the future of their coach, Carlo Ancelotti. Whilst Torino look to escape another season in Serie B and matches with Ternana and Treviso, sixth place in Serie A is considered a humiliation for mighty Juve. A lot can change in 50 years.

In the half-century since the Superga disaster, Torino have won the title just once (in 1976), spending the late 1990s in Serie B. The 1998–99 season saw things take a turn for the better, with the club clinching promotion back to Serie A, but the past few years have been grim for Torino fans. Whilst their club have languished in the second division, faced mountainous debts, suffered falling attendances and endured an inquiry into alleged tax evasion, city rivals Juventus have dominated the European game, reaching numerous European finals and attracting some of the world's best players to the Stadio Delli Alpi. An elaborate graffito on the roadside on the way to Superga depicts the Juventus zebra doing something unspeakable to a startled-looking Torino bull – an unsavoury image, but one that could be said to encapsulate the current situation. However, the *ultras granata*, Toro's most fanatical fans who take their name from the club's wine-coloured shirts, remain fiercely loyal.

Sportswriter Lapo Novellini of the *Gazzetta Del Piemonte* and *Football Italia* magazine is a native of the city and well-versed in Juve–Toro rivalry. 'Torino was founded back in 1906 and has always been in the hearts of the citizens of Turin,' he tells me. 'Of the city's two teams, Torino are by far the most beloved by their fans. Juventus have always been the team of the Turin upper class, whilst Torino fans have always been found more in the working or middle classes of the region. Torino's fans have always been rather against "the machine" that in Turin has always been represented by the Fiat company – the nation's largest car manufacturer, owned by Giovanni Agnelli, "The Lawyer", who is honorary president of Juventus.

'Torino have fans all over Italy, not in such large numbers as Juventus, but it is fair to say that the team is very popular among those that believe that the working class can sometimes go to paradise. Supporting Torino is a very distinctive thing: it is not just about football, it is about being against "those that win all the time, often without merit" – a label that any *granata* would stick on Juventus.

'The reasons behind the lasting effect that the crash has had on three generations of *torinesi* stem from the fact that the Grande Torino team, almost unbeatable, had become a new hope for all the people of Torino coming out of the Second World War. The Torino supporters have always honoured the memory of the team and each one of them still bears in his or her *vecchio cuore granata*, "old granata's heart" – the loving memory of a team that went beyond football boundaries to become the symbol of a whole city.'

Turin was once a grand city – indeed, it was the first capital of Italy after the unification of 1860 – but its streets are now choked with traffic and many of its buildings are shabby and in ill repair. The gridlock imposed upon the city by Michael Caine's mini-driving henchmen in *The Italian Job* is now repeated daily in the city's streets as the neat baroque road layout proves incapable of accommodating the heavy traffic of a modern city.

During the early evenings, the city's beautiful people don their designer clothes and walk around the piazzas. They don't seem actually to be going anywhere (stand still for a few minutes and before long the same people will walk by in the same order), but stop any one of them at random and you can guarantee that the proceeds from their clothes and jewellery would keep Crystal Palace in business for another couple of seasons.

Despite these nightly displays of opulence, Turin is not a rich city like, say, Milan. Away from the central piazzas decrepit apartment blocks crowd dark, narrow streets. Shutters dangle alarmingly from windows; the chipped plasterwork looks as if someone has roamed the streets with a blunderbuss, randomly letting off salvos of grapeshot at once-fine buildings.

Turin's demise as an administrative centre was countered by the rise of industry, with over 50,000 Turinese now employed by the Fiat car company. Fiat's owners, the startlingly rich Agnelli family, provided the cash that turned Juventus into the massive institution they have become. Juve have been the dominant club in the city for most of its football history. Torino, formed by disaffected members of Juventus, can only ponder on what would have happened if the plane carrying that 1949 side had landed safely. Their short, but glorious, domination of the Italian game is the only time they have superseded Juve in even the Turin pecking order, let alone the game as a whole.

The rivalry between the two sets of fans is intense. Parallels can be drawn with Manchester. Juve draws support from all over Italy, particularly the south; they have always offered high wages and signing-on fees; they have attracted overseas imports, from John Charles in the late '50s to Zinedine Zidane today. Torino's following comes mainly from within the city itself (ironically, many Torino fans work for Agnelli at Fiat, the fruits of their labours thus helping to bankroll their hated rivals), whilst big signings are rare. Denis Law spent an unhappy time with Toro in the early '60s, but in general the club have had to rely on home-grown talent.

'Torino and their fans' destiny seems to be one of sufferance,' says Lapo. 'Any true *granata*, though, won't change a second of that for any of Juventus's glory.'

Juventus and Torino now share the vast Stadio Delli Alpi on the outskirts of the city. The stadium where Paul Gascoigne watered the pitch with his tears in 1990 is unpopular with both clubs, as views are poor, access is difficult and the players complain of a lack of atmosphere. At the match with Napoli three days before the anniversary of Superga, around 25,000 people gathered to watch Torino beat Napoli 3–2 thanks to an injury-time goal by Serie B's top marksman Marco Ferrante. This result all but assured Toro of promotion, but the cavernous stadium subdued the atmosphere. Both clubs are keen to return to their former homes: Juventus to the Stadio Comunale and Torino to Campo Filadelfia, the scene of their greatest triumphs.

'Torino left their traditional home in 1963 because it had become too small for the big matches of Serie A,' explains Lapo. 'They moved to the Stadio Comunale, formerly the Benito Mussolini Stadium, which they shared with Juventus until the building of the new Stadio Delle Alpi that became both teams' home after it was completed for the World Cup in 1990. It's a fact that, for Torino's fans, the Filadelfia has always remained "their" ground, just as the Comunale has always been more associated with Juventus.

'The prospects of the club's return to a redeveloped Campo Filadelfia are yet to really take off, because the City of Turin's governing body is still assessing the project. The club, meanwhile, have changed management, which has contributed to a slowing-down of the process. It is probably fair to say that it will take at least three more years before Torino are back at their own ground.'

A 20-minute walk from the city's Puorto Nuovo station, the Filadelfia sits forlornly between apartment blocks inside a red-brick perimeter wall. A flimsy corrugated fence bars the main entrance. Slipping through a gap and into the old stadium, I find virtually nothing left of the stage where one of Europe's greatest-ever club sides played out their greatest triumphs. All that remain are two corner-sections of terracing and two small pieces of grandstand. At the rear of one of these, faded paintwork still guides you up an impressive sweeping staircase to 'sectors A, B, C and D'.

At the foot of the stairs stands a vast stone football on a plinth, with a barely discernible painted message. From my limited Italian vocabulary I can deduce that it was presented to the club by a local sportswear manufacturer. On the other side of the staircase a matching ball lies smashed among the weeds on the floor. I climb the staircase but it leads nowhere, the ornate, rusting banisters tailing off in ugly curves of twisted metal at the lip of a sheer drop of around 15 feet. I feel as though I'm on the wreck of the *Titanic* – such grandeur, long neglected and unused, yet still with an eerie feeling that everyone has just left. There's a vaguely humiliated atmosphere hanging over the place, as if the old stadium has lost its dignity.

Arriving at the pitchside, I find traces of the players' tunnel, where 11 bewildered teenagers stepped nervously on to the field just eight days after the crash, filling dead men's shoes in a 2–0 victory over Fiorentina. The title had been awarded to Torino anyway, a unanimous decision by the other clubs, but they still fulfilled their final four fixtures with a youth team. Sportingly, their opponents did likewise; fittingly, Torino won all four matches.

Looking across the pitch 50 years to the day after the disaster, I am conscious of the eerie silence. Despite being closely surrounded by apartment blocks on three sides, I hear no noise, no shouting, no radios, no traffic – just the mournful roar of a jet aircraft passing overhead in the low cloud above. The silence is exacerbated when I think of the crowds that used to gather here, roaring on Il Grande Torino to victory after victory, dropping cigarette ends and apple cores at their feet, cursing the roofless nature of the stadium in bad weather. At the end of the game the crowd would disperse, happy in the glow of victory, whilst the players headed for the showers (one tiled wall of which now stands exposed at the back of the remains of the grandstand).

Wading through the knee-length grass and dandelions of the pitch, avoiding old lumps of ironwork and timber, I arrive at what would roughly have been the centre-spot. Here began some of the greatest performances ever seen at club level, where Toro remained undefeated for six years. On this pitch, in 1947–48, Torino dropped just a solitary point at home on their way to their emphatic title win. From this spot in 1947 poor Alessandria were forced to kick off ten times on the receiving end of what remains Serie A's record victory. From here Valentino Mazzola, such a popular figure that he was known simply as 'Captain Valentino', would stand with the ball at his feet, roll his sleeves up to his elbows and bellow 'avanti!' to launch another relentless attack.

On the open side of the ground, the hills on the city's outskirts can clearly be seen. In the far distance one can just about make out Superga.

On 4 May 1999 a number of events took place to commemorate the anniversary of the crash: a service at the cemetery where the team is buried together; a private mass at Superga attended by Torino players and officials past and present; and a public mass in the city's cathedral. As the centrepiece, a match was arranged between a Torino-past-and-present team – which included Christian Vieri and Gianluigi Lentini – and a League Representative XI which featured the frightening strikeforce of Ronaldo and George Weah.

'For anyone growing up in Turin, 4 May is always something special,' said Lentini, once the most expensive player in the world. 'It's still fascinating to watch the footage of Il Grande Torino on the television.'

Marco Ferrante, Torino's modern Mazzola, pledged his support to a return to the Filadelfia by revealing: 'It is my dream to play at Campo Filadelfia in the top flight.'

At 5.05 p.m. on 4 May the city fell silent. The Superga disaster still looms large over the city of Turin. That day the front page of the Turin-based sports daily, *Tuttosport*, carried on its front page a photograph of the 1949 team under the simple headline, 'IMMORTALI'. Shops created window displays in memory of the disaster.

When Manchester United were decimated by the Munich crash, at least the manager and some players survived to rebuild for the future. Within ten years United had won the European Cup that the Munich team had coveted. Torino lost everything and have never recovered. Despite reaching the 1992 UEFA Cup final, where they were unlucky to lose on the away-goals rule after hitting the crossbar twice during a goalless second leg at Ajax, Torino have never come close to emulating the achievements of the great Superga side.

The effect on the Italian national side was also profound. Italy had won the last two World Cups before the war and had been much fancied for the 1950 tournament in Brazil. The Italian party, hastily assembled under the direction of Ferruccio Novo, refused to fly to South America and at the end of their long sea-voyage were eliminated at the first hurdle. It was to be 1970 before Italy progressed beyond the first round. Valentino Mazzola's son Sandro appropriately featured in the squad that reached the 1970 final.

Vittorio Pozzo wrote in *Stampa Sera* of the Torino team shortly after the disaster:

> It had passages of play as shining and resplendent as precious metals. It had won the love and enthusiasm of the crowds. In its best moments it had surmounted every possible obstacle in its way, scoring goals with the facility that a millionaire gives away thousand-lire notes. It bore a fine name, the name of one of those clubs which, passing through joy and grief, had succeeded in building Italian football out of nothing, a monument of imposing size and of social significance.
>
> They almost made up a caste, these players who filled our city with their presence and their deeds. They should be buried together so that they can remain together in the future as they have lived together, won fame together, and died together. So that they can continue to form a team in the afterlife too. So that it will be more natural, simple and human to remember them all when thinking of the greatest tragedy ever to have stricken football anywhere in the world wherever it is played.

The silhouette of the basilica at Superga watches over the city, providing a constant reminder of the tragedy. As dusk falls over the Campo Filadelfia, 50 years to the day after the crash, I lean on a rusting crush barrier high up on a weed-strewn crumbling corner terrace, and can almost sense the ghosts of that wondrous team still passing and moving, shooting and scoring.

Rest in peace, *campioni.*

4.

FAROE ISLANDS: EUROPE'S FOOTBALL OUTPOST

Stóra Dímun is one of the more remote Faroe Islands, which is saying something. In fact only three people live permanently here on what is little more than a big rock: sheep-farmer Jákup Dímun, his wife and his aunt. Dímun's family took their name from this small, rocky island of steep inclines and hazardous drops to the sea and he is the seventh generation of Dímuns to farm the island. His family has been here for over 500 years living in the typically Faroese turf-roofed farmhouse on a scarce piece of flat ground. He relies on a weekly helicopter flight from Atlantic Airways, the Faroese national airline, for supplies and most of his human contact with the rest of the world. It is on one of these flights that I arrive.

Clamping one hand to his head to stop his hat from being whipped into the choppy sea nearby, he yanks open the door to the helicopter and motions at me to disembark. Vague greetings are shouted, lost in the thump and clatter of the rotors. We scamper, half-crouching, across draught-flattened grass and the helicopter lifts off again, returning to collect me in an hour after delivering to an island further south. As the noise diminishes we can finally make ourselves heard; the first question the farmer asks is, 'Did you see the football?'

Four days earlier the Faroese national team had gained an unlikely 1–1 draw with Scotland in a Euro 2000 qualifier and Jákup Dímun had watched the game on his television. He will park himself in front of the set again in a few hours' time when the Faroes take on Bosnia-Herzegovina. Even here, in the middle of the north Atlantic on a craggy piece of rock only a few hundred yards across, someone is looking forward to watching a football match.

The Faroese love their football. The crowds of 4,500 which watched each of the Scotland and Bosnia games represent 10 per cent of the Islands' entire population – roughly the equivalent of 5.5 million people turning up to watch England play at Wembley. The exploits of the national team, in the decade since they entered international competition in explosive style, have revitalised a country that has suffered economic turmoil and near-bankruptcy during the same period. Football has also raised international awareness of the existence of the Islands: before football the Faroes were probably known only for incurring the wrath of Greenpeace with their controversial whaling activities.

Their recent emergence on to the international football stage from comparative isolation also makes the Islands a microcosm of the modern game. How far has commercialism infiltrated the previously amateur game? What does the future hold for football in the Faroe Islands with the benefit of a decade's international experience?

I spent a week there, mainly because the national airline Atlantic Airways only flies once a week to and from Aberdeen. A few months earlier it had been in Aberdeen that I first encountered the Faroese, during the Euro 2000 qualifier at Pittodrie. Scotland defeated the islanders by two goals to one that night, a result that pleased the visitors more than the home side. Over 500 Faroese had made the trip; the Islands' cruise ship was chartered specially. It was moored at Aberdeen for three days but there was a well-stocked bar on board and many Faroese set foot in Scotland only long enough to see the game. Others, though, hit the shops – like most of Scandinavia the Faroe Islands are comparatively expensive, so many bargains were to be found in the streets of Aberdeen.

Early in the game Neil Sullivan had been lucky to escape with a booking after he raced from his goal to clatter Faroese striker Todi Jónsson outside the penalty area. Scotland had taken the lead in controversial circumstances: a ball was cleared into the stands and a replacement quickly thrown back into play. Meanwhile the original ball was returned from the crowd, so two footballs were bouncing around the Faroese penalty area. Craig Burley curled one of them into the bottom corner whilst the visitors' defence froze. Scotland added a second after half-time, but John Petersen's penalty with four minutes remaining led to an anxious finale for Craig Brown's side. At the final whistle the visiting supporters gave their team a standing ovation. They remained in place long after the players and most of the Scottish fans had departed, still singing the praises of their heroes' battling performance. As they left, eventually, the Faroese serenaded the empty stadium with a rousing version of 'We Are The Champions'.

Danjál Mariusárson, a 32-year-old chef and restaurant manager from the Faroese capital, Tórshavn, had predicted the correct result to me beforehand in an Aberdeen bar. 'I think it will be 2–1, but I'm not sure which way,' he had said. 'I hope it is us, but 2–1 to Scotland would still be a great result.'

His friend Louis Wilson, born in the Islands of an English father and Faroese mother but now resident in the more temperate climate of Kingston-upon-Thames, had displayed similar soothsaying talents by predicting the same correct score as we entered Pittodrie. 'The first match I remember watching was in 1957 against the Shetland Islands in Tórshavn,' he told me as we made our way to our seats. (Pittodrie operates a non-smoking policy in the stands, so we had to feel our way through the fog emanating from the toilets where the Faroese were sucking frantically on fistfuls of cigarettes.) 'It was on a gravel pitch and I can't remember the score. I know the Faroes won, though.' Gazing across the lush Pittodrie turf shining under the floodlights in front of the bright red Pittodrie seats, he fell silent for a moment and said: 'It's unbelievable to be here tonight. You could never imagine it. It's like . . . science fiction.'

On the bus back to the quayside after the match both men dissected the game. 'The midfield wasn't offering options to the defence,' reckoned Louis. 'We couldn't get it out of the last third. I was happier with the second-half performance. We weren't too convincing in the first.'

'In the last few games we've played really well in the second half,' concluded Danjál. 'We seem to be better organised. We lost, yes, but we lost with honour and can hold our heads high.'

The discussions of what went wrong continued long into the cold Aberdonian night, and long after Danjál and Louis had seen their acquaintances safely back to the harbour.

A few months later I find myself in a small plane barrelling out of the sky towards the Faroes. The Atlantic Airways aircraft aims between two rocky promontories and heads for Europe's shortest runway. The plane touches down and the brakes go on. Before my face is buried in the back of the seat in front, I'm sure I see anchors hurtling past the window.

Until their entry into European football I had never heard of the Faroe Islands. Approximately halfway between Scotland and Iceland, they are easily missed on a map, eighteen tiny islands dropped into the north Atlantic – a place, according to legend, formed when God cleaned out his fingernails after creating the Earth.

An archipelago of islands on which you are never further than five kilometres from the sea, the Faroes are usually shrouded in rain, mist, fog, drizzle or any combination of the four. But it was in unusually clear weather that the little Atlantic Airways plane landed at Vagar, in the west of the islands. Vagar is the only Faroese airstrip for the simple reason that it is the only island with a flat piece of land large enough to support a runway (albeit a frighteningly short one).

From the airport it's an hour-and-a-half bus ride to the capital, Tórshavn, one of the smallest capital cities in the world with a population of just under 14,000.

The journey from the airport shows off some of the best of Faroese scenery: craggy green hilly pastures speckled with sheep (in Faroese the islands are called Føroyar, or 'islands of sheep'). Thin waterfalls tumble down sheer basalt cliff faces into a labyrinth of babbling streams and you hardly see a living soul that isn't clad in shaggy wool and wearing a dozy, quizzical expression. The rocky terrain cannot support permanent crops, there are no areas of woodland and only 6 per cent of the land is given over to arable use. Thanks to the terrain, vegetables do not feature heavily in the Faroese diet: what you find in the supermarket is imported from Denmark. There are no railways, no standing army and only a small police force, but then crime is a rare thing in the Faroes.

During the Middle Ages the Faroes came under the jurisdiction of the Norwegian assembly, the Gulating. In 1814, Norway was annexed to Denmark and the Faroes passed into Danish jurisdiction. Keen to preserve their identity, the Faroese tended to resent Danish rule, and then in 1940, with Denmark occupied by German forces, a British warship commander instructed the Faroese to raise their own flag in place of the Danish one. A 1946 referendum called for unlimited sovereignty independent of Denmark, and a compromise home-rule settlement came into effect in 1948.

In the late 1980s the Faroes had one of the highest standards of living in the world, with a consumption rate ten times that of Denmark. However, a decline in fish stocks during the early 1990s led to a sudden and catastrophic economic crisis (96 per cent of Faroese exports were fish products). The state bank, supporting a national debt of DK9.4 billion, was forced to call in the receivers, and the Faroese government was obliged to go cap-in-hand to the Danes to the tune of DK1.8 billion.

The Danes imposed severe austerity measures, slashing public spending, pushing up taxes and cutting wages in the public sector. Over half the country's fish-processing plants closed and unemployment in Tórshavn had risen to one person in five by 1993. An international boycott of Faroese produce in protest over whaling methods at the same time didn't help matters.

This boycott concerned the *grindadráp*, a ceremony in which the Faroese lure a pod of pilot whales to shore and set about them on the beaches with harpoons and knives. As a quarter of the meat consumed on the islands is whalemeat, the Faroese maintain it is a traditional part of their culture dating back to Viking times. Their maritime situation dictates that the sea is their market-place. Whatever the justifications or otherwise, the boycott came at the wrong time for the economically crippled islands.

The Copenhagen-imposed cost-cutting worked, however. Fish stocks improved accordingly and oil was discovered between the Faroes and the Shetlands. The population, falling due to emigration to Denmark during the economic crisis, levelled out to a steady 45,000 and today the Faroes are back on their feet.

In the midst of all this hardship the football team emerged on to the European scene. Before the 1990s, Faroese football was a simple affair and strictly amateur. The concept of a player moving between clubs was almost unheard of: it was accepted as the natural order of things that a young footballer would join his local club at youth level and stay with them for the duration of his career. No player was on a contract because nobody needed one. Football was, and is, phenomenally popular and there is still one football team for every fifty males on the islands. As the bus to Tórshavn passes through villages populated by no more than a couple of hundred people, the main landmarks in each are a church and a gravel football pitch. The men's game supports a league structure of five divisions as well as further regional leagues, and the women's game is arguably more popular in terms of participation than anywhere else in Europe.

The Faroese national association, the Fótbóltssamband Føroya, was formed as recently as 1979, with FIFA membership following a decade later. Following entry into the European arena, football in the Faroes underwent enormous changes. Money reared its ugly head, a club hierarchy developed and overseas players arrived. Most of the imported talent comes from central or eastern Europe, and such is the foreign presence in the Faroes' domestic game that foreign players could make up two whole teams in the ten-club top flight. In return, Faroese players began to venture abroad to the professional game in Norway, Iceland and latterly Scotland. The national team became a major source of national pride, and the FSF lured a former European Footballer of the Year (Allan Simonsen) to the north Atlantic as its national coach.

Midnight approaches as the bus enters Tórshavn, but this being summertime in the north Atlantic, the sun is still up. Danjál is waiting amongst the long shadows at the bus station and we adjourn to his restaurant to discuss – over hefty steaks so rare that I'm sure mine said 'ouch' when I put the fork in – the state of the game in the Islands.

Danjál is a supporter of Havnar Bóltefelag, or HB, from Tórshavn, traditionally the Islands' most successful club. They share the town's Gundadalur stadium with their rivals Bóltefelagið 36 (B36) and have recently appointed a Romanian coach.

'Faroese football now has some eastern European trainers who have brought with them new ideas, particularly about fitness,' he says. 'The spirit is quite different now as well and the domestic game has improved immensely. The fact that the Faroes play in European club and international competitions has helped develop our game in the last decade.

'In Tórshavn there is a bit of a rivalry between HB and B36, a little like Manchester United and Manchester City in England. B36 have a new Yugoslav trainer and HB have brought in Ion Geolgau, a former Romanian international. He's introduced a new regime and the players are noticeably much fitter. They train six times a week now as well as having full-time jobs. He works them really hard. For the month before the season started they didn't even touch a football. If a player injured his leg and said he couldn't train, Geolgau would reply, "Well – there's the gym. Go and work on your upper body!"

'Also, if the players couldn't train one evening because of work commitments or whatever, Geolgau would say, "Come in at seven in the morning and I'll do an hour with you." It sounds horrific but you could see the difference in the players. After a couple of months they had so much more energy; you could see it in the way they played.

'In Faroese football, as everywhere else it seems, there are always clubs who are at the top and clubs who are always changing divisions because those bigger clubs have the money to lure the better players away. Here there used to be a strict loyalty that you'd stay with your local club – you couldn't and wouldn't play for anyone else. Now, since we have entered Europe, things are becoming more professional and the same clubs dominate the league. Whether that's good for the game or not, I'm not really sure.'

Since the 1980s football in the Faroe Islands has been transformed from sport to industry, swamped by an avalanche of sponsorship, advertising, endorsements and an increased competitiveness clopping after the carrot of European competition. The lure of European football has led to the Islands' richer clubs clambering over each other to reach the financial honeypot that lies beyond the rocky shores of this Atlantic outpost. Even though they always fall at the first hurdle in European competition (Faroese clubs have conceded an average of just under four goals a game in Europe and are yet to win a two-legged tie), the financial rewards of mere qualification are enough to boost bank balances to a previously unimaginable degree, and four clubs are already nosing ahead of the rest.

'B36 and HB are from the capital Tórshavn, and KI is from the second city, Klaksvík,' Faroese football writer Emil Jacobsen had told me before I arrived in the Islands. 'The fourth club is GI from Gøtu, not a particularly well-populated town, but they have managed to keep a relatively high standard due to their four successive domestic championships between 1993 and 1996. This brought them into European football with its financial rewards like those earned from their matches against Glasgow Rangers a few years back. This is one of the reasons that GI "keeps up" with the other three.

'I think the general feeling among the clubs is that this commercialisation is an inevitable process. It has happened, or happens, almost everywhere else as well. The main concern among the supporters of the big clubs is how this will affect their own youngsters, who see players from other clubs step into the team while they end up in the reserves or on the bench. The home-grown players of the big clubs – especially of B36 and HB – are moving to the smaller clubs, where they get first-team action every weekend because they can't get into their own team.

'This particular aspect of it is not unhealthy, but the main problem is the financial part. Professional football is brand new in the Faroe Islands, and some of the clubs are better at it than others. This could lead to financial ruin for some, but we don't know that for sure yet.

'From a sporting point of view, there has been a lot of debate about the size of the First Division. At the moment it consists of ten teams, but there is a big difference between top and bottom. In 1998 we had results like 10–0 and 11–1, and even though we have not had any scores like that recently, it is obvious that this does not lead anywhere. The small clubs are naturally against a reduction in the league because they will miss the games against the big clubs.

'It is very difficult to say whether the trend will be reversed. But personally I feel that the big clubs in a few years' time will go back to nurturing their own talents more and stop looking so much at the other clubs. As an example, when HB won the championship in 1998, only three or four of their players were actually from Tórshavn, which is by far the most populated town on the islands. Naturally the supporters were happy to win the championship, but there was another feeling of "hang on, this isn't HB". If the clubs listen more to their supporters, maybe this will stop in the forthcoming years, or at least slow down.

'The biggest problem these days seems to be how to cope with the new times – contracts, player salaries, bonuses etc. All of these things did not exist in the Faroes a few years back, but since we joined FIFA and UEFA, the money issue plays an increasing part. For teams like B36, HB and KI it is essential to get European qualification, otherwise the players will want to leave, or the club can't get the money to pay them.'

When the islands emerged blinking on to the European stage in 1990 they were a blank canvas, unspoilt and unsullied by the ravages of the commercialism sweeping through the world game. Not long after the innocents bit into the apple of temptation marked 'FIFA membership', the fig leaves of sponsorship and player-poaching began to cover the private parts of amateurism.

At the time FIFA membership was first mooted in the mid-'80s there was some opposition. Most clubs and individuals approved, however, and the Faroese were accepted into UEFA just in time to enter the draw for the 1992 European Championship qualifiers.

'There is much discussion about smaller nations playing in international competition,' says Danjál, waving a forkful of steak in the air to prove his point. 'You can say it's better for the bigger nations to play each other, but we as a small nation can only improve by playing the better teams. Football in general would improve this way. It might not be so interesting for England to come here to the Faroes, but to us it would be a huge occasion. I dream of seeing the Faroe Islands play at Wembley even though we'd probably lose heavily.'

To lose heavily was what the Faroese expected from their first-ever competitive international against Austria in September 1990. Their warm-up campaign had consisted of a 2–0 win over the Shetland Isles, a home defeat to an Iceland 'B' team and a 6–0 drubbing at the hands of Danish club Brøndby.

Austria were fresh from a reasonably successful 1990 World Cup finals campaign, where they had been unlucky to lose 1–0 to the hosts, Italy. The match was to be played in the Swedish town of Landskrona because the Faroe Islands had only artificial pitches (the Faroese climate and geology making a grass surface unviable). Striker Toni Polster predicted that the Austrians would rack up double figures against the minnows from the north Atlantic. Just 1,200 fans saw the game, including a smattering from the Faroes.

A battling performance by the Faroese – none of whom had much experience of playing on real grass – meant that the Austrians were restricted to just one clear chance before half-time when bobble-hatted goalkeeper Jens Martin Knudsen saved athletically from Kurt Russ. But in the second half the Austrians began to lay siege to the Faroese goal, in which Knudsen was having the game of his life.

Just after the hour Torkil Nielsen, a timber salesman from

Sandavágur who had become a father for the first time two days earlier, burst through the Austrian defence and lashed the ball past Michael Konsel in the Austrian goal, right into the back of the net. The Faroese went wild. Back home, television and radio relayed the momentous events to a population agog.

The panicky Austrians threw everything at the dogged Faroese but found Knudsen in the way whenever they broke through the Islanders' rearguard. When the final whistle went, the Faroese players danced with delight and disbelief, the Austrian players left the field to look up the word 'hubris' in the dictionary and Austrian coach Sepp Hickersberger went to look for a new job.

It was a remarkable start to the Faroes' international career and one that sent pictures of the goalkeeper with the bobble hat all around the world. Jens Martin Knudsen was at the time a fork-lift truck driver at a fish factory in Runavik. Like most Faroese footballers, he joined his local team (NSI) as a youngster. The bobble hat had been knitted by his grandmother to protect a head injury sustained in a schoolboy game. Now in his mid-thirties, Knudsen has been the Faroes' first-choice goalkeeper ever since that victory over Austria. He played for GI Gøtu, one of the Faroese 'big four', in 1994, before turning professional with the Icelandic club Leiftur in 1997. With over fifty caps to his name, Knudsen is the Faroes' most-capped player; but he lost his place in the national side after being sent off in the Faroes' opening Euro 2000 qualifier against Estonia.

Sadly, he no longer wears the bobble hat. When Allan Simonsen took over as national coach in 1994, one of the first things he did was to ban Knudsen's idiosyncratic headgear. As long as people lampooned Knudsen's bobble hat, felt Simonsen, the less likely they were to take his team seriously. But at the time, the victory over Austria made Knudsen's hat the most famous piece of knitwear in world football. In fact it became the subject of one of the Faroes' few crimes, when two Norwegians let themselves into his house (to say they broke in would be an exaggeration as no one locks their doors in the Faroes) and swiped the famous article not long after the Austrian game. They were eventually apprehended at the airport and the hat was returned to its anxious owner.

A month later the Faroes visited Copenhagen for their first match as an independent entity, against Denmark. Despite having been granted home rule and autonomous status after the Second World War, the Faroes actually remain under Danish jurisdiction. Danes have often looked down upon the Islands, resenting the subsidies that the Danish government grants their north Atlantic neighbours and feeling that their nation is needlessly subsidising the group of islands situated the other side of the British Isles.

For the Faroese, strongly desirous of full independence, the match at Copenhagen's Idrœtspark was a rare opportunity to face the Danes on equal terms, the Faroese national anthem playing alongside that of the Danish, and 11 Faroese taking on 11 Danes over 90 minutes of football.

The Danish fans whistled and sang throughout the Faroese anthem. Over 38,000 people packed into the stadium, including a Faroese contingent boosted by Danish-based expats to around 5,000. Despite falling behind to the team that would go on to become European champions less than two years later as early as the ninth minute, the Faroese were not long in arrears. As Peter Schmeichel failed to gather a Torkil Nielsen cross, eighteen-year-old midfielder Allan Mørkøre poked the ball over the line for a shock equaliser. The visiting fans erupted. Back in Tórshavn the turf roofs nearly blew off the buildings.

Eventually the Danes rallied to win 4–1, but the Faroese had not been disgraced. A 1–1 draw with Northern Ireland followed and the Faroes had proved they were no pushovers. Since then, however, they have failed to live up to their early promise.

It's early hours in the morning by the time I leave Danjál's restaurant and meander through the purplish twilight to my accommodation. The Faroese air is so clean you can almost taste it and the chill wind allows you to feel its purity right to the bottom of your lungs. I fall soon into a deep sleep.

It turns out that I've been lucky with the weather. 'Four seasons in one hour' is a local saying, but the next morning the sun is still shining as I head into Tórshavn. Down by the harbour on the old main street of Tórshavn which leads to Tinganes, the original ancient settlement from which the capital grew, I visit the tourist office.

John Eysturoy is the closest Faroese football had to a star in the late 1960s. A bustling centre-forward with HB, Eysturoy remembers a different game from today as he gazes out of the window of his office overlooking the harbour in the capital. He works for the Faroe Islands Tourist Board, at the heart of a relatively new and potentially lucrative industry in the Islands. After the fish fiasco of the early '90s the Faroese are looking to be less dependent on the sea. Most of the Faroese catch is exported: bizarrely, even though the Islands are surrounded by waters teeming with fish, what fish you can buy in the shops is usually shrink-wrapped and imported from Denmark.

Ironically the Tourist Board building was designed as the headquarters of a bank which was then declared bankrupt during the economic crisis. Inside I meet and shake hands with Eysturoy – who played for the Faroes national team in the days when their fixture list included the might of opponents such as Anglesey, Shetland, Greenland and Orkney – and begin to chat about the Islanders' favourite subject, football.

'We were just enthusiastic footballers in those days,' he recalls. 'Of course we were proud to represent the Faroe Islands against other teams, and we played to win, but we played more for enjoyment than success. I can remember playing for the national team in Shetland in 1967. The ferry crossing took 22 hours, but I think we won. Whatever the result, we had many drinks with our opponents afterwards. That was always the Faroese way.

'It was a very different game then. We had to buy all our own national team kit and wash it ourselves. After a couple of washes, all the shirts would be different colours. The pitches were gravel or mud, the facilities were poor, but we just played for the love of the game. We would even set up herring boxes as goals down by the harbour and play football for hours, just because we enjoyed it so much. We never even thought about playing professionally, not like today. But that's progress, I suppose.'

Professionalism was only legalised in the Faroe Islands in 1998, in response to the number of players going abroad to join professional clubs without their home club receiving a penny in return. Eysturoy's modern counterpart, Allan Mørkøre, had that morning made the newspapers by becoming the first Faroese footballer ever to be sold for a transfer fee. In a similar mould to Eysturoy at his peak, this stocky, competitive striker had covered every inch of the pitch during the Faroes' 1–1 draw with Scotland four days earlier. Mørkøre is one of the modern Faroese game's stars and has been ever since he flicked the ball past Peter Schmeichel in Copenhagen in 1990. In 1997 he left his home-town club KI Klaksvík to join HB (generally acknowledged as the 'Manchester United of the Faroes') on what, for a semi-professional player training to be a teacher, was a lucrative contract.

Mørkøre was one of the first players to move between domestic clubs and was then the first to be sold. No one epitomises the modern Faroese game better than Mørkøre. The burly 28-year-old had made no secret of his desire to make money from playing football and to pursue his career abroad. The IBV club of Iceland had to part with a sum equivalent to £20,000 to secure his services; and although he is by no means the first player to take off from the Islands' tiny airstrip for the professional promised land, the Mørkøre transfer represents a watershed for Faroese football. It's all a long way from John Eysturoy and his herring boxes.

From the harbour I make my way north to Tórshavn's stadium at Gundadalur which is shared by the capital's two leading clubs, HB and B36. Next door a new stadium is being built with a grass pitch, to bring the national team's matches to the capital. International matches and European club games have previously been played on the Islands' only grass pitch, over an hour's drive away in Toftir.

HB and B36 are two of the most powerful clubs on the Islands, and they have embraced the concept and financial rewards of European football with vigour. Both have their own stand along one side of the ground, with an empty 'no-man's land' lying in-between. Despite the fact that average attendances rarely rise above 800 (although 1,500 had watched HB's 4–2 win over their rivals two weeks earlier, representing more than a tenth of the town's population), both stands are dominated by executive boxes plastered with the logos of the businesses that rent them.

'Obviously, a strong club like B36 cannot survive on gate income alone,' says B36 chairman Kristjan á Neystabø inside the clubhouse, 'so we must look elsewhere for money. Football is very popular in the Faroe Islands, we are one of the more successful clubs, and businesses like to be associated with success. It is not difficult for us to attract sponsors.'

In the early 1990s, having lived in the shadow of HB for many years, B36 adopted a much more assertive approach to recruiting players: 'B36 was started by players who were not good enough to play for HB, but in the late '80s and early '90s we decided that we must take up the cudgels against them and have built ourselves up since then. We began to look for the best players from all around the Faroes, not just from Tórshavn. That was the only way for us to progress and now we are one of the strongest teams. Obviously we have a small population here, so to remain a strong team and reach Europe, where the real riches are, we have to take the best players from the small clubs. There are more job opportunities in Tórshavn than in the villages, so it is easy to attract the best players from around the islands. After all, if we don't get them, HB will.'

Despite the rivalry, HB and B36 maintain strong links. 'The boards of both clubs work very well together,' says á Neystabø. In fact I'm going for a meeting shortly with my counterpart at HB to discuss building a sports hall here between the two clubhouses. That's a big project, and we've formed a company split fifty-fifty between HB and B36. It's necessary for us to work together because we've always shared the facilities.'

The issue of overseas players is one of the main talking-points in Faroese football today. B36 have a Yugoslav coach and a Yugoslav player. For á Neystabø, these players make sense economically as well as on the field: 'Most of the overseas players who have come to the Faroes have had a positive influence and clubs have, by and large, had good experiences with them. They are not so expensive and seem to like staying in the islands.

'Our coach, Tomislav Sivic, has brought with him strong ideas, especially in terms of strength, discipline and physical fitness. Also, with our smaller more insular society it's easier for coaches to have new ideas. If a Faroese coach went to, say, an English or Scottish club then no one would know him and it would be harder to implement ideas. Here it is different.

'European competition helps too. We have some good young players who need to develop and face fresh challenges. I was behind entry into Europe one hundred per cent, I was convinced it was a good idea. Some people opposed it, but now I think everyone is convinced.

'Standards here will not get much higher, but from our point of view we need to find the best players from the smaller clubs. As I have said, if we don't get them HB will, or Klaksvík or GI will. As a result the small clubs will struggle. Teams like HB and B36 will always be strong, like Manchester United in England will always be strong.'

Á Neystabø's counterpart at HB, 36-year-old Gunnar Mohr, concurs. Having spent his entire career at HB, Mohr retired from playing in 1997. As a member of the legendary squad which beat Austria in 1990 ('I was the substitute but I didn't get on to the pitch') and as HB's chairman since 1992 (a rare example of a club chairman who pulled on his boots for the team every Saturday), he is well qualified to comment on the changes in the Faroese game.

Mohr's newly built house overlooks Gundadalur, where heavy industrial machinery clanks away at the construction of the new national stadium throughout our conversation. The new grass pitch means that HB and B36 will be able to play their European home games at home, rather than trekking across to Toftir.

'Yes, it's very sad for the small clubs that they lose their best players, but HB are the strongest club and we have to ensure that we have the strongest team,' says Mohr. 'We have to make sure that we can play in Europe, because it presents new challenges and brings in a lot of money for the Faroese clubs from UEFA. In two years we will be erecting floodlights which will cost DK6 million. We need money to play in Europe and we need to play in Europe to earn the money.'

Mohr tells me that he approves of the increased commercialism of Faroese football – he helped recently to secure HB a major sponsorship deal with the largest Faroese bank – but I detect a slight sadness in his demeanour at the way the good old days have vanished so quickly.

Later in the week I visit the home of EB/Streymur, a club based in the village of Eiði (pronounced 'eye-ee'), at the northernmost tip of Streymoy, the largest of the Faroe Islands. Their ground is without question one of the most beautiful football settings in the world, overlooked by green-sloped mountains and with the Atlantic Ocean crashing against the rocks a few yards from the touchline. Inevitably the pitch is artificial and the ground consists of little more than a clubhouse and a rail around the playing surface. Breathtaking location it may be, but that's scant consolation when EB/Streymur also hold down bottom place in the Faroese Second Division. The product of a 1993 merger between two Third Division clubs, EB/Streymur enjoyed a brief foray into the top flight, but now find that the polarisation of the Faroese game is crippling their already limited resources.

'Only 400 people live in Eiði,' says chairman Magnus á Stongum, 'so we have great trouble finding players. Since Faroese football has become more professional, there is definitely growing pressure on small clubs like ours. In our first season after the merger, we lost three of our best players to the bigger teams, which makes it hard for us to survive. If we get a good player, we are automatically in danger of losing him. We can't afford to put him on a contract, so when another club comes in there's nothing we can do. It's a very big problem.

'We concentrate on finding youngsters. That's our only chance of improving in the second division. But without contracts, and with the big clubs sniffing around, we hope that they become good – but not that good!'

His club has also fallen victim to a rule change that seems designed to preserve the big clubs' monopoly. When EB/Streymur were promoted as Second Division runners-up in 1994, the top two clubs went up automatically. But since 1996, only the champions go up: the team finishing second plays off against the team second from bottom in the First Division.

'Since they changed the rules we have finished second twice, but lost the play-off both times. For us to develop, it is vital that we reach the First Division. That way, perhaps we can keep our players. Also there is just no money in the Second Division. Our crowds can drop as low as thirty, and you can't survive on gates like that.

'Times are changing in the Faroe Islands and it's hard to predict which way things will go. If we only have three or four clubs dominating the game, the excitement will disappear and we'll lose the interest of the public. When the same clubs dominate the game and receive all the money from European competition, this concentration of power takes all the spirit out of football. People say that it's good for developing our football at international level, but in my opinion we can't progress much further than we have. I don't see us qualifying for a major tournament.'

The Second Division side haven't joined the queue to bring in foreign talent either. 'No, we haven't joined that particular bandwagon, because you have to provide the player, and possibly his wife, with a job. We can't do that here. Also, for a player to settle abroad he has to feel comfortable, and we just don't have the facilities of, say, Tórshavn. There are no dances here at weekends, for example. Whilst many of these players have helped to improve the Faroese game, it's not something we have the resources to explore. The whole situation is very difficult for us.'

As I leave the village, two small boys are playing football in the street. One wears an HB tracksuit, the other a Manchester United shirt.

It is from clubs like EB/Streymur that HB, B36, KI Klaksvík and GI Gøtu plunder talent. I ask Gunnar Mohr whether it is good for the game that EB/Streymur should be left to struggle while those fortunate enough to play in Europe grow stronger and richer.

'I think it is important that we have strong teams in Europe,' he replies, 'but yes, I feel sorry for the little clubs. They often ask when we visit, "How can we compete with you?" I can't really answer them. The club you mentioned from Eiði, they really have a lot of problems . . .'

But this week is all about the national side. On the day of the Scotland match there is a mass exodus from Tórshavn. A convoy of cars, vans and buses snakes along the winding roads from the capital across to Toftir, where the 6,000-capacity national stadium sits hewn from the hillside. One end of the stadium is overhung by a craggy rockface, the other falls away to the sea below. Behind the main grandstand is the Islands' only athletics track, built for the 1989 Island Games and now home to Toftir's team B68, who play on the artificial surface in the middle of the track.

Never a major force in Faroese football, B68 nonetheless took the import of overseas players to its extreme early in 1999 by signing four Brazilians. It was a major event when the Latin Americans arrived at

Vagar; and before long Marcelo, Marlon, Messias and Lucio were soon winning over the Faroese football public.

'I remember interviewing them in February, when it was still snowing and freezing cold,' Emil Jacobsen tells me. 'They said they liked it here, that the people were nice and the weather – well, that was something they'd have to get used to.' Climate aside, the main problem the quartet faced was adapting to playing on artificial surfaces. They were also alarmed by the amount of fitness training they had to do minus the ball. 'In Brazil we concentrate more on technique,' panted Marcelo soon after his arrival.

Toftir, population 700, is a far cry from their home city of Rio, where they had played in the Brazilian second division. However, they have immersed themselves in local life, cheerfully taking to their employment in a local fish-canning plant and learning Faroese. Marcelo made the biggest impression, scoring eight goals in his first fifteen games, but Lucio suffered a serious knee injury in his first match and was to miss most of the campaign. Messias, meanwhile, came on as substitute early in the second half of the same match and was promptly sent off.

But for all the quartet's enthusiasm for, and platitudes about, their new locality, the main question surrounding their appearance in the Faroes was – obviously – *why*?

'It was a good opportunity to get away from Brazil and gain experience in Europe,' said Lucio.

'We want to play well for B68 and be spotted by a bigger European club,' added Marlon. 'If that happens, then we won't say "no thank you".'

'I think they like it here,' says Emil Jacobsen. 'It's a big difference from their own country. When they arrived in January the temperature in Rio was 40 degrees. Here it was around zero. But they have coped well with all the changes and I think that they would all like to stay, given the opportunity.'

While the Brazilians ply their trade on the artificial surface, Toftir's grass pitch plays host to the national team and Faroese club sides' short-lived European campaigns. Built at the height of the Faroese economic crisis, a grass playing surface was essential for the future viability of the FSF. Upping sticks to Sweden every time to play a home match was emptying the Faroese coffers when they should have been filling. Supporters travelling to Sweden were spending money that should have been staying in the Faroes. Toftir provided a timely and much-needed fillip to the Faroese game. It also put the small town on the Faroese map, a map which the Tartan Army were trying to make sense of in order to track down their heroes.

It was a depleted Scottish contingent, more Tartan Platoon than Army, which rolled up in Toftir. Scotland's match against the Czechs in Prague four days later was a top-of-the-table clash, and the difference in importance and in prices between the Faroes and the Czech Republic was enough to convince most of the Scots to choose the latter.

A crowd of over 4,000 filled the stadium, trickles of people coming over the hills from all directions. The atmosphere was one of the most convivial I have ever experienced in international football. The Scots mingled with the locals and the Faroese kept up a barrage of noise thanks, in the main, to Viking-style horns that echoed back from across the bay behind the goal.

As the match got under way, the Scots looked out of sorts and had trouble finding their rhythm. They were fortunate to go ahead after half an hour, Allan Johnston turning in a close-range shot when Faroese goalkeeper Jakup Mikkelsen palmed a cross straight into his path.

The Faroese were looking strong, however, and contained the visitors without too much alarm. As at Pittodrie, though, they had trouble working the ball out of defence and their only clear chance fell to Todi Jónsson, who scuffed his shot when well placed.

The Faroese cause was helped by the unlikely figure of Matt Elliott: following an exchange of words with Jónsson as they awaited a throw-in, he slapped the FC Copenhagen striker around the face. Jónsson went down as if he'd been strafed by gunfire and Elliott headed for the dressing-room, a mouthful of invective from team-mate Tommy Boyd ringing in his ears.

In the second half the Faroese players tried to capitalise on their numerical advantage, but it wasn't until the 92nd minute that burly defender Hans Fróði Hansen – rejected by Motherwell a few months earlier – powered a header past Neil Sullivan and into the bottom corner. The stadium erupted in a cacophony of cheers and horns that would have been heard back in Tórshavn. Tórshavn means 'Thor's harbour', and the roar from Toftir would have been enough to raise the Norse god from his slumbers.

In the injury-time that remained, Uni Arge could even have won the match for the home side; but having burst through the left of the defence, he skied his shot high, wide and out of the ground. Nevertheless this was arguably the Faroes' greatest result since Austria. Tórshavn's only pub had its biggest party for years, as ecstatic Faroese and sanguine Scots partied long into the night. And you didn't need to be fluent in Faroese to understand the headline on the front page of the Faroese newspaper *Sosialurin*: 'HANS FRÓDI SLØKTI SKOTSU!' it crowed, devoting ten pages to coverage of the match.

Four days later the convoy headed for Toftir again. The Faroese had a rare sniff of victory in their nostrils and Bosnia-Herzegovina were to be the victims. Just under 5,000 people turned out to see a thrilling 2–2 draw, and if John Petersen had not seen his second-half penalty saved by FK Sarajevo's Mirsad Dedic, the Islanders would have been celebrating an unlikely four Euro 2000 points in as many days.

After this match I catch up with an ebullient Allan Simonsen. The Faroese coach since 1994, Simonsen has enjoyed a glittering playing career at the pinnacle of the European game with Denmark, Barcelona, Borussia Mönchengladbach and Charlton Athletic. For someone with his pedigree, the Faroe Islands' hot-seat was a curious posting, but it's a job he has taken to with enthusiasm and loyalty. Simonsen is a diminutive figure on the Faroese bench, standing amongst towering substitutes in his hooded tracksuit with a clipboard clutched permanently to his chest. The awestruck respect he has gained from the Faroese players and public is fully deserved, for this week's results have proved what an influence he has been on the Faroese game.

Danjál has told me that the reaction to Simonsen's appointment was euphoria. 'Since we are kind of a Danish colony, we always followed the Danish team before we had our own,' he said. 'Allan Simonsen was a very famous Danish player, so we were very, very happy when he was appointed. He's instilled an attacking philosophy in the team. Previous coaches packed the defence in an effort to keep the score down, but Simonsen has a different attitude – forget about the big names, just play our own way, try to go forward at every opportunity.'

As Simonsen waits to join the squad for their post-match meal, he tells me, 'The Faroese approached me in Denmark and I decided to take the job. The first few matches were disappointing, but I knew it was a long-term project and that we would develop over a period of years rather than weeks. This week has for sure been the highlight of my time as Faroese coach. With a little more luck we would have won both games, but one day the luck will be on our side.

'Results like the Scotland match and today mean a lot to the Faroe Islands,' he continued. 'It's a very big surprise in football when results like that happen. But we have been developing a lot lately and

FACE-OFF: LUXEMBOURG V. BULGARIA, MARCH 1999.

UNDER THE MOON: HRISTO STOICHKOV IN LUXEMBOURG.

ABOVE: CAMPO FILADELFIA, THE HOME OF IL GRANDE TORINO, ABANDONED SINCE 1963.

LEFT: THE TORINO MEMORIAL AT THE POINT OF IMPACT, SUPERGA BASILICA.

TOP: THE FAROE ISLANDS TAKE ON BOSNIA-HERZEGOVINA AT THE TOP
OF A MOUNTAIN, JUNE 1999.

ABOVE: 'WE HAVE TROUBLE ATTRACTING PLAYERS HERE; THERE ARE NO
DANCES IN THE VILLAGE.' THE GROUND OF EB/STREYMUR, EIÐI,
FAROE ISLANDS, POSSIBLY THE MOST BEAUTIFUL FOOTBALL
SETTING IN EUROPE.

TOP: FLYING THE FLAG IN THE FAROE ISLANDS.

ABOVE: LAST-GASP EQUALISER BY HANS FRODI HANSEN (FAR LEFT) TO EARN THE FAROES A MEMORABLE POINT AGAINST SCOTLAND IN TOFTIR.

MATTHIAS SINDELAR, FROM STREET URCHIN
TO THE PRIDE OF A NATION.

AUSTRIA VIENNA (PURPLE AND WHITE) ON THEIR WAY TO A 5–2 WIN
OVER GRAZER AK, SEPTEMBER 1999.

MODERN VIENNA RISES BEHIND THE HISTORIC HOHE WARTE STADIUM,
BIRTHPLACE OF THE *WUNDERTEAM*.

TOP: WASPISH BEHAVIOUR: INTER BRATISLAVA'S PAŠIENSKY STADIUM, A MONUMENT TO SOVIET ARCHITECTURE.

ABOVE: YELLOW FEVER: WHIPPING UP THE ATMOSPHERE AT THE PAŠIENSKY.

I've always known that we are capable of springing a few surprises.'

He sees the commercialism enveloping the Faroese game as good for the international team. 'A lot has changed in Faroese football, particularly over the past three or four years: the game has definitely become much more commercial. I see that as a positive thing, because without the money that has come into the game, I wouldn't be able to do things like taking the players away to training camps to relax before internationals. Without the money, the game couldn't develop in the Faroes.

'With players playing professionally overseas, like Todi Jónsson at Copenhagen and Julian Johnsson at Sogndal in Norway, our team can develop physically and mentally. Plus, they have the advantage of playing regularly on grass – something that they can't do at home.'

Simonsen knows the limitations of a national side drawn from a total population that would only half fill Wembley. 'My hope for the Faroese game is that we can become stable and pull off a few surprises. Ultimately I would like to see Faroese football develop towards the middle of the rankings, but I can't see us qualifying for a major tournament for at least ten years,' he says. 'But if more of our players gain experience abroad then who knows what we might achieve?'

It appears that, like almost everywhere else, the commercial development of Faroese football is irreversible. When they entered European competition the Faroes were unsullied by high finance. Just a decade on, the real world has set up camp on the Islands and refused to budge.

Before I leave the Islands I drive out to Tjørnuvík, to the north. It's an ancient Viking settlement surrounded on three sides by towering cliffs and the fourth by the sea. Today, one light burns in one of the village's few houses. Looking out to sea, it's a straight uninterrupted line to the North Pole. It's midnight. A deep orange stripe of sunlight traverses the horizon between the grey sea and cloud cover like a fiery tear. Picked out in silhouette are the standing stones of Risin and Kellingin, the giant and the witch. According to Norse legend Risin was an Icelandic giant who wanted to bring the Faroes closer to his home. One night he secured a rope to a rocky promontory near Tjørnuvik and, with his wife, a witch, tried to drag the islands to Iceland. The Faroes wouldn't budge, the sun came up and the two would-be thieves were turned to stone.

In the same way, commercialism is attempting to steal the soul from one of the last bastions of sporting integrity. But then again, who would have been aware of the Faroe Islands if they had not ventured into European football? As I drove back through the twilight ready to depart the Islands the next day, I recalled Danjál's words on the subject back in Aberdeen. 'Thanks to the football team,' he said, 'at least people know now that the Faroe Islands are nothing to do with Egypt.'

5.

AUSTRIA: THE LIFE AND MYSTERIOUS DEATH OF MATTHIAS SINDELAR

Vienna's Central Cemetery has a lengthy list of subterranean dignitaries entombed within its walls. Musicians, composers, actors, politicians – and those rich enough to try reversing the maxim 'you can't take it with you' by commissioning ostentatious mausoleums to vanity – are crowded into plots that make up a forest of tombs stretching as far as the eye can see.

The Viennese have quite an obsession with death. The city has the highest suicide rate in the world. There is even a museum devoted to the craft of the undertaker. The Zentralfriedhof is enormous and the grass leading to the final resting-places of Beethoven, Schubert and so on has long been worn away by an endless procession of tourists.

Close to the main entrance, facing a pathway ill trodden by jabbering overseas visitors in search of Vienna's traditional cultural heroes, sits an unpretentious grave. So tightly packed are the graves that it is barely possible to get close to the headstone without stepping on a neighbouring one. From the shiny black marble headstone, a green relief sculpture of a face looks out a little spookily. At the base of the headstone stands a small stone plinth on which sits a sculpted football.

A few dried flowers surround it. Autumn's crinkly brown leaves and a layer of dust coat the marble length of the grave, which is striped by the weak sunshine streaming almost apologetically through the trees; and for a moment I regret not bringing some kind of floral tribute to brighten up the dusty tomb. The name on the stone is legible only to those who know what they are looking for, as it is a chiselled, gold-painted representation of the incumbent's swirling signature.

The man lying in the grave drew over 20,000 people on to the streets of Vienna for his funeral over 60 years ago. In heavenly, magical terms, theatre and music critics had praised his performances in print and in the swanky coffee-houses around the Ring (the circle of linked roads which loops around the centre of Vienna). But this wasn't a great composer, musician or actor, although he was certainly a virtuoso in his own right.

His name was Matthias Sindelar. One of the greatest footballers who ever lived, he was the star of one of the greatest national teams ever assembled and was also viewed as a beacon of anti-Nazism during the early part of the Third Reich. Many people have never heard of him. Indeed, he seems almost to be one of European football's best-kept secrets outside his home nation. Yet throughout the late '20s and early '30s, in the Viennese cafés where poets, critics, musicians and artists gathered to discuss the latest works of high culture, Sindelar's goals were discussed as pieces of high art.

In December 1998, almost 60 years to the day since his untimely death, Matthias Sindelar was voted Austria's Sportsman of the Century. Given that most of those people voting would not even have been born when he graced the pitches of Europe, this accolade speaks volumes for how highly Sindelar is regarded in Austrian, and particularly Viennese, sport.

Matthias Sindelar gave a nation identity at a time of economic hardship and political upheaval. When Austria found itself embroiled in depression and civil war, Sindelar led the national team to the brink of winning the 1934 World Cup. When Austria disappeared from the map following the German *Anschluss* of 1938, Sindelar led a hotch-potch team against the best players of unified German Austria and beat them. However, as the Nazi regime tightened its grip on the nation – just when his people needed him most – Sindelar died. Suddenly and mysteriously.

If anything symbolised the death of Austria and the decline of Vienna as a cultural haven, it was the death of the country's finest-ever footballer. A man of principle, deeply opposed to the new regime, he registered his disapproval in the best way he knew: through his extraordinary football talent.

This talent was honed in the streets of Favoriten, then a working-class district in the south of Vienna. Born on 10 February 1903 in the village of Kozlau, Moravia (now part of the modern Czech Republic), the young Matthias and his family moved to the Austrian capital in search of a better life. The population explosion that increased the number of Viennese inhabitants five-fold, between 1848 and 1919, led to an insatiable demand for new housing: stonemasons such as Matthias's father were assured of work. Favoriten was renowned for its large number of brick factories, and the indigenous population disparagingly referred to the immigrant families who populated the district's warrens of streets as 'Brick Czechs'.

The young Sindelar crafted the incredible skills which were to take him to the top of the world game on the scrubby wasteground of Favoriten. With other working-class children, he would tie up a bundle of rags with string and play endless games of football until the sun had long disappeared behind the belching chimneys and the sky had turned from blue to deep red to inky darkness. Before long, word spread through the district of the extraordinary skills of the sinewy lad with the high forehead and shock of blond hair – how the other boys could not get near him thanks to his balletic poise and lightning reactions. At the age of 15, a year after his father had been killed in action on the Italian Front during the First World War, Sindelar was turning out for the local junior side, Hertha. A troublesome knee injury eventually required surgery, and Sindelar spent the rest of his career with his right knee heavily bandaged. Many have attributed his evasive, intelligent style of play to a fear of receiving a career-threatening blow to the troublesome joint. His performances for Hertha attracted the attention of many clubs and in 1924 Sindelar joined the Wiener Amateure. Two years later the club became FK Austria Vienna.

FK Austria are traditionally the club of the Jewish middle class. Vienna had a burgeoning Jewish population in the early part of the twentieth century. Attracted by the high standard of education available in the city, by 1915 the Jewish population had reached 175,000. Jews dominated many of the professions: in 1936, for example, 62 per cent of Viennese lawyers were of Jewish extraction. Vienna's Jews were the backbone of the city's bourgeoisie, contributing to the famous cultural life of the city – Mahler and Schoenberg in music, Wittgenstein in philosophy and Freud in the field of psychoanalysis.

Sindelar's first season at FK Austria coincided with the introduction of professionalism, pioneered by the visionary Austrian coach and administrator Hugo Meisl. His first season also saw Austria Vienna's first League Championship. Two years later Sindelar inspired FK Austria to another championship.

Sindelar forced his way into the international team against his native Czechoslovakia in September 1926. On his début, Sindelar scored the winner in a 2–1 victory in Prague followed a fortnight later by a brace of goals in the 7–1 mauling of Switzerland in Vienna. In November that year, the striker netted his fourth goal in three matches in a 3–1 win over Sweden; and when he scored the sixth and final goal against Hungary in April 1927, Sindelar had chalked up five goals in as many games.

After that, Meisl appeared reluctant to utilise the FK Austria striker: a B international against Yugoslavia in 1928 and a match against the Czechs in Prague represented Sindelar's only international outings between 1927 and 1931. The Austrian press clamoured for his inclusion and eventually, tired of being harangued by Sindelar's supporters every time he entered the Ring Café – the cultural and spiritual home of Austrian football – Meisl included the FK Austria striker in the team to face Scotland at the Hohe Warte stadium in May 1931.

This match has attained almost mythical status in Austria. Scotland boasted one of Europe's strongest teams at the time and had pioneered the short-passing game favoured by the Austrians. Although slightly under-strength, the Scots arrived in Vienna with a fantastic reputation, whilst Austria had won just two of their previous eight internationals. A 45,000-crowd gathered at the Hohe Warte, in expectation more of seeing a breathtaking Scottish display and defeat for the home side than of witnessing an unlikely victory. But the Austrians ran riot, beating the Scots at their own game and winning 5–0. Sindelar contributed one goal to the total and set up another. Scotland had no answer to the remarkable performance of the Austrians. Those 90 minutes of sheer brilliance were to live long in the memory of all who witnessed it.

Visiting the Hohe Warte today is a sobering experience – in more ways than one, in my case. It's situated to the north of the city at Heiligenstadt, an area better known as the location of Beethoven's house. The great composer's former residence is now a wine-tavern, an institution unique to Vienna. I spend a balmy autumn evening there in the open courtyard, drinking tumblers of coarse, home-produced white wine, while the place where Beethoven wrote his final symphony echoes to the strains of a red-cheeked drunken accordionist roaming the tables performing depressing Austrian folk-songs (which, this being Vienna, are mainly about death). Stumbling back to my *pension* afterwards, I feel that, had the great composer been present at his former lodgings that evening, his deafness would for once have been a very great comfort to him.

The next day, as the hot sun pounds at my wine-shrivelled brain, I return to Heiligenstadt and commence the climb to the Hohe Warte (which doesn't translate as 'highest viewpoint' for nothing). Cursing myself for leaving my crampons at home, and for having those last five tumblers of wine, I circle the stadium almost in its entirety, find a way in, and eventually stand high at the top of the terracing looking down on the old ground. Three-quarters of it remains probably just as it was that day in 1931: row upon row of uneven wooden steps, now infested with knee-length grass and weeds. Along one side of the pitch runs a modern, soulless grey concrete grandstand, for the Hohe Warte is still home to First Vienna, a once-great club now in the lower divisions.

It is easy to imagine this as the Austrian national stadium, full to bursting with ecstatic Viennese as goal after goal went in against Scotland. Even from up here in the 'gods', I can imagine Sindelar's shock of blond hair leaping for crosses. In the distance, above the grandstand, a panoramic view of Vienna's modern towers and skyscrapers opens up through the heat haze. The immaculately manicured pitch looks a little incongruous, set amongst the undulating bowl of terracing strewn with coarse grass, but everything about the Hohe Warte points to the past. Everything except the concrete monstrosity of the grandstand opposite.

That Scotland match saw the official birth of what became known as the *Wunderteam*, a rare flowering of talent which would dominate the game in Europe over the next three to four years. Playing exquisite football, using short passes and intelligent movement off the ball, the *Wunderteam* tore opponents apart with a ruthlessness disguised by their elegant, fluid style.

Sindelar, the most recognisable and highly regarded member of a great team, was prime material for superstar status. Six feet tall, with distinguished features and a muscular physique, he belied his nickname of *Der Papierene*, or 'Man of Paper'. He hypnotised opposition players and spectators alike with his tireless, intelligent running off the ball, his beguiling skills with the ball, and his clinical finishing. He really was a player like no other – blessed with the craft of the skilful centre-forward. Where most teams of the age preferred the physical, direct approach, requiring brawny front-men capable of barging the goalkeeper over the line (sometimes taking the ball with them), Sindelar was the pioneer of a more artistic style. He almost danced the ball into the net rather than thunder in shots at every opportunity. With Matthias Sindelar, brain triumphed over brawn every time.

Sindelar's face appeared in advertisements for wristwatches, milk and yoghurt. He even appeared in a feature film called *Roxy and her Wonder Team*. The Filmarchiv Austria still sells a poster featuring him in its gift shop – displayed alongside images of James Dean and Marilyn Monroe, better-known examples of those who shone brilliantly before an untimely demise.

The *Wunderteam* took on and beat all comers. A week after the Scotland exhibition, the Austrians travelled to Berlin and turned over Germany 6–0, rattling up five more without reply during the return in Vienna a few months later. This was the first match at the newly constructed Prater stadium and 50,000 spectators gathered there to watch Sindelar chalk up a hat-trick against a nation who would become a more ominous foe in the ensuing years.

The Prater today is a modern, well-appointed stadium. It is also home to the offices of FK Austria (although they play most of their matches at the smaller Franz Horr Stadion across town) and seats 49,000 people, but it is dwarfed by the surrounding park, the famous Volksprater on the banks of the Danube. Dominated by the huge Riesenrad Ferris wheel – where Holly Martins harangued Harry Lime above a war-ravaged city in *The Third Man* – a walk through the park to the stadium is a pleasant experience along wide, leafy boulevards. A far cry from approaching, say, the New Den.

At the FK Austria offices I meet Michael Adler, the club's young, enthusiastic *Marketingleiter*. Unlike many modern football marketing executives, Adler has a deep feel for the history of the club, and almost bundles me physically into the boardroom to show me the pictures and trophies accumulated during FK Austria's illustrious history. He opens a drawer to reveal piles of old players' identity cards. They include greats such as Ernst Ocwirck, nicknamed 'Clockwork' by the English after his ruthlessly efficient performances against them. Tossing the cards back and closing the drawer, Adler shrugs and says that the offices are full of fantastic memorabilia like this but there's not the space to display it.

The Prater houses a museum to Austrian football, but this has been closed for a year now. Adler has no idea why. 'Maybe too many people were coming to see it,' he adds, drily. Austrian football is in the doldrums: perhaps the authorities don't want to remind people too much of the glory days. Huge trophies fill the shelves around the dark oak-panelled walls, some of which would surely require three men to lift them. A lap of honour would necessitate enlisting a cart and at least a couple of sturdy horses.

Sindelar's picture adorns many walls, including the main club office. His face gazes down, there, on the club's employees to provide a constant reminder of the true nature of football, lest the club have ideas about selling out.

To some extent they have done so. The famous FK Austria Vienna have been officially titled, for the last few years, FK Austria

Memphis. This is not some bizarre tribute to Elvis (although I wish it was), but a deal with a cigarette firm. The club's insignia is now the Memphis logo with 'FK Austria' written above in significantly smaller letters.

As we leave the office to dine on the inevitable *Wienerschnitzel* at a park restaurant, Adler gestures out towards the pitch.

'Looks nice, doesn't it?' he says. 'Not enough seats, though.' Despite being of a similar size to Wembley, the Prater's capacity is much smaller due, says Adler, to the seats being too big. However, at the time of this conversation, Austria's national side is hardly likely to pull in the crowds, losing 9–0 to Spain and 5–0 to Israel in the Euro 2000 qualifiers. ('Just to remind you, this is football, not skittles,' said one Austrian sports reporter before giving out the Spain result.)

The Prater has been totally reconstructed since Sindelar led the line in the walloping of Germany and is now a smart, modern stadium – one that is used for the FK Austria–Rapid Vienna derby and big European matches as well. In 1995, the Prater hosted the European Cup Final. It's an impressive stadium, but one that seems a little incongruous now that Austrian football is in decline.

The *Wunderteam* had no such worries, and continued to dominate the European game through 1931 and 1932. The home match with Hungary in April 1932 is regarded by many as Sindelar's finest match. Playing back at the Hohe Warte, Austria turned over their neighbours and former imperial allies by 8–2: Sindelar scored a brilliant hat-trick and had a hand in each of the other five goals for a fantastic personal triumph.

In December of that year came the *Wunderteam*'s sternest test: a match in London against the English, who had played just two matches against continental opposition on their own turf (Spain and Belgium), but had seen them off with convincing victories. England's reputation as the nation that gave the game to the world went before them; but in truth they were already lagging behind the rest in terms of technique, training methods and tactics. Nevertheless, England's lofty dismissal of World Cup participation and parochial attitude to the rest of Europe still made them an enigma. As Willy Meisl, brother of Hugo, wrote in his book *Soccer Revolution*: 'What the English could not know was the incredible inferiority complex under which the early continental sides laboured when they stepped on to a British football field. For them it was sacred soil. They were so overawed they could barely put their foot down.'

Such was the interest in the game that loudspeakers were set up on

Vienna's beautiful Heldenplatz, in front of the old imperial Hofburg Palace. Where Austro-Hungarian Emperors addressed the assembled throng from the vast, ornate imperial balcony in the previous century, 20,000 people turned out in 1932 to listen to live commentary of a football match taking place hundreds of miles away.

The *Wunderteam* was only the third foreign nation to be invited to England. And despite their record, when they stepped out at Stamford Bridge, Europe's finest team expected to lose. However, after about half an hour, and having fallen two goals behind, the visitors began to realise that the English team were mortal after all They started playing the flowing football for which they were renowned: the longer the game went on, the more the Austrians dominated, and in the final 20 minutes England barely had a sniff of the ball. Somehow the hosts clung on to win 4–3, but few in the stadium doubted which was the better side.

(England's unblemished home record lasted another 21 years, until Ferenc Puskas and his magical Hungarians waltzed their way into the history books.)

Characteristically Sindelar contributed a fine goal in the match at Stamford Bridge. The referee that day was the famous Belgian Jean Langenus, who had officiated at the first World Cup final two years earlier. He said that Sindelar's goal was 'a masterpiece, which no one has scored against a team like England either before or since. He picked up the ball in his own half, moved up the field in that elegantly elusive fashion before doubling back and hooking the ball into the net with a tremendous shot.'

The Times called Sindelar 'one of the greatest players in the world' and referred to Austria's 'moral victory'. The *Daily Mail* called him 'a genius'. Soon after the match at Stamford Bridge, none other than Manchester United offered the Austrian striker a lucrative contract, but were turned down flat. It would take a miracle to tempt Sindelar from his beloved Vienna.

He was a man of simple tastes who, despite his phenomenal success, continued to live in the heart of Favoriten with his mother, who ran a laundry service from their apartment. Quellenstraße is a long road, a line of latitude across Favoriten. The apartment block at number 75 – where Sindelar lived on the ground floor until the last months of his life – looks from the outside much as it would have done in his lifetime. It's a characterless, architecturally uninteresting building. But then Favoriten was never one of Vienna's most salubrious areas.

Despite the Stamford Bridge setback, and a surprising 2–1 home defeat to the Czechs in April 1933, the *Wunderteam* continued to dismiss all other teams: Belgium by 6–1, France 4–0 in Paris, and Italy

4–2 in Turin. Then a 6–1 victory over Bulgaria sealed a place in the 1934 World Cup where the Austrians were widely expected to confirm their rightful place at the head of the international football table.

Circumstances began to conspire against them, however. Whilst the football team took the nation to new sporting heights, Austria as a country was plunging into turmoil and hardship. In the World Cup year of 1934, unemployment in Austria stood at a whopping 38 per cent. The Austrian Nazi Party, encouraged by native Austrian Adolf Hitler from across the German border, launched a terror campaign which culminated in open civil war as bombs and bullets thudded and zinged around Vienna's streets. The Austrian Chancellor Dollfuss declared the Nazi Party illegal and brought Austria into direct conflict with Germany, whose Chancellor had written as the second sentence in *Mein Kampf*. 'German Austria must return again to the German motherland'. Austrian Nazis assassinated Dollfuss at his desk.

Against this turbulent background Sindelar took the *Wunderteam* to Italy for the World Cup. Such were the financial constraints at the time that the team could not afford to take a trainer or masseur with them; and the late finish to the Austrian season meant that it was a tired and demoralised Austrian squad which struggled to a 3–2 first round win over France in Turin and a narrow 2–1 victory over Hungary in Bologna.

This set up a semi-final tie in Milan with the hosts, Italy. The 1934 World Cup was meant to be a showpiece for Mussolini's regime and the home side was expected to do the right thing and carry off the Jules Rimet Trophy. That year the Italian dictator, then in a much stronger position than Hitler, had mobilised his troops on the Austrian border after the attempted Nazi coup. But no such assistance could be expected on the football field.

Sindelar was up against the notoriously physical Argentine-born defender Luis Monti. They had encountered each other before: two years earlier the Italians had come to the Prater and been beaten 2–1 with Sindelar scoring both goals. His winning goal passed into legend. A corner swung over from the right and Sindelar met it with his head. Instead of powering it goalward, however, he lobbed the ball over the head of one defender, then repeated the trick, nodding the ball over another Italian before heading the ball past the goalkeeper into the corner of the net. It was a goal of impudent genius, one that humiliated the opposition. One of the defenders who had been rooted to the turf whilst Sindelar slipped by to collect his own header was the same formidable Luis Monti.

The big Argentinian hadn't forgotten the incident, and saw this match as the opportunity for retribution. Before the game he told the Italian coach Vittorio Pozzo, 'When I see Sindelar, I see red.'

Heavy rain leading up to the match left the pitch a quagmire, ill-suited to the artistry of the Austrians. Within the first few minutes, Sindelar was rendered little more than a passenger after a robust challenge from Monti. This treatment continued throughout the match, culminating in a sly kick to the Austrian's ribs as he lay prone on the turf after yet another brutal tackle. Exhausted, battered and hampered by the muddy pitch, the *Wunderteam* succumbed to a single dubious offside goal and bade farewell to their chance of crowning their formidable reputation with the Jules Rimet Trophy. It was only their third defeat in nearly four years, though a 3–2 reverse in the third/fourth-place match with Germany followed it four days later. But Sindelar missed the game through injury.

After the World Cup, the *Wunderteam*'s best days had passed, but Sindelar – who had turned 31 during the World Cup – was still Austria's shining light despite his advancing years. In a nation wracked with political and financial problems, Sindelar's performances for the national side and for FK Austria provided valuable respite from the gloom. Unrest continued to grow in the country and the Austrian Nazi party began to increase its influence. Hitler had made no secret of his desire to assimilate Austria into the German Reich; Mussolini gradually withdrew his tacit support for Austria's situation; France was embroiled in political turmoil itself and could offer no help; and Britain said it could provide nothing more than diplomatic assistance in the event of overt German pressure.

By 1938, the *Anschluss*, or reunification, of Germany and Austria was all but inevitable. Schuschnigg had taken over from Dollfuss as Chancellor, but Hitler was gradually turning the screw to allow the right-wing politician Seyss-Inquart into power. This was a man who had vowed not to take up arms against the Germans because he 'refused to spill German blood'.

Feeling shunned by the rest of Europe, and eyeing Hitler's sweeping economic reforms in Germany, the Austrian public gradually came around to the idea of *Anschluss* with Germany. Eventually, in March 1938, Austria was taken over not by military force but by a few telephone calls; and on 12 March, German forces advanced unopposed across the border. Hitler followed soon afterwards, entering the country at his birthplace, Branau-am-Inn.

It is a matter of great national shame to Austrians that Hitler was not so much opposed as waved through Austria on his way to Vienna. There was not one single gesture of defiance, not one bullet, barely a shout of opposition – in fact most crowds cheered and gave the Nazi salute as the Führer's open-topped car travelled further into Austrian territory. At Linz an estimated 80 per cent of the town's populace took to the streets to watch Hitler pass.

On March 15 the Führer appeared on the balcony of Vienna's Hofburg Palace and addressed a Heldenplatz crowd of around a quarter of a million. Where six years earlier, 20,000 spellbound Viennese listened enthralled to their national team giving the English a lesson in football, over ten times that number cheered Hitler's speech which, ominously, did not mention the word 'Austria' once. The Führer addressed the crowd as 'fellow Germans'.

To this day, Austrians are embarrassed to discuss the way in which they greeted their entry into the Third Reich, an occasion which sealed the death of Austria. Two weeks after Hitler's Heldenplatz speech a plebiscite was held on whether to accept German sovereignty. Of an electorate numbering 4,484,000, a total of 4,453,000 voted 'yes' and just 11,000 said 'no, thank you'. Austria's Jews were not permitted to vote.

In hindsight, the Austrians felt isolated. The rest of Europe had apparently turned their backs and 400,000 unemployed in Vienna alone saw Hitler's rhetoric and hard-hitting reforms as the last way out. Little did they realise that this was the end of Austria. Goebbels famously had a map of Europe painted on the wall of his countryside chalet that drew no border between Germany and Austria. The painting had been completed in 1934, four years before the *Anschluss*.

Vienna's Jews, all 175,000 of them, immediately feared for their safety. Anti-semitism had long been a problem in Vienna – as far back as 1897 the politician Karl Lueger had been elected mayor on a ticket which suggested that jobs should be allocated on grounds of racial origin. Before long, Jews were excluded from the professions and universities. FK Austria, with its largely Jewish administration and background, was soon singled out for attention.

There were two reasons why the German authorities had it in for FK Austria. Their Jewish associations were the prime concern, of course. But there was also the fact that the 'Viennese School' of football displayed by FK Austria – which put the more direct, physical Germanic style to shame – rankled with the Nazis who regarded sporting prowess as a major factor in their concept of the 'master race'. Consistent humiliation by Austrians on the football field didn't sit well with Nazi philosophy.

Immediately after the *Anschluss*, the FK Austria board met at the Ring Café to discuss the future. The Reich's anti-semitic stance was already well known, although Hitler's attitude to the Jews had yet to reach the extremes of outright extermination. The largely Jewish board decided that it would be safest if they emigrated as soon as possible, to France or Switzerland. Almost immediately after the Germans arrived in Vienna, the Austrian Nazis had begun plundering and looting Jewish properties. So enthusiastically criminal was the looting that even the German authorities acted to curb its worst excesses.

In time the authorities commenced an organised operation to drive the Jews from Austria. In August 1938 the Central Office for Jewish Emigration was set up in the centre of Vienna, administered by Adolf Eichmann. Within four months 79,000 Jews had left the country, and many more were arrested following the 'Crystal Night' of 9 November 1938, when over 6,500 Jews were arrested in Vienna after the assassination of the German Ambassador to Paris by a young Jew.

Within weeks the players and officials of FK Austria had dispersed. Austrian football attempted to continue some sort of normality. However the overriding difference was that Jews were no longer allowed to compete and Jewish clubs were taken over or closed down – the Viennese Hakoah club, for example, and even the Slav-based Slovan. Hakoah's record was expunged from the Austrian First Division for the 1937–38 season; all the other teams were awarded 3–0 victories.

Hakoah had been formed in 1909 to confront Austrian anti-semitism and confound the prejudicial view of Jews as weak and more interested in money than sport. Hakoah (meaning 'strength') won the first professional league in Austria in 1925. A friendly match with West Ham United in 1922 drew 50,000 people to Vienna to see a 1–1 draw. The following year Hakoah travelled to east London for a return fixture and defeated the FA Cup finalists 5–0.

On 17 March 1938, just five days after the Germans had crossed the border, FK Austria were banned temporarily from competing in the Austrian League. Half the players and most of the officials were planning to leave the country anyway, if they hadn't already done so, and the stadium was requisitioned as a barracks. Jews who wished to participate in sporting activities were limited to playing each other; 'aryans' were forbidden to compete with or against Jewish sportsmen and sportswomen.

The former FK Austria player Hermann Haldenwang, who had long been a member of the Austrian Nazi Party even when it was outlawed by the ill-fated Dollfuss, replaced Michl Schwarz as President. The non-Jewish FK Austria players, who continued to train, recalled that Haldenwang even wore his Nazi armband to training. One of his first moves in charge of the club – renamed Ostmark until public outcry resulted in a reversion to FK Austria – was to replace the portrait of the erstwhile President Schwarz with one of Hitler. However, the remaining officials had the last laugh:

Schwarz's portrait was placed on the back of the Hitler image and the former president was restored to his rightful place whenever Haldenwang left the room.

The new boss was nothing if not thorough. Committee member (and gentile) Egon Ulrich was summoned before Haldenwang one day and told that he had to leave. Ulrich asked if his work had been substandard and was told that he was being dismissed because he was Jewish. Ulrich corrected the President, only to be told that he must go because even if he wasn't Jewish, his name sounded as though he might be.

Sindelar, meanwhile, a committed Social Democrat, was becoming increasingly uneasy about the prevailing climate. His response to being forbidden to associate with Jews was to march straight up to Michl Schwarz and tell him publicly: 'We have been told to not even acknowledge you. I will always give you my time, Herr Doktor!'

Within days of the *Anschluss*, a match to celebrate the reunification of Germany and Austria was organised hastily for the Prater. The Austrians were absorbed into a 'Greater Germany' team, which meant that despite having qualified, Austria would not take part in the 1938 World Cup.

The best Austrian players were assimilated into the German side, with the rest lining up for an 'Ostmark' side. Sindelar had drifted out of the national team, due to his advancing years and recurrent pains in his troublesome knee, and was put in charge of the opposition. He struck a small blow for his beloved Austria by insisting that this team should wear red and white, the colours of the now redundant Austrian flag. But they were warned not even to score a goal against the German side, let alone consider winning the game. Therefore 60,000 people gathered at the Prater not realising that they were supposed to witness a sham of a football match. The reality turned out to be quite different.

Even at the age of 35 it was obvious that Sindelar was still the best player on the pitch. Consistently he danced through the German defence, only to fluff his shot in almost comical fashion – making it obvious to the crowd what his team had been instructed. After he had skied yet another shot high and wide into the crowd from close range, the Viennese finally caught on and the match became a festival of anti-Nazi feeling.

In the second half Sindelar continued his magnificent solo display and finally could stand it no longer. Having hit a shot against the goalkeeper, he curled the rebound delicately into the corner of the net. The stadium erupted. Shortly before the end of the game his team-mate and closest friend, Sesta, launched an impudent lob from 45 yards which flew over the goalkeeper's head and into the back of the net. Sindelar could barely contain his delight. Running to the VIP area, filled with disgruntled Nazi dignitaries, the striker danced pointedly a jig of delight. He had struck a blow against fascism in the best way he knew how – with his nimble feet.

Immediately the Germans sought to take Sindelar to the World Cup, but he was adamantly not interested, crying off with injury or saying he was too old. Essentially, Sindelar did not want to play for Germany. Years later the coach of the German side, Sepp Herberger, said of Sindelar: 'He acted like the great bloke I knew him to be, which was one of the reasons he was so revered in football circles. He asked me politely to leave him out of the squad, and when I asked him again and again, I got the impression that there was more to it than injury and age. I sensed that it was his dismay with and hostility to the political developments that played on his mind and were behind his refusal. Finally I understood, and gave up asking. When I told him, it was almost as if a heavy burden had been lifted visibly from his shoulders.'

Later that year Matthias Sindelar finally moved out of his mother's apartment, taking over a café on Luxembourgstraße (which bisects Quellenstraße in Favoriten). The café had been confiscated from its Jewish owner and, despite the prevailing economic conditions that saw gentiles plunder Jewish businesses, Sindelar paid him the full pre-*Anschluss*, pre-depression market price. The Nazi authorities recorded the fact that Sindelar was reluctant to display their posters, either putting them out of sight or 'losing' them altogether. Friends noted that he was becoming more and more disillusioned. He had lost his two Austrias, the nation and the football club, and his friends and colleagues had been scattered around the continent by the evils of fascism.

On the morning of 23 January 1939, Matthias Sindelar was found dead. His body lay on the bed of his girlfriend of a few days, Camilla Castagnola, who lay dead alongside him. Within hours the police said that the couple had died of carbon-monoxide poisoning from the apartment's gas cooker. Rumours began almost immediately: the Gestapo had murdered him; it was a tragic accident; it was a suicide pact borne of disillusionment with the political climate . . .

The police investigated the possibility that Sindelar was murdered for a further six months, until the Nazis forcibly terminated the investigation. All official records and documents pertaining to the death of Austria's greatest sportsman disappeared soon afterwards and were never recovered. Thus it cannot be known whether the gas tap had been left open, or whether the pipe was leaking.

It's a romantic theory – the great sporting hero committing suicide rather than play for and live under a regime whose politics he abhorred. Certainly the renowned Austrian poet Friedrich Torberg thought so, in his poem 'Auf Den Tod eines Fußbalspieler' ('On the Death of a Footballer'). The poem reads beautifully in the original German, and loses something in translation, but of Sindelar's demise Torberg writes:

> He was always good at tactics,
> And so he thought for days on end.
> His sense of strategy gave him the feeling
> That the gas-tap was his opportunity.
> The gate through which he then passed
> Loomed before him, silent and dark.
> He was a boy from Favoriten,
> And his name was Matthias Sindelar.

The newspapers speculated upon the role of Camilla Castagnola, a half-Jewish former prostitute who had known Sindelar only for a few days when they died together. 'All the signs point to the fact that this fine man, this model sportsman suffered death by poisoning,' said *Die Kronen Zeitung*; 'to find the motive, one must look into the soul of that woman, the only one potentially guilty of this death. However, the mouth of Camilla Castagnola is closed forever.'

Back in the offices of the Prater, Michael Adler pores over a map of Vienna to point out the location of Castagnola's apartment. 'You know,' he says, 'it's a great story, that Sindelar killed himself in opposition to the Nazi regime. But his old team-mate Tomas Stroh once told me a different version.

'Apparently, Sindelar had taken up with Camilla Castagnola after splitting up with a long-term girlfriend. A few days later Sindelar and his former girlfriend decided to get back together and on the night he died, Sindelar had met Camilla Castagnola to finish with her. Stroh said that earlier in the day Sindelar had told him that this is what he intended to do. Maybe she took the news badly and decided that neither of them should live without each other.'

The next day I take a tram, which passes for part of the way along the route of Sindelar's funeral procession, to the Franz Horr Stadion to watch his modern counterparts at FK Austria take on Grazer AK in the Austrian League. The match marks the official opening of a new stand, despite the fact that it has been in use for the last five weeks. Perhaps the fact that it's just two weeks before the Austrian elections has something to do with it. 'We wanted to name the stand after Matthias Sindelar,' says Michael Adler, 'but the city wouldn't allow it – instead it's named after some politician.'

Two politicians in ill-fitting suits perform one of those farcical kick-offs that used to take place before testimonial matches, give extensive interviews to television and depart the pitch waving to a disinterested crowd.

In front of barely 5,000 spectators FK Austria run out 5–2 winners. A blond Austrian international striker with a high forehead scores a memorable hat-trick: a diving header, a goal resulting from a rebound from his own shot and a brilliant solo effort, dribbling through the home defence and rounding the keeper to tap into an empty net. Christian Mayrleb's three goals, of which a certain predecessor would have been proud, provide rare pearls in a poor-quality match.

Vienna's refusal to allow the naming of a new stand after Sindelar is just one proof that the Sindelar legacy is hard to find. Two days after the match I come across the FK Austria 'Fanshop' tucked away off the enormous shopping street the Hauptsraße Landstraße. Wandering in, I am assailed by a variety of souvenirs in the club colours of white and vibrant violet. Alarmingly, there is a CD of songs recorded by the club captain, Toni Pfeffer. The cover is a cartoon representation of Pfeffer crooning into a microphone. I am about to stagger backwards through the door with my arms thrown about my face, when my attention is caught by a coffee cup and saucer set high on a shelf. Through the cellophane I make out a familiar face. Under the words 'FK Austria' and 'Legend' is a picture of Matthias Sindelar, immortalised on Korean-made porcelain. I couldn't resist it. It's looking at me as I write this.

It's not as tasteless as it sounds. Indeed, what better souvenir could there be pertaining to the great man? After all, it was in the coffee-houses that his performances were praised to the skies.

Back at the Zentralfriedhof, I am barely six feet from the remains of one of the greatest footballers ever to pull on a pair of boots. The truth behind his mysterious demise will probably never be known. If anything the mystery contributes to the legend. Little footage survives of Sindelar in action, so his achievements are passed down orally. Later, back in England, Robert Diermair, a fanatical FK Austria fan and archivist, sends me a video recording of what's left, including an extraordinary goal from a Mitropa Cup final against Bologna. The vantage point is high behind the goal, but Sindelar's loose-limbed frame is easy to discern. He sends a looping shot into the top corner from nearly 40 yards.

For those who remember him, however, the great goals become greater with every telling, the runs become ever-more exquisite, the perfectly placed shots gain ever-greater precision. Another defender is beaten with every recounting, shots edge further back with each telling. But those who remember are decreasing in numbers.

Nevertheless, one thing is for sure. Even as the recollections grow foggier, the legend of Austria's finest-ever footballer will remain writ large in the annals of the game. And Matthias Sindelar deserves to be spoken of in the same breath as Vienna's other cultural icons.

The centrepiece of the town's main park is a gold statue of Johann Strauss, the man behind wallpaper music with titles like 'Chit-Chat Polka'. The statue and the composer's visage appear throughout the city. I attend a concert of Strauss music in the Strauss Capelle and become bored almost immediately with the endless 'oom-pa-pa'. The Viennese obsession with the classical equivalent of Black Lace amazes me. As I walk back from the concert (two encores of the 'Blue Danube Waltz' almost have me diving headlong out of the nearest window) through the streets of Vienna, airbrushed faces stare out of election posters. A fortnight later the far-right Freedom Party of Jörg Haider becomes the third-biggest force in Austrian politics. Haider has praised some of Hitler's economic policies and described former Waffen SS men as being 'of great character'.

A few months later, on Sunday, 23 January 2000, a small group of Austrian football dignitaries gather at Sindelar's grave. They brush the dead leaves from the black marble and place a wreath of flowers at the foot of the headstone. Their breath clouds on the crisp winter air as they stand in silent tribute. They come here every year on this day to remember their nation's finest-ever footballer. That morning's newspapers carry reports about the collapse of coalition talks and the latest opinion polls that show Haider's Freedom Party ahead of the rest. If there had been a general election this week, the chances are that Haider – who uses phrases first coined by Goebbels in his political oratory – would have won.

The image of Sindelar's face on the headstone is streaked with rivulets of lime, the legacy of years at the mercy of the Austrian weather. To the people gathered there that day those streaks must have looked like tears.

6.

SLOVAKIA: INDEPENDENCE DAYS

Until the Iron Curtain clanged shut after the Second World War, the people of Vienna looked upon Bratislava almost as a suburb. Now, as the capital of modern Slovakia, this city teeters on the western edge of its nation, a mere 50 miles along the Danube from Vienna. Between the wars the Viennese could hop on a train, spend an evening at the theatre in Bratislava and return home the same night. However, the frostiness of the Cold War gradually ensured that the two cities might as well have been 1,000 miles apart.

When Rapid Vienna made the same journey in September 1999 for the first leg of their UEFA Cup First Round tie with Inter Bratislava, they would confidently have expected to return to the Austrian capital with the same level of contentment as their theatre-going ancestors. Austria's strongest team of the modern era with 30 championships to their name, Rapid were up against the club acknowledged traditionally as Bratislava's second team – a club which has undergone no less than five identity changes since the war, and one suffering from the severe financial restrictions of a struggling game in a young, economically impaired nation.

Rapid's place in the first round of the UEFA Cup came as consolation for their defeat by Galatasaray in the final qualifying round of the Champions League. Inter's progress was a little less glamorous: they reached this stage by defeating the Albanian side Bylis Ballsh over two legs in the preliminary round of the UEFA Cup.

As their club-liveried air-conditioned luxury coach pulls up to the entrance to Inter's Pašiensky stadium for a training session on the evening before the match, Rapid's pampered squad look through the tinted windows at the featureless shallow concrete bowl lined all around with bench seating. So spartan is the ground that I circle it twice before locating the main entrance.

I arrive just as the Austrian players are sauntering on to the pitch, laying out cones and placing markers on the turf. I sit high up in the bleachers with Inter's president, Juraj Oblozinský; the new president of the Slovak Football Association, František Laurinec; and the Slovak national team coach, Josef Adamec. Oblozinský and Laurinec both tell me separately in hushed tones that Adamec once scored a hat-trick for Czechoslovakia against Brazil, a feat likely to secure immortality in any football nation.

We murmur appreciatively at the casual skill of the Austrians, particularly that of Yugoslav international Dejan Savicevic, recently arrived in Vienna from Milan. This is the player Inter fear most. We wander along the benches to where Inter's coach Josef Bubenko sits alone watching the Austrians with furrowed brow, hoping to gain some clue as to their game plan from the half-hearted two-touch games in front of him. If he wanted to be inconspicuous then the startling Hawaiian shirt he's wearing is an ill-advised choice. He grunts the curtest of greetings and offers the briefest of handshakes. He looks worried. He *is* worried: two hours later, on returning to the Inter training camp, he suffers a major heart attack.

After the session I accompany Laurinec and Oblozinský, who is also Laurinec's deputy president at the Slovak FA, to a bar on the other side of the Danube. 'You like to drink beer?' was the first thing Oblozinský asked me when we met, obviously well briefed about English journalists. They make an intriguing double act. František Laurinec is middle-aged with a kindly face and unkempt greying hair. His suit doesn't quite fit his slightly podgy frame.

Oblozinský, however, is a figure in contrast to his president. A fit man in his 40s, tanned and slim, he wears beige casual slacks and a tight-fitting designer black T-shirt. His glasses are also designer. At least I assume they are – they certainly look expensive. We glide into town in his 528 series BMW, the air-conditioning a welcome respite from the hot late-summer Slovak weather. His mobile phone matches the walnut design of the dashboard. 'Nice car,' I comment as we pull away. He just shrugs. Juraj Oblozinský obviously has made a lot of money in the decade since the fall of communism.

We cross the Danube and glide to a halt in a restaurant car park. Emerging into the September heat we take seats at the bar in a restaurant on the leafy river bank.

Laurinec and Oblozinský have taken over at the Slovak FA only recently. Such was the discontent with the old regime that one Saturday many Superliga teams took to the field wearing black armbands, mourning the slow death of Slovak football. The final straw came after the national team's spineless 3–0 capitulation at home to Portugal in the Euro 2000 qualifiers. Laurinec, a former employee of the Slovak FA, and Oblozinský stepped in after the resignation of the previous president. Much is expected of them.

With independence thrust upon it in 1993, Slovak football was always going to struggle. The economic hardship that followed the split with the Czechs, and the absence of matches with the big Prague teams and the large crowds they produced, put the game in Slovakia at an instant disadvantage. Various structures were attempted; the league format seemed to have been tinkered with every season.

'We were not satisfied with how things were going,' says Oblozinský, 'and the public was not satisfied. Everyone had high expectations after independence but reality can be a sad place. We started to implement some changes when we took over, but it's a short time to see results.

'We've changed the organisation of the Slovak FA and founded an Association of Professional Clubs. We're also trying to make a new structure for the league so we will have a ten-club division at the top. We revitalised the national team as well, changing the coaching staff from the first team downwards. It's a difficult process but we're trying to improve everything from the way clubs are organised to training methods.'

As we speak, the Czech Republic are about to complete their Euro 2000 qualifying campaign by winning ten games out of ten. Slovakia, meanwhile, lie a distant third in their group behind Portugal and Romania. 'It's the result of reality,' says Oblozinský. 'Portugal and Romania are strong teams. We try to spring surprises but in reality we are not as strong as they are. Maybe the World Cup qualifiers will bring us more luck, but it depends mainly upon the quality of the team we put out. We've a new generation off the field as well as on it and we hope that this new start can bring in fresh ideas. There are four or five really great national teams in Europe at the moment, but I'm sure that we can give the rest serious problems.

'It is difficult for Slovaks to appreciate the difference between Slovak results and Czech results,' he continues. 'The Czechs happen to have a particularly strong generation of players at the moment, and their football infrastructure is stronger. We must remember that the Czech Republic has a population of ten million, whereas ours is half that. But the success of the Czechs gives us something to aim at.'

Laurinec and Oblozinský are prepared to be patient: theirs is a long-term vision for the success of Slovak football. After all, they have already had one golden age. The Czechoslovakia team that won the 1976 European Championships was predominantly a Slovak one, and Czechoslovakia's only European club trophy success was Slovan Bratislava's 1969 Cup-Winners' Cup victory over Barcelona.

'There is a new generation of young players coming through,' says Laurinec, sliding another bottle of Zlaty Bazant beer towards me.

'Our youth team is arguably the best in Europe and our under-21 team is also very good. The Czech Republic has had great success with their current generation of players, and we are now in the same situation as they were a few years ago. So who knows, maybe Slovakia will do the same as they have.

'There are a lot of young players who could make the national team now, but we are grooming them for the future. Some of these players are the best in their club sides already, so we can afford to be cautiously optimistic.'

With the economic difficulties facing the former communist states, the success of football in Slovakia becomes important in terms of attracting investment and gaining international recognition.

'The Slovak FA is an organisation independent of politics, but it does have a kind of power,' says Laurinec. 'Everybody from our country's president down likes football. It's the number-one sport in Slovakia and success in football has a big effect on the public. We've been successful in other sports such as ice hockey and tennis, and now it's important that football should do the same. The problem is that economic resources here are limited and there is competition between football, ice hockey and tennis for what little sponsorship is available.'

Certainly it appears that the Czech Republic has come off better in most areas – football included – since the 'velvet divorce' of 1993. 'It's funny,' says Oblozinský; 'everybody knew about Czechoslovakia. Some people think it still exists and people still talk about it. Football success would help to show that there is an independent Slovakia. I was on business in the USA recently and there were many people there who didn't know Slovakia existed, let alone where it is. One of our responsibilities in football here is to make progress in public relations and international awareness.'

Inter's games with Rapid Vienna give Slovakia a rare opportunity to shine on the football stage. Progress is important in terms of awareness and also finance. Whilst Rapid represent a big scalp for the taking, the chance to draw a big club from one of Europe's top football nations – Germany, Spain, Italy or England – will also boost Inter's coffers considerably.

It's something that has not escaped František Laurinec. 'The results of these matches are very important for Slovak football,' he says. 'We don't have so many teams taking part in European competition and our clubs cannot afford to bring in players from overseas. So the teams we put out in European competition are almost entirely Slovak. This is a good thing because it gives our young Slovak talent valuable experience in international football, which can only benefit the national team in the long run.

'I feel that there are not enough young Slovak players abroad. We don't have any players in the top European teams, so our national team has no players with regular international experience. I think that I would prefer Slovak players to play regularly for top European teams – it's no good going to a poor side, or going to a big club and not playing regularly.'

At the time of our conversation, only half a dozen players from the national squad are playing abroad, and one of those is at Slavia Prague. Goalkeeper Alexander Vencel is at RC Strasbourg in France; Vladimir Kinder at Middlesbrough; the star of the national team, Peter Dubovsky, is at Spanish club Real Oviedo (but he later died, tragically, in July 2000); Lubomir Moravcik at MSV Duisburg in Germany; and Marian Zeman at struggling Vitesse Arnhem in the Netherlands. Of those players, only Zeman and Vladimir Labant (the one at Slavia) are under 28.

Laurinec's vision is long term. I ask him where he sees Slovak football in ten years' time.

'I'm sure we'll have seen a big improvement,' he says. 'I've stabilised the political and economic situation of the FA and the period of acclimatisation after the split with the Czechs is over. We know what our level is and what it should be and have important work to do with the clubs. Only as a result of long-term hard work will we see results, and hopefully those results will bear fruit on the wider European stage.'

Despite the obvious limitations of being a country half the size of its neighbour, the Slovak public still has problems accepting what they perceive as the great strides being made by the Czechs whilst their own nation appears to make no progress. Juraj Oblozinský is sanguine about the situation.

'After the "velvet divorce" everyone expected the same level of success as when we were part of Czechoslovakia, but reality has set in. Now we are more realistic but realise that the fans still have expectations. The majority of people know we have work to do if we want success – it's not about luck, it's about hard work.

'The Slovak FA is quite big. We have 230,000 members, of whom 170,000 are players – serious numbers for a country like Slovakia. We have made great improvements in schools football and the junior clubs and are able to encourage the good young players to fulfil their potential. We're trying to maintain close relationships with the first division chairmen and attempting to arrange for coaches to gain experience abroad.

'We've organised public forums to gain feedback from the supporters. Slovak football is ingrained in our culture. Go to any village in Slovakia and you'll find a church, a school, a bar and a football ground.'

Eventually our discussion draws to a close. Oblozinský and Laurinec have to return to the Pašiensky for a meeting. As he drops me at my hotel, the sleek car stirring a great deal of interest among the shabby apartment blocks that surround us, Oblozinský enlarges upon the problems facing Slovak football.

'Everything depends upon sponsors. Many clubs in Slovakia are forced to sell players, but Inter is in a slightly better position as we are probably the only club without serious financial problems. We have a good sponsor, and a year ago I managed to sell our midfield player Vladimir Gresko to Bayer Leverkusen. With the proceeds I'd brought in seven new Slovak players within a fortnight. That's the main difference between clubs in eastern and western Europe: money. I've had offers for our players from Spain, Germany and Italy. Peter Nemeth is attracting a lot of interest and he is probably our biggest talent. If he's on form tomorrow night then perhaps we can get a result.'

Riding high in the league, Inter are emerging steadily from the shadow of their neighbours, Slovan, whose stadium is just across the road. Traditional underachievers, Inter's only Czech title success came in 1959 during a spell when they were known as Red Star Bratislava. Since independence Inter have always been there or thereabouts in the Slovak League, but it wasn't until 1998–99 that they posed a serious threat to their city rivals, finishing just two points behind Slovan.

The contrast between the two clubs is enormous. Slovan all but represent Slovakia on the football field. Their crest is a potted version of the Slovak flag, they have provided the bulk of the Slovak national team since independence and they have won the first three post-independence Slovak titles. The Slovak FA even has its office within the Slovan complex. Slovan traditionally have been the biggest club in Slovakia and thus have always attracted investment and support. Slovak Gas, the biggest state-owned company in Slovakia, provides much of the club's funding.

Inter, by contrast, have led a rootless, itinerant existence, changing their name and colours until settling on yellow and black – the corporate colours of oil company Slovnaft, who bankroll the club. Finally, though, with Slovan struggling after the assassination of their and Slovak Gas's president, Inter are emerging as a force to be reckoned with in Slovak football. Top of the league, with Slovan floundering in the chasing pack, this is Inter's biggest opportunity yet to assert themselves in their home city, let alone the nation as a whole. A great deal rides upon the result of the game with Rapid.

With such a short hop from Vienna, the visitors contribute around 2,000 travelling fans to the attendance of 6,500 – a respectable attendance for modern Slovak football. Resplendent in green replica shirts, the Austrians spill out of every bar in the approaches to the stadium.

The Inter press reception area turns out to be an army surplus tent. On the right is a big barrel of cold Slovak beer, and on the left a steaming pot of the best goulash I have ever tasted. Inter are certainly trying to make a good impression on their first foray into the international spotlight.

Inside the ground the atmosphere is noisy despite the comparatively small crowd and open stadium. Inter's *ultras* occupy the flanks of the main stand; Rapid's spread along the opposite touchline.

As the teams emerge on to the field from the corner of the stadium the odds appear to be stacked heavily against the home side. Their coach Bubenko is lying in his hospital bed watching the match on television whilst his assistant Ladislav Petrás takes charge for the biggest game in Inter's recent history. Rapid look confident. So confident, in fact, that they leave Savicevic on the bench.

It's a move that appears well founded as Marek Pensa raps the outside of an Inter post in the opening minutes, a chance he probably should have converted. It's all Rapid as managerless, nervous Inter find it difficult to hit their rhythm.

The score remains blank, however, and Rapid's frustration becomes more tangible as the half progresses – serving only to instil confidence in the home side. As the minutes pass, Inter in their yellow and black shirts are buzzing around the Rapid penalty area like wasps. Just before half-time they win a free-kick 30 yards from goal. Stocky midfielder Marian Lalik steps up and thunders a rising shot off the inside of the left-hand post and into the net. It's a stunning goal, scored on the stroke of half-time – perfect goal, perfect timing – and Inter's fans erupt.

Unsurprisingly, Savicevic is thrown on for the second half, but once again it's the home side who dominate. Rapid have no answer to Inter's relentless attacking and never look like netting a crucial away goal. Only the home side's poor finishing prevents Inter from taking an unassailable lead to Vienna for the return.

It's a great victory for the underdogs and a notable achievement for assistant coach Petrás in the absence of Bubenko. Marian Lalik's goal will be repeated endlessly on Slovak television in the coming days.

Swept up in the celebratory mood of the home fans, I head for the old town. Once there, dodging between rattling trams and descending a dingy staircase, I enter a subterranean bar called KGB, lured by the initials and the sign outside depicting a froth-capped beer-glass. Whilst for many these initials still conjure up images of late-night visits from grim-faced men in raincoats, the abbreviation in this instance stands for Krcma Gurmánov Bratislavy, the Gourmet Club of Bratislava.

It's a favourite haunt of Tomáš Král, Inter's 22-year-old International Officer who has been looking after the Rapid team during their visit and who had offered to show me around town.

The KGB bar is a favourite haunt for Tomáš and I soon track him down: the Rapid beach-towel presented to him by the defeated Austrians as a thank-you for his help is sticking out of the top of his rucksack. The bar is possibly the most flagrant example of how Slovak youth is asserting itself in a post-communist, post-independence atmosphere. A bust of Lenin sits above the bar wearing an American GI's cap and a similar plaster representation of Leonid Brezhnev stares sightlessly at an illuminated advertisement for Gauloise cigarettes.

Where a decade ago their compatriots were toppling Lenin's image from plinths across the nation and setting about him with picks and chisels, the young people of this even younger country have found their anger channelled into dry humour. Not too many years ago nobody would have dared to mock the KGB, let alone lampoon the image of its ideological fathers, but today it's a far more effective statement than raw demolition.

Portraits of long-forgotten stony-faced Communist party digni-taries line the windowless walls of this popular underground den. Slovak pop music thunders out of the speakers, a curiously effective mixture of thumping dance and electronic turbofolk. The conversation shouted above the music is all about Inter's victory; the bar is in jubilant mood. The KGB has the feeling of something new, something daring. Perhaps it's the way that the staff sit cross-legged on the bar between serving customers, or the way the patrons eye me as I try to make sense of the drinks menu with the confident smirk of newly discovered national identity. Oh look, a tourist, bless him . . .

'The revolution took place ten years ago now,' says Tomáš as a portrait of Yuri Andropov looks sternly at me from over his shoulder. 'That means that not all the young people can particularly remember it. Those who can, like me, think that it had to happen sometime. There have been negative sides to it – the mafia, crime, drugs and so on – but there are easily more positives, like freedom of speech, freedom to travel, basically a whole new attitude amongst the younger generation.'

Of all the eastern European cities, Bratislava was always ripest for such developments, more so in fact than Prague. It's always been a multicultural city: in 1918 Slovak inhabitants of the city then known as Pressburg were outnumbered by other nationalities – despite the purges of the fascist Tiso era during the Second World War and the targeting of the Germans after the war. Today it's the Hungarians who suffer prejudice, denied many basic civil rights in a 'backsies' revenge for the repressive 'magyarisation' of the nineteenth and early twentieth centuries. Slovakia's 0–0 draw with Hungary in Bratislava during the Euro 2000 qualifiers was played out under a cloud of simmering hatred.

It's hard to imagine such divisions whilst strolling through the fairy-tale architecture of the old part of Bratislava. Once the capital of the Hungarian Empire, the city was the location of the official division with the Czechs in 1993. The fall of the Berlin Wall and the collapse of communism stoked flames of nationalism amongst Slovaks, who had long felt as though they were second-class citizens behind the Czechs.

After the election of the left-wing Movement for a Democratic Slovakia under the dubious figure of Vladimír Meciar in 1992, Slovakia declared its sovereignty in June 1992. On New Year's Day 1993, the 'velvet divorce' (so called because of its relative lack of acrimony) brought an independent Slovakia into existence and Bratislava was a capital city once more.

As an outpost of the Soviet empire, the city had been spared the worst ideological and architectural excesses of the era. Its proximity to western Europe (from Bratislava Castle, in the heart of the old town, with the aid of a sturdy catapult I'm sure I could twang a pebble into Austria) meant that Bratislavans could receive Austrian television and radio. In effect they were probably the most westernised citizens in the eastern half of Europe before 1989.

But when, in Vienna, I asked someone if there was much rivalry between the two cities, he shrugged and said that the Viennese didn't know much about Bratislava because of the Iron Curtain. Vienna has the third-highest standard of living in Europe, whereas its near neighbour has an unemployment rate of 20 per cent, most of whom have been out of work for a year or more. In 1999 alone, 40,000 jobs were lost in the Slovak construction industry. In such conditions, football has suffered with attendances dropping down into three figures for many top-flight matches. Only games involving Inter, Slovan, the disproportionately well-supported Spartak Trnava and Košice attract anything like respectable attendances.

While most of Bratislava's old town was spared from Stalin's wrecking ball, the legacy of the era is plain to see. Across the Danube from the old town is the district of Petržalka, sometimes referred to as 'Bratislava's Bronx'. Row upon row of identical featureless rectangular apartment blocks line up towards the horizon like vast tombstones. The product of the Soviets' laudable campaign for universal public housing, Petržalka's rank ugliness serves only to emphasise what a jewel the old part of the city is. Yet Petržalka, ugly, faceless Petržalka, is the area where most of Bratislava's fashionably dressed youngsters – now free to hop on a bus to Vienna to stock up on clothes – return after debating music and art in the wine bars and clubs of the old city. Back to anonymity, broken-down lifts and the way things were.

Juraj Oblozinský had shown me the Petržalka stadium, a modern arena with brightly-coloured seats that belied the surroundings. Petržalka is in fact Slovakia's oldest professional football club. They have played here for almost exactly a century, but are some way behind Inter and Slovan in status. Indeed, Petržalka play their matches on a Sunday morning to avoid clashing with Bratislava's big two.

The two sides of the city are joined by the Nový Most, a remarkable concrete construction that bridges the Danube at Bratislava. Constructed during the Stalin era, the bridge's central support pillar leans back like a cobra about to strike. Built to commemorate the 1944 Slovak National Uprising, when the communists overthrew the fascist puppet-ruler Josef Tiso, the Soviet planners drove the approach road through the old Jewish quarter, flattening it entirely. Since the collapse of communism the Slovaks have erected an abstract sculpture memorial on the site of the old synagogue. If you look at it from a certain angle, you can make out the Star of David facing the sky, a nod to the clandestine nature of the Jewish way of life under the Soviets and the Tiso regime. The concrete monstrosity of the Nový Most rising from the Danube above the old bell-shaped towers of the old town will serve as a constant reminder of the way things used to be.

Yet today, and looking forward, Bratislava is like a blank canvas. One can almost feel the excitement about the future permeating through the city's bars and cafés, an international outlook. The city has a vibrant art scene and the centre is littered with impudent sculpture: a smiling man with a huge bald head emerges from a manhole, Napoleon leans on a bench gazing pensively across the main square. At night a green laser is fired from the twelfth-century St Mark's Tower, bouncing around the streets from strategically placed mirrors.

Artistic freedom has been seized with controlled vigour and is expressed in many different ways.

Beneath the Nový Most on the old town side, a wall has been covered with a fantastic graffito-art representation of the new Bratislava. 'THIS IS THE REAL BRATISLAVA' it says, depicting grey Soviet faces under fur hats giving way to colourful images of young people and recognisable city landmarks.

'Bratislava is the capital of Slovakia, so it's the centre of Slovak culture,' says Tomáš. 'We are similar to the Czechs but still different. We're more hospitable, sensible and emotional than they are. Our country is a lot smaller and there haven't been many tourists yet, so it's still easy to feel that you've stumbled on a completely new part of the world.'

Certainly a stroll through the old town is reminiscent of Prague in the days between the fall of communism and its overrunning with tourists. The cobbled central square, the Hlavné Námestie is home to a number of craft stalls and cafés and every hour the clock on the Primate's Palace chimes a melancholy glockenspiel melody.

Bratislava is not all peace, love and understanding, however. When my rickety chair collapses under me in the ubiquitous Irish theme pub – The Dubliner – nobody really takes any notice. A couple of people smirk as I dust myself down, examine the Guinness stains on my trousers and try to put the seat back together again; but otherwise the incident is forgotten immediately.

I learn later that on almost the exact same spot, three weeks earlier, someone else slumped unceremoniously to the floor of this popular bar in the centre of Bratislava. This was no clumsy foreigner, but a young man with blood spurting from a bullet wound to his left temple. Nearby another man lay dead, his brother wounded. The man whose blood mixed with the sawdust and spilled beer where I fell was 26-year-old Tomáš Arnold, out celebrating his graduation. He died a lingering death in hospital the next day, innocent victim of an inelegant mish-mash of mafiosi, blackmail, protection rackets and indiscriminate amateur hit-men that is an unfortunate part of post-communist free enterprise.

When Tomáš Arnold entered The Dubliner, his life was opening up before him. A promising career in finance beckoned, he had an eight-month-old daughter and he'd just discovered his wife was pregnant again. That night he walked inadvertently into Bratislava's sleazy underside. Caught in the crossfire of a bungled gangland hit, he succumbed to the elements of a twilight world in which he had neither interest nor involvement, but which exists alongside the city's vibrant youth culture and developing democracy. But, for a population of just five million which suffers over 12,500 violent crimes each year, the death of a graduate among the fake Irish paraphernalia in the heart of Bratislava's beautiful old city is just another example of the problems facing the ineffectual Slovak government.

Whilst I was in the city, the Slovak Prime Minister changed sides and the newspapers reported a remarkable exchange between two politicians in parliament. A member of the far-right Slovak Nationalist Party, a gynaecologist by profession, attacked a member of the ruling Slovak Democratic Party for alleged drunkenness and public urination. The accused replied that the nationalist should 'stick to what he knows: female sex organs' and went on: 'I could even maintain that I have a better insight to those organs than he has.' And these people are running a country hopeful of joining the EU in the near future.

The financial sector is not faring much better. The state-owned bank reported that, due to a 'miscalculation', the two million Slovak crown profit it reported for 1998 was actually a *four billion Slovak crown deficit*.

The police shrink meekly before the mafia and haven't helped their cause by an apparent disinterest in the rising number of racist attacks by roaming gangs of skinheads. On the day of my undignified tumble in The Dubliner, three skinheads had beaten a Chinese diplomat into a coma on a crowded Bratislava bus.

The skinheads have attached themselves in the main to Slovan. A visit to their Tehelné Pole stadium can often be a little like stepping back in time to The Den, *circa* 1978. Close-cropped youths in calf-high DMs, bleach-spattered jeans and flying jackets adorned with Nazi insignia gather behind the goal. Fortunately for Inter, Slovan's identification with Slovakia means that the skins gravitate there rather than to the Pašiensky.

Another recent incident saw a Peruvian student set upon by thugs at Bratislava's language school. When his friends rushed their injured colleague to hospital the car was soon stopped by police. Faced with a battered and bleeding young man in the back seat, and the students' frantic descriptions of what had happened, the police chose only to fine all the car's occupants – victim included – for not having the correct identification papers.

Tomáš Král himself told me that he had been pulled over for speeding by two policemen a couple of weeks earlier. The offer of a pair of tickets for Inter's next match immediately prevented the incident being taken further.

While bruised students stump up fines for trivial offences and police officers trade amnesties for match tickets, organised crime continues its profitable business largely unchecked. The day after my run-in with the local carpentry I walk across Bratislava's central square. A sleek black four-wheel drive vehicle with smoked windows rolls slowly, confidently and illegally across the cobbles and disappears down a side-street. It isn't hard to guess the nature of its occupants. Two police officers look pointedly in the other direction.

Back in the KGB bar, however, the mood is ebullient. Tomáš is pleased with the result but feels that Inter will come unstuck in the return.

(A few days after my return to England I learn that Inter went to Vienna and won 2–1. 'The best point was that no one from Rapid thought it could happen, but it did!' gushes Tomáš down the telephone. 'It's like Andy Warhol said: everybody is famous for 15 minutes at some time in their life!' In the next round Inter crash out 0–7 on aggregate to the French club Nantes, a tie in which their opponents had just 11 chances over both games. So highly regarded was Inter's short, glorious cup run that for the away leg – when they were already 3–0 down from the tie in Bratislava – the Inter party, including about 50 supporters, travelled on the Slovak government's official aircraft.)

For all its problems Bratislava is a refreshing city to visit. The gorgeous architecture of the old town and the positive feelings for the future of the younger generation, despite the machinations of politicians and the mafia, set the city apart from many European capitals.

Tomáš Král sets out his vision for the future: 'I hope good times are coming for Inter and Slovakia. I hope that Inter can win the championship, that Slovakia will join the EU and NATO, and finally that we get the same chances and opportunities as young people from the west.'

The odds are against Slovak football, with its small population and little available funds for investment. But Inter's short, glorious venture into the UEFA Cup will have given them heart, as will the success of nearby Slovenia in qualifying for Euro 2000 with a population less than half that of Slovakia's. At the end of the season, with Inter winning the Slovak league-and-cup double to earn a crack at the Champions League, that club's efforts – plus those of Messrs Laurinec and Oblozinský, as well as the success of the Slovak under-21 team – may just put Slovakia on the football map before too long.

Before dawn on the day I leave the city, I climb up to Bratislava Castle to watch the sun rise. There's been a fortress on this hill for 1,000 years, and the treaty that divorced Slovakia from the Czech Republic was signed yards from where I am standing. The sky turns from a gloomy darkness to rosy pink, casting a soft light over the steeples and cranes of this historic yet developing city. To my right, across the Danube, the sky over Petržalka is still, appropriately, a featureless grey. Turning around, I look across the ramparts towards Austria. As a new dawn breaks, western Europe opens out in front of me. A feeling Inter Bratislava and the patrons of the Krcma Gurmánov Bratislavy know only too well.

7.

FRANCE: FINE CLARETS AND CHEEKY REDS

When David Trezeguet lashed Robert Pires's cross into the roof of the Italian net in Rotterdam to win the European Championships for France, he executed the strike with a relaxed confidence that mirrored the national mood. With a calm swing of the boot, the Monaco striker bulleted the ball past Francesco Toldo to add the Henri Delaunay trophy to the Jules Rimet-inspired World Cup won by France on their own patch two summers earlier. When the team returned to Paris the next day, football had come home in the truest sense – for if the British invented football, it was the French who set about organising it into the game we recognise today.

From the far-sightedness of Rimet and Delaunay in the early days of FIFA to the all-round perception of Zinedine Zidane, vision has played a major part in French football history and, as we shall see, one small club chairman also has a vision to make his club the biggest in France. That long-term vision, stretching back to the formation of FIFA and UEFA and the creation of the European Cup, reached its zenith at Euro 2000 as France became the champions of both Europe and the world. For once no one could argue with the qualities of the winners.

Half a million French poured on to the Champs-Elysées within minutes of Trezeguet's fizzing strike. Three hours after the ball hit the net, as midnight struck in a jubilant Paris, France assumed the presidency of the European Union. The nation was indisputably number one in Europe. The French economy is booming, and its health and welfare systems are in fine shape. Renault has launched an impudent bid for the Japanese car giant Nissan, while Vivendi, once a run-of-the-mill water company, has just taken over the American entertainment giant Seagram.

With the maximum working week reduced recently to 35 hours, there has rarely been a better time to be a French worker since the nobility were having their heads removed from their shoulders 200 years ago.

It seems that even a higher being was smiling on the French team. An estimated 35,000 gathered at the Place de la Concorde the day after the final to welcome home the champions. The heavens had been wide open all morning, but as the team assembled on the balcony of the Hôtel Crillion the rain stopped, the clouds parted and golden shafts of sunlight became snared in the arcs of champagne being sprayed over the assembled throng below.

'Our victory marks the triumph of a certain conception of the game: had Italy won, it would have taken football back ten years,' said man-of-the-match Thierry Henry. 'We always try to go forward and we play to have fun. Attacking football was the winner.'

Christophe Dugarry, whose noble gallic nose suffered an inordinate amount of damage during the tournament, said: 'There's nothing higher than this – maybe we should all stop now.'

Whilst bearing the presidency of the European Union, France wants to persuade other countries to follow its example in issues such as social rights and welfare. What the French have succeeded in demonstrating is that there is more to life than hard work. Nowhere was this better observed than in the de Kuip stadium that July night. As the Italians knuckled down in laborious style, even as the injury-time minutes ticked away before Sylvain Wiltord's equaliser there was still a perceptible spring in the French step.

But it was in that magisterial strike from Trezeguet that France as a team and a nation was best summed up. It was hit with a mixture of calm assurance and a *joie de vivre* that said if it ballooned out of the ground it wouldn't be the end of the world. And when the ball flew into the net, Trezeguet's expression was a delightful mixture of joy and disbelief: 'Hey, look what I did!'

Fourth Division Calais displayed similar traits when they came within minutes of winning a UEFA Cup place by reaching the 2000 French Cup final. The part-timers were the leading lights of a number of lower-division clubs who had left a trail of bigger clubs in their wake during the French knockout tournaments, in a triumph for football democracy.

In the early hours of an April morning a coachload of boisterous young men made its way through the French countryside towards the French port. The ever-so-slightly sozzled collection of sales-men, students, teachers and gardeners were heading for home accompanied by a soundtrack of clinking bottles and the odd raucous song. This motley collection of tradesmen and businessmen was the Calais team returning from their victorious French Cup semi-final victory over the reigning French Champions, Girondins de Bordeaux.

In an upset equivalent to, say, Harwich & Parkeston beating Chelsea, Calais became the first Fourth Division team to reach the final in the history of the competition. The fact that the victory was achieved 100 miles away from their home town in neutral Lens is astonishing enough. But the achievement is magnified further by the fact that the part-timers scored three goals in extra-time against a collection of super-fit professionals and internationals to reach the final at the Stade de France.

Only one aspect of the fairy-tale didn't go quite to plan: if Monaco had beaten Nantes in the other semi, Calais would already have had a place booked in the UEFA Cup. With Monaco having already clinched a place in the Champions League by winning the French League the previous weekend, their cup-final opponents would have been guaranteed a place in Europe the following season. However, Nantes' 1–0 victory over the champions still left the little club just 90 minutes from Europe.

For the semi-final at Lens' Felix Bollaert stadium, 40,000 fans bought tickets – half the population of Calais. But with Lens having beaten Second Division Cannes and Lille and First Division Racing Strasbourg on their way to the last four, few gave the provincial seasiders an earthly against the aristocrats from Bordeaux.

Goalkeeper Cedric Schille commented before the game, 'We have proved that there is not such a big difference between amateurs and professionals over the course of a single match, but Bordeaux are like an Everest we have to climb. We will try.'

Despite Bordeaux rattling Schille's crossbar shortly after half-time, Calais' stout rearguard helped to keep the match goalless for 90 minutes. Surely, though, the superior fitness of the team that competed in this season's Champions League and featured four players destined to be included in Roger Lemerre's Euro 2000 squad would be decisive in extra-time against the amateurs? The French press certainly thought so – the early editions of the following day's newspapers, which went to press while extra-time was still in progress, reported Bordeaux's progress to the final.

Eight minutes into the first period of extra-time, Calais substitute Cedric Jordeau leathered a clumping 20-yarder into the top corner of the net. Shortly after the turnaround, however, Lilian Laslandes slipped the ball past Schille for the equaliser. Many lesser teams may have crumbled at this point, but within five minutes Calais had regained the lead through Mathien Millieu. With two minutes remaining, Calais' leading marksman Mickael Gerard broke away as Bordeaux threw everyone forward and wrapped up a remarkable 3–1 win.

Club president Jean-Marc Puissesseau gasped, 'I have to keep pinching myself to believe we're in the French Cup final. We climbed aboard the bus in a daze as if we couldn't quite grasp what the team had achieved.' Claude Simonet, president of the French Football Federation, described the result as 'a breath of fresh air for football'.

As the players and officials were treated to a banquet at a local casino until long into the night, Calais' Spanish-born coach Ladislas Lozario mused, 'We have a different concept of modern football, a long way from the big money. But I can assure you that this success won't change anything. We won't get big heads.'

It was an embarrassing defeat for the aristocrats from Bordeaux. Thanks to the wine trade, Bordeaux is one of the most prosperous cities in France and sits on the fringes of the Dordogne, an area popular with British expats. There has been a strong British presence in Bordeaux since the twelfth century, when the future English king Henri Plantagenet married Alienor of Aquitane. Over the centuries gallons of claret have been exported from Bordeaux to Britain. In return we gave them Clive Allen.

In 1999 Bordeaux won the French Championship for the first time in 12 years. Their season had got off to a flyer and their brand of entertaining football was spearheaded by Sylvain Wiltord and Lilian Laslandes, who scored 50 goals between them. It took an 89th minute winner at Paris St Germain on the last day of the season to clinch the title, but most pundits agreed that Bordeaux were worthy winners. At last they were laying to rest the ghost of Claude Bez and the fraud convictions that set the club back several years during the '80s.

In 1999–2000 Bordeaux struggled to recapture their crown, but then French champions never hold on to their titles. The French league is notoriously open, such as in 1997–98 when the title was a two-horse race between previously unremarkable provincial teams Lens and Metz.

In October 1999 Bordeaux faced Monaco at Parc Lescure – their sternest test of the season so far – keen to demonstrate that their 1999 success had not been a fluke. I arrived in Bordeaux to find the boulevards that ring the city clogged with traffic. The prosperity enjoyed by the port in the seventeenth and eighteenth centuries is discernible in the classical architecture and road layout of the city, whilst the Parc Lescure is a monument to a different age. Fronted by a huge arch, the stadium was built in art deco style in the 1930s and was one of the major venues of the 1938 World Cup. Now a national heritage protected monument, the stadium was renovated for the 1998 World Cup and currently seats just over 35,000 people. There's a relaxed atmosphere inside. Bordeaux crowds prefer to enjoy their football rather than work themselves into a frenzy (save for a dedicated band of *ultras* still adjusting to the all-seater nature of the stadium.

The Monaco match was a near sell-out and, fittingly, the two teams produced one of the best matches of the season. Laslandes gave Bordeaux an early lead that Simone soon cancelled out. Within two minutes Laslandes, in the form of his life, had regained the lead for the home side from the penalty area.

The second half was evenly matched until, with a quarter of an hour remaining, Sylvain Wiltord made the score 3–1. Simone replied with five minutes left but the home side hung on for the points. It had been a fantastic game displaying all that is good about French football: quickness of thought, speed of movement, skill and attacking styles from both teams. It was a match to have connoisseurs purring.

However, at the end of the season Bordeaux missed out on the league as well as the cup: vanquished Monaco carried off the title. Meanwhile Calais' run to the final ended in controversial circumstances. In front of nearly 80,000 people at the Stade de France, the part-timers took the lead late in the first half but were pegged back late in the game. In the final minute a Nantes player tumbled over in the penalty area and the referee pointed to the spot. It was a controversial decision, but the top-flight side converted from the spot. There was just time for Calais to hit the woodwork at the other end. The dream was over, but Calais accepted their controversial defeat with grace; the Nantes captain invited his opposite number to collect the trophy with him.

Calais' run overshadowed other great cup performances from lower-division sides – not least those of a suburban Paris team from the third division with distinguished roots and a bizarre plan to become a leading light in the European game.

Imagine if Barnet moved to Wembley. Imagine if the troubled Bees forsook doomed, ramshackle Underhill for the rebuilt, state-of-the-art national stadium. It's a fair bet that even with developers revving their bulldozers and checking their watches outside Underhill, the club hasn't yet entertained that idea. Yet, just three hours from Barnet by Eurostar, such an unlikely situation is a tangible prospect, for tiny Third Division Red Star 93 from the Paris suburb of Saint-Ouen are pursuing a move to the Stade de France. Despite playing to crowds of around 700, Red Star and their colourful chairman are convinced that a move to the national stadium will lead to the historic club becoming a major force in European football.

Formed over a century ago by none other than Jules Rimet, Red Star's history has been one of mergers, financial hardship and lower-division football. There was a brief golden age in the 1920s, when the club became the first team to win the French Cup on three consecutive occasions, but otherwise it's a been a story of struggle for the Parisian minnows.

Despite numerous conglomerations with most of the other clubs in Paris (and even, in the late 1960s, Toulouse – the geographical equivalent of Clydebank solving their current problems by merging with Bristol City), Red Star have survived often against strong odds. In 1978, bankrupt and playing parks football, the club was saved by former player and self-made businessman Jean-Claude Bras, who was to become the pivotal figure in the move to the Stade.

By 1998 Red Star had hauled themselves back up the ranks and reached the French Second Division. The World Cup was galloping over the horizon, the spanking new Stade de France was complete and PSG (Paris St-Germain) were expected to take up residence at the new national stadium in time for the 1999–2000 season. At least that's what the investors in the Stade had been told. PSG had other ideas. A combination of municipal and supporter pressure led to a decision by PSG to stay at Parc des Princes – after all, as the local authority pointed out, if they had moved across town then they would no longer be Paris St Germain but Paris St Denis.

This left the French government with an expensive and embarrassing headache. So sure had they been that PSG would move in, they had agreed to an annual penalty clause of £5 million payable to the Stade's investors in the event that the stadium stood empty. The situation became so dire that there was talk of pulling the ground down altogether.

At this point Jean-Claude Bras threw the Red Star hat into the ring – mooting that his club, pulling in its loyal 700 for home matches, should move into the new 80,000 capacity stadium as part of his masterplan for little Red Star to dominate the French game and take on Europe.

Paris has a strangely apathetic football history. Despite the French and European games having much of their organisational roots there, the demise of Racing Club in the '60s left the capital with no major football club. The creation and rise of PSG and their installation at Racing's old ground, the Parc des Princes, gave the capital a strong club. But it's been a shaky history.

Although PSG are developing a substantial fan-base now, their recent struggles and the lack of a serious rival in the city has left Paris a passionless place in football terms. PSG's 1996 European Cup-Winners' Cup win brought the crowds on to the streets, however, and France's victories in the 1998 World Cup and Euro 2000 produced jubilant scenes reminiscent of the Liberation. But when the fuss had died down and creeping reality set in again, the Stade was empty and little Red Star still held the most feasible bid for tenancy.

A relieved French Sports Minister, Marie-George Buffet, was in favour of Bras' idea provided that financial and administrative criteria could be met. Bras was so convinced his plan would come to fruition that in summer 1998 he released most of the first-team squad and fired the coach in preparation to receive the big names he anticipated would be queuing at his door.

Ten days before decision day, with Bras choosing curtains for his swanky new office at the Stade, the Red Star president was arrested and charged with fraud. Although the charges were unrelated to football, Bras' arrest certainly hampered the club's application. Marie-George Buffet scrutinised the budget put forward by Red Star and reluctantly vetoed the move until the club was on a more sound financial footing.

Hence at the start of the 1998–99 season, Red Star were left without a ground, manager or team for the start of the campaign. The club had quit their historic but decrepit Stade Bauer in their home district of St Ouen and a rapidly arranged move to a stadium close to the Stade de France at least gave them somewhere to play. However, the hastily assembled squad lurched towards inevitable relegation.

Despite the setback of dropping into the Third Division, known as the National, Red Star's move is still palpably on. The potential of the idea was demonstrated by a one-off experiment in 1998. Red Star hired the Stade de France for their home league match with resurgent St Etienne. It was a bold move and one that paid off when 48,000 people showed up – easily the highest attendance in the history of the French Second Division. The size of the crowd demonstrated that there most definitely is potential for another big club in Paris.

If Red Star can tap into the vein created by the 1998 World Cup and Euro 2000 and move into the Stade, who knows what they could achieve? Where they score over PSG is in tradition, for PSG have no history and therefore no traditional fan-base. Red Star has that tradition – at their centenary hundreds of former players gathered on the pitch at the Stade Bauer for an emotional reunion – and to attract nearly 50,000 to the St Etienne match was a phenomenal achievement.

'If there'd been enough of us to make ourselves heard, the regulars could have sung, "Where were you when we were shit?",' joked fan and English expat John Hanson.

In 1999–2000 Red Star signalled their intentions of joining the élite by knocking out three top-flight clubs from the French cups. An astonishing 3–1 victory away at St Etienne (re-established in the French First Division), despite Red Star having their goalkeeper sent off, was followed by a 1–0 win at Sedan in the League Cup. Then a stunning goal from the highly rated midfielder Karim Fellahi was enough to knock Le Havre out of the French Cup.

In the quarter-finals Red Star faced mighty Lyon. Another scalp looked likely when the Parisian club led by a goal to nil with ten minutes remaining, but Lyon burgled two late goals and Red Star were out. It was back to normal in the league soon afterwards.

───────────

Red Star's current home is at the Stade Marville, a municipal sports stadium in a public park on the northern outskirts of the city. Emerging from the St Denis Porte de Paris métro station, the Stade de France looms immediately over your shoulder. The Marville, a 20-minute walk through the run-down suburb, is quite a contrast. The Stade de France was built in St Denis as part of a regeneration plan for the area. Passing along long dark boulevards, with the occasional shop and dingy bar the only signs of life, you eventually arrive at a large public park. Tonight, behind the swimming pool, Red Star face Clermont Foot in the Third Division, a game they need to win to stay in contention for the promotion places disappearing rapidly over the horizon. As I pound the streets along with a small gaggle of Clermont fans – one of whom, it turns out, loves England so much he went to London and bought a black cab – I can see the ground but can't find a way in. A little like Red Star and the national stadium.

Having discovered a rare gate that isn't padlocked, we enter the Parc Marville and make our way into the stadium. It's a soulless place. Low bench seating curves around a running-track and (remarkably in these times) a 12-foot high fence separates the crowd from the arena. Most of the spectators sit high at the back of the ornate grandstand along one side, while the Clermont fans occupy a covered stand opposite.

It's a freezing Saturday night and barely 500 people are in the ground. The visitors, with a huge banner draped over much of the seating, and several drummers, do their best to create some sort of atmosphere; but it's a tall order in a ground that makes even Selhurst Park seem like a hotbed of passion.

The match is dire, the only highlight being the performance of Karim Fellahi, who is head-and-shoulders above everyone else on the field. A mind-numbing 0–0 draw ends Red Star's hopes of a swift return to the Second Division and would appear to put off the proposed move to the Stade as well.

A week later, however, Red Star are again trotting out at the national stadium. Despite their centenary having been celebrated in 1997, the club has hired the Stade de France for a 'centenary' tournament. The programme for the evening sees Red Star play Racing Club in a league fixture, followed by a triangular tournament of 45-minute matches featuring Athletic Bilbao, St Etienne and a team from the Ivory Coast. It's another freezing night, but a crowd topping 30,000 sees Red Star beat their local rivals 2–1 and Athletic Bilbao carry off the Centenary Trophy.

If 48,000 will turn up for Second Division matches, and 30,000 for games in the Third, Hanson and his long-suffering cohorts can only wonder at the crowds who would flock to the Stade to see First Division and European football. Jules Rimet surely would approve. For now, though, there are immediate issues to contend with.

'The priority now is to get Red Star back into the Second Division next season,' says Hanson. 'Although we are still the official candidates for the Stade residency, Racing Club de Paris are seriously trying to move there too. Racing, however, are more laughable than Red Star: their home gates are around the 250 mark, and although they have an outside chance of promotion from the Third Division, there are other clubs in a better position to go up.

'The traditions and history behind the club certainly helped to put bums on seats for the centenary match,' Hanson continues. But other than the occasional burst of sentimentality in the press the *chouchous* for nostalgia tend to be Stade de Reims.

'I think the centenary tournament was a genuine movement of the people of Seine-Saint-Denis, but having St Etienne, Athletic Bilbao and the Ivory Coast helped too. The Marville has a nice setting in the park and the pitch is a wonderful playing surface, but as a football stadium it's hopeless. The stands are too far from the pitch, access by public transport is nearly impossible and there just isn't the same relationship between the fans and the players as there was at the Stade Bauer. The old stadium was part of the legend, the history of Red Star, and basically you don't just piss on your history like the club did.

'Red Star were already due to leave the Bauer temporarily when Bras had a change of heart and decided to launch his campaign to install Red Star as the resident club at the Stade de France. The ground was falling down and no longer met the safety standards of the French football authorities. Some of the stands date as far back as the 1920s. We were originally due to move in at La Courneuve during the reconstruction, but then Bras went for the Stade and the rest is history. Personally, I believe the Stade de France plan is a publicity stunt, but that's just my opinion.

'Bras did after all save the club, investing his own time and money into something he obviously cared about. In my opinion he genuinely loves Red Star and I don't think he's in it for personal financial gain, maybe not even for the ego trip, although it appears that the lofty position of president may have gone to his head a bit. He might have lost touch a little with the regular supporter, but he runs the club as he sees fit. Bearing in mind he's on limited resources, I think he does OK. One thing you can't take away from him is his belief in the Centre de Formation and on bringing youth through. Other than that, he does have vocal opponents on the terraces.'

One product of the matches with St Etienne has been the forging of strong links between the two clubs. It's not quite the bizarre merger with Toulouse ('a marriage of convenience,' says Hanson: 'Toulouse were in the First Division, Red Star in the Second and the club used the misfortunes of Toulouse as a fast-track to the top flight') but the arrangement suits Red Star.

'Basically St Etienne help us out financially,' says Hanson, 'especially with the running of the youth scheme, the Centre de Formation. In return they get first pick from the best of the young players we provide. Not gratis, of course – they still have to pay us – but if two or three clubs are interested in one of our players, St Etienne get first refusal. As well as cash, they'll also lend us players, young players trying to break into the big time who need to gain experience.'

Red Star's cup runs have also boosted the club's coffers. 'We earned around half a million pounds from the cup exploits. Bearing in mind our budget for the season was around one and a half million, this obviously helps us out financially. In terms of kudos the cup runs have got us on the television and in the newspapers and people at work who've shown no previous interest in football chat to me about Red Star and the cups. It's good for the players, too, as it's put a lot of them in the shop window for the bigger clubs. Blackburn Rovers sent scouts to the league cup semi-final.

'Clubs in France operate under strict financial controls, so the cup runs have helped. They've enabled us to continue to improve the Centre de Formation so we can keep turning out players like the hugely gifted defender Abdoulaye Meëté who's now at Marseille – watch out for him.'

Political developments in the city would appear to offer Red Star different options, should the Stade de France plan come to nothing.

'There's a new mayor in the town hall at Saint-Ouen,' says Hanson, 'and a change of stance on the municipal stadium means that Red Star could once again return home. At the moment the Stade Bauer cannot be used at all – all three remaining stands are closed for safety reasons and the thing is becoming a dangerous eyesore.

'However, bearing in mind that Paris could be in the running for a future Olympic Games, there is a possibility that the Bauer could be redeveloped as part of the Olympic bid. Things need to happen soon, though, and it's vital we get out of the National. Red Star remains a professional club; but you can only stay professional for two seasons in the National, then you have to revert to semi-professional status. So with not going up this year, we have to go up next season to remain fully professional.'

From the brink of calling one of Europe's best stadia 'home', to playing in a public park and struggling to cling on to professional status. It's been a crazy couple of years for Red Star, the club so steeped in French football history that they were formed by the game's greatest-ever administrator. Even France's Euro 2000-winning coach Roger Lemerre used to play for them. In summer 2000 they made a big-name signing, 36-year-old Tony Cascarino, who arrived at the club 'determined to win things'. Whatever happens, he's bound to have an eventful time in the red shirt of Red Star.

As French football booms like never before it's a pity to see a club at the very heart of its tradition fall on such hard times. But with the enigmatic and elusive Jean-Claude Bras at the helm, who knows, maybe a Red Star–Marseille European Cup final within the next decade isn't such a mad idea. The chances of it happening rely as much on the machinations of Parisian civil bureaucracy as on events upon the football field, but in French football today the mood is that anything could happen.

'But we'll have to wait and see,' says John Hanson, 'French politics works in mysterious ways . . .'

8.

SPAIN: THE LANGUAGE OF FOOTBALL

The Guggenheim Museum is an astonishing-looking building. The centrepiece of a rejuvenated Bilbao, the titanium-coated jumble of smooth curves and sharp angles sits glinting on the riverbank exuding modernist cool amid the industrial bustle of this city in northern Spain. The titanium plates and curves give the building a scaly, fish-like appearance, architect Frank Gehry's nod to the industry on which Bilbao has developed and until recently depended. Completed in 1997 at a cost of £66 million, or about £37 from every local taxpayer, the museum was designed as much to attract investment to Bilbao as to provide the local population with a major centre of modern art.

As art and architecture critics from around the world salivate over the Guggenheim's extraordinary design, Jeff Koons's 40-foot high terrier constructed from flowers which guards the entrance and the breathtaking variety of modern art within, few realise that the futuristic museum stands on a little piece of football history.

This flat piece of land next to the river Nervión was known previously as *Campo Los Ingleses*, the Field of the English. For it was here in the late nineteenth century that English miners and dockworkers, brought to Bilbao to aid the city's rapid economic development, would meet to play football. The banks of the Nervión provided a rare flat piece of open ground in the crowded, quickly industrialising city hemmed in on all sides by steep hills. Curious locals would gather to watch the foreigners puffing after a leather ball for hours on end; before long Athletic Club Bilbao was formed, adopting the red-and-white stripes of the workers' favourite team, Sunderland.

Yet despite their anglicised name and origins, today Athletic Bilbao has come to represent another nationality: a people craving independence and self-determination who are often described as the aborigines of Europe.

Visiting Bilbao you realise before too long that there's something different about the city. Old men sit outside bars wearing matching dark blue berets, speaking to each other in an impenetrable tongue that no Spanish language student would begin to understand. Road signs are written in Spanish but also in a language which, with its proliferation of Xs and Ks, would rack up record scores at Scrabble. It's a unique language, apparently unrelated to any other which, despite its suppression during the 40-year reign of General Franco, is now spoken fluently as a first language by a third of the population. Nine out of ten children learn the language at school. Men pass their free time playing *pelota*, a sport where players slap a hard ball against a wall with callused, swollen, leathery bare hands. A look into gloomy mesh-covered recesses between doorways often reveals a bright vista beyond, as beret-sporting men loiter in groups and watch others whiling away an afternoon on the public *pelota* courts.

Outside municipal buildings fly the flags of Spain and the European Union, but also a curious flag that looks to be a red, green and white interpretation of the Union flag. This is the *ikurreña*, emblem of the Basque Country, a loose federation of seven regions covering the north of Spain and the south-west of France. An ancient people, the Basques retained their identity and territory undisturbed for thousands of years thanks to the inhospitably mountainous nature of their terrain (even the Romans gave up trying to subjugate the Basques, although 'Astérix the Basque' never made it into comic book history). In medieval times they cornered the whaling market, with Basque ships chasing whales as far as Iceland. There is even a school of thought convinced that the Basques were the first to reach North America. When Columbus eventually arrived a couple of hundred years after the Basques perhaps did, his crew was predominantly Basque. The Basques are proud, industrious and fiercely independent.

Spain was not a unified entity until 1469. However, within that federation of provinces the Basques, Catalans and (to a lesser extent) the Galicians never lost the characteristics that distinguished them from Spaniards. These regions became known as the *nacionalidades históricas* and their legacy still permeates Spanish society.

Basques were always at the forefront of industrial development on the Spanish peninsular, considering themselves to be more diligent and hardworking than the rest. They were the first to establish a banking system when the Banco de Bilbao was founded in 1857. The roots of Basque nationalism reach back through the centuries, but it was during the region's rapid industrialisation during the late nineteenth century that these nationalist feelings were moulded into organised movements. The religion-sparked Carlist wars of the 1870s saw the Basques lose their ancient foral rights that gave them control over their own financial affairs.

Bilbao, the most heavily industrialised of the Basque cities, began to grow and transform. Its population rose from 20,000 to 100,000 between 1850 and 1900 as workers from the poorer regions of Spain gravitated to the Basque provinces in search of work.

Much nationalist sentiment was invested in the indigenous, largely impenetrable language, Euskara. It was Arturo Campión, a writer from the Basque district of Navarro, who asserted in 1884 that 'Euskara is the living witness that guarantees our national independence' and 'will never be enslaved'.

Athletic Bilbao emerged as a major focus and figurehead for Basque nationalism. In spite of its anglicised beginnings, since 1919 the club has operated a strict policy of signing only Basque players. Indeed, one of the early leaders of the Basque National Party, which in its extreme early days opposed intermarriage between Basques and Spaniards and the use of the Spanish language, was José Antonio Aguirre. One of the great figures of Basque nationalism, Aguirre led the nationalist movement to a less confrontational outlook and co-operated with the left-wing movements springing up in Madrid. Aguirre is one of the most significant figures in the history of Basque nationalism.

But between his political activities, Aguirre was also a regular in the Athletic midfield during the 1920s. Fans nicknamed him 'The Chocolatemaker', because of his familial links to a local confectionery factory.

Despite the Basque-only handicap, the club has a long history of success. They have won the Spanish League eight times and the Copa del Rey on a record 23 occasions. Perhaps the dogged determination of the Basques to defend their homeland has had something to do with Athletic producing a string of great goalkeepers. Two of Spain's most famous custodians, José Angel Iríbar (who defended the San Mamés goals between 1962 and 1980) and Andoni Zubizaretta, are Bilbao Basques, as were greats such as Blasco and Lezama. In 1998 the club reached the Champions League, an achievement that assured virtual immortality for Athletic's popular coach Luis Fernandez.

Not a Basque himself (the Basque-only policy does not extend beyond the playing staff), Fernandez was a member of the great French international side of the early '80s before going on to coach Paris St Germain, with whom he won the 1996 Cup-Winners' Cup. He joined Athletic soon afterwards and took them to the Champions League qualifying places at the first attempt. His attacking policy won him many admirers and not just in Vizcaya.

There have been hard times for Athletic, however. In 1936 the fascist leader Francisco Franco staged a swift *coup d'état* in Spain. For the first few months the Basques enjoyed a great deal of autonomy, with Aguirre sworn in as leader of a Basque government in the shade of the legendary Tree of Guernica (the most spiritually important symbol of Basque nationalism). Schools were given Euskara dictionaries and traditional Basque sports were revived.

However, Franco's net widened, and with the help of German troops the dictator invaded the Basque Country. So ill-equipped were the Basques that where the fascists dropped bombs the Basques threw rocks. But the Basques, despite their disadvantages and despite being considerably outnumbered, fought hard against the latest foe to covet their resources and autonomy.

A key moment came in April 1937: German Junkers planes bombed the town of Guernica on market day when the streets were crowded with people. Hundreds were killed, but Franco blamed Basque communists until as recently as 1970. Pablo Picasso immortalised the scene in his painting, *Guernica*. This is one of modern art's masterpieces, but one that has strangely never appeared in the Guggenheim. Its current home, the Reina Sofia Museum in Madrid, claims the painting is too delicate to transport to Bilbao – but many think the museum authorities won't loan it for fear that the Basques just wouldn't give it back.

The Basques dug in around Bilbao after that air attack. Barbed wire and trenches surrounded the city, but after a siege lasting three months the fascists eventually took it. Of 16,000 people arrested as suspected rebels, 1,000 were executed. Thousands of others were deported to German labour camps.

Franco outlawed Euskara. The provinces of Vizcaya, of which Bilbao is the capital, and Guipúzcoa lost all their rights to autonomy. Many Athletic players were killed during the civil war. It was during this period that Athletic and Barcelona became heavily associated with Basque and Catalan separatism.

With the Basque language outlawed, the football ground at San Mamés – known as 'La Catédral' due to its advanced architecture for the time – became a hotbed of nationalism. Athletic matches were the only place where Basques could find safety in numbers and sing Basque songs and hold Basque conversations without fear of arrest. Before each match the players were supposed to give the fascist salute and sing the Francoist anthem, 'Cara al Sol', at the conclusion of which they were required to chant, 'Arriba España, viva Franco'. Unsurprisingly, this didn't happen too often at the San Mamés, where the matches became allegories for the Basque battle for independence from Spain. Real Madrid, the team Franco supported, came to represent the oppressive regime in the eyes of the Basques; even today, Real are assured of a fierce reception whenever they play in Bilbao or further along the coast at Real Sociedad in San Sebastián.

A Euskadi representative team began to tour Europe publicising the Basque plight. For this they were roundly condemned by FIFA, and Athletic – who provided most of the players – were vilified by the rest of the Spanish game, most of which was now controlled by the Francoist military. Atlético Madrid became Atlético Aviación and Athletic were forcibly renamed with the Spanish moniker Atlético de Bilbao. It never caught on.

Amongst Aguirre and the members of his 'government in exile' there was a feeling that Franco's regime was built on shaky foundations and would crumble before too long. However, the dictator was to be rescued by the Cold War. The spread of communism in eastern Europe gave Franco an unlikely ally in the United States which released $62 million of funding to Spain. Soon afterwards Franco's coffers were boosted further by $226 million in return for allowing the US to establish military bases in Spain. Rejuvenated, Franco redoubled his efforts to bring the Basque Country and Catalonia into line.

Between 1956 and 1975, Franco's government had declared 11 states of emergency. Ten had been in the Basque region. At the end of the 1950s the paramilitary group ETA, whose initials translate as 'Basque Homeland and Freedom', commenced its campaign of retaliation against what it felt was the campaign of state terrorism waged against the Basque Country.

ETA's biggest success to date is the assassination of Franco's deputy, Admiral Luis Carrero Blanco, known as 'The Ogre', in Madrid in December 1973. The car bomb that killed Carrero contained 165lb of explosives and was timed to coincide with the commencement of a round of Francoist 'show trials'. The death of Carrero was seen at the time as a major blow against the regime of ageing *caudillo*. In September 1975 Franco had five political prisoners, including two suspected ETA activists, executed – an action which received widespread condemnation. Fifteen European nations withdrew their ambassadors from Spain, Mexico called for Spain's expulsion from the United Nations and the Spanish Embassy in Lisbon was set on fire. At the San Mamés, Athletic goalkeeper José Angel Iríbar – always an outspoken proponent of Basque nationalism – persuaded his team-mates to take the field wearing black armbands.

Within weeks, Franco was dead. But any hopes the Basques may have had for the end of repression were shattered when the newly restored monarchy of King Juan Carlos appointed one of the dead *caudillo*'s henchmen as head of state. Suppression of demonstrations continued unabated. The hated Guardia Civil killed 16 Basques in the first year after Franco's demise.

In 1978 ETA's political wing, Herri Batasuna, was founded, giving a political voice to the paramilitary organisation. Basque separatism received a blow in March 1996, however, when the right-wing Popular Party, whose policies are arguably closest to those of the Franco regime, were voted into a coalition government. Their leader, Jose Maria Aznar, had narrowly escaped death the previous year when ETA blew up his car. There is vociferous opposition to ETA's violent stance, but the movement – which many believe could have a membership as low as 30 out of a Basque population of 2.4 million – continues to draw attention to the Basque cause by keeping itself at the forefront of the headlines.

Since the death of Franco the Basque region has succeeded in wresting back a degree of autonomy from the Spanish state. It has been allowed to run its own treasury and police force. In fact, the Basque region today has more autonomous powers than those devolved to the Northern Irish government by the British.

Athletic are still a tangible symbol of Basque nationalism, even though Bilbao is probably the most culturally diluted city in the region. Wherever you go in Bilbao you won't be far from the Athletic Club crest. A pennant hangs from the mirror of every taxi, every bar has a framed photograph of the team on its wall and even the waiter who served me my *alubias rojas* (a traditional Basque dish made from red beans) in a Bilbao restaurant wore an Athletic pin badge on his black waistcoat. Indeed, as soon as you emerge from customs at Bilbao airport you are faced with a café, a newsagent . . . and an Athletic souvenir shop.

I have come to town for the visit of Barcelona, a match between the two clubs most identified with separatism, on the weekend of the Spanish general election.

The stadium at San Mamés is a major landmark with the huge white arch that spans the length of the main stand visible from most parts of the city. It is situated to the west of town, at the end of one of Bilbao's ramrod-straight main thoroughfares. The huge club crest that adorns the fascia of the stadium can be seen from the heart of Bilbao.

On matchdays, red-and-white-clad fans gather up to three hours before kick-off outside the numerous bars in the surrounding streets, reading the match programme (which is written in both Basque and Spanish) and inspecting the wares on offer at the countless merchandise stalls. Every Athletic souvenir you can think of is available, as well as scarves and replica shirts of the Euskadi 'national' team which had beaten Nigeria 5–1 in a friendly at the San Mamés three months earlier.

The issue of national teams is an important one for the Basques and the Catalans, who also play an annual fixture as a national side, beating Yugoslavia in Barcelona just before Christmas. Catalans and Basques are notoriously cool in their support for the Spanish national team. Both regions have long pressed for their own national sides, citing the existence of separate Welsh, Scottish and Northern Irish sides as evidence that their claims are justified.

The Belgian lawyer Jean-Louis Dupont, the man who defeated the European football authorities as the legal representative of Jean-Marc Bosman, believes that both regions have a strong case and has been preparing a legal document in support of separate national sides. FIFA's own statute book appears to support his case: Article 1.5 states that a 'football association in a region which has not yet gained independence may, with the authorisation of the national association of the country on which it is dependent, also ask to become affiliated to FIFA'.

'I was consulted on the legal aspects of the feasibility of the Catalan project and the political aspect is not my business,' Dupont tells me from his office in Brussels. 'Still, the important political data is that, even if the states oppose, since at the end of the day football is only a private business, FIFA and UEFA have the last word – although obviously they will take into account the views of the states concerned.

'The project is still very active. I've read that the foundation leading the project has launched a public concourse in order to select the Catalan national jersey.

'The legal cornerstone is that international federations are consituted by members. The question here is who can be a member. The answer is that some international federations are "associations covering a territory that has a seat at the United Nations". In other words, these federations, such as the International Olympic Committee, use the classic international public law criteria.

'In other international federation, membership is open to "an association covering a territory that the international federation considers as being sufficiently autonomous in sport matters in order to be a member". In other words, these federations retain their autonomy when it comes to deciding who can be a member, and they refused to be "handcuffed" by international public law. FIFA is a good example of this and has allowed a modern approach by, for example, granting membership to Palestine.

'So in this second case the legal door is open to the likes of Catalonia and the Basque Country to claim membership. However, it must be noted that the international federations falling into the second category could always shift to the first category.'

Barcelona's Spanish international Pep Guardiola said recently, 'I am a Catalan and if there is a Catalan national team, that is where I would like to be.'

Naturally the Spanish authorities are against the move: the Basque and Catalan regions alone account for 20 per cent of the population and, by implication, of the nation's sportsmen and sportswomen. The Spanish Football Federation spoke out against the moves, arguing that as neither the Basque Country nor Catalonia has its own league, they cannot compare themselves to the British nations. Yet Liechtenstein has competed in every international tournament since 1994 despite the fact that it has no league of its own and its seven registered clubs play in the Swiss lower divisions. Perhaps the Spanish are also nervous of the potential strength of the Basque and Catalan sides. Jordi Cruyff was in the Catalan squad. So was Albert Ferrer. For the Basques, Athletic's Julen Guerrero and Jose Etxeberria are both regulars in the Spanish national team. Spain would be crucially depleted at a stroke, should the Basque and Catalans succeed in their secessions.

Catalonia's win over the Yugoslavs could certainly be described as a 1–0 thrashing. The Catalans missed around a dozen chances in the first half alone and, disappointing though the Yuogoslavs were, it was still a result to make the European community take note. In the corresponding fixture last year, Nigeria were seen off to the tune of five goals without reply, whilst in December 1997, the Catalans gained a creditable 1–1 draw with Bulgaria.

The Basques may not have a current crop of players as rich in talent as the Catalans, but the way they demolished the Nigerian side – which was admittedly missing players such as Nwankwo Kanu, Jay Jay Okocha and Sunday Oliseh – gave the Basque supporters hope for the future of their national team. If Dupont succeeds in pushing through legislation granting them permission to field a team in international competition, it will be a major step forward for Basque separatism.

Athletic fan Mikel Fontecha is not so convinced. 'To me, the matches of the *selección* matter less and less with each game,' he tells me. 'I don't feel much for the Euskadi shirt or the Spanish one.

'To me, Athletic is the important thing,' he continues, outside the San Mamés. 'Athletic is everything to Bilbao, you cannot separate the one from the other. Athletic are everywhere in the city. Go to any bar and you'll see a poster, a scarf, a shield or a photograph. You can see here – it's still two hours before kick-off and the party is starting already.

'And a Euskadi team would include Real Sociedad players, whom I hate to death. Well, obviously that's hatred in a sporting sense – I don't want anyone to die – but I'm hoping that Sociedad will be relegated this season. There's a big thing made of how we are all brothers. To watch Basque television coverage of the derby matches, you'd get the impression from the commentators that it's almost like a friendly. But it's nothing like that at all. I'll never go back to San Sebastián to see another derby. They don't give us tickets; then, if you do get in, you're showered with stones and spittle. To beat Athletic is everything as far as they are concerned.'

I ask him his opinion of Athletic's Basque-only policy.

'That's one of the main factors behind Athletic's fanatical support,' he says. 'It's what makes us different from other clubs. OK, it may put us at a competitive disadvantage, but there are many fans here who would rather see us relegated to the Second Division than see a non-Basque or a foreigner in an Athletic shirt. I think a good youth policy can reap great rewards, whatever the club's situation.'

The signing in 1996 of the French Basque defender Bixente Lizarazu (who used to celebrate victories at his previous club Bordeaux by parading the Basque flag) caused outrage among some sections of the club's support. Many feared it would pave the way for the Basque-only policy to be phased out. These fears are as yet unfounded.

Tonight's opponents, Barcelona, present a stark contrast. Although identified throughout their history with Catalan nationalism, Barça have always included a strong overseas presence in their line-up – from Hungarian Ladislao Kubala in the 1950s, through Johann Cruyff, to the modern Dutch contingent. They go into tonight's game fresh from a successful Champions League group campaign and looking to gain ground on leaders Deportivo La Coruña at the top of La Liga.

Despite their political similarities, there is a history of antipathy between the two clubs. This mainly thanks to the challenge by Athletic's Andoni Goikotxea on Barça's Diego Maradona in 1984, which nearly ended the Argentinean's career and earned its perpetrator the nickname, 'Butcher of Bilbao'. An undignified and prolonged verbal spat between then Barça coach César Luis Menotti and his Athletic counterpart Javier Clemente ensured that ill-feeling continued long after the incident. Thankfully relations have thawed a little in the intervening years, although Athletic's fiery coach Fernandez almost came to blows with Luis Figo and Guardiola after a match at the San Mamés in 1998.

San Mamés is a compact, cramped arena, an all-seater since 1997 with a 36,500 capacity. There has been talk of the club leaving La Catédral for a new larger, purpose-built stadium. It surely must be an intimidating place when Real Madrid come a-calling.

Barcelona enter the arena to deafening whistles from the home crowd, a shrieking which intensifies as the visiting players line up in the centre-circle and wave to all four corners of the ground. Athletic dominate the game for long periods, with Julen Guerrero almost opening the scoring with a delicate chip after just three minutes. Guerrero is the star of the Athletic team, a floppy-haired attacking midfielder whose number eight adorns most of the replica shirts worn by a significant proportion of the crowd. On eight minutes, however, Philip Cocu is allowed a free header to put the visitors ahead.

Athletic storm back, dominating the midfield and creating havoc in the space in front of Barcelona's back three. Their competitive and aggressive attacking play seems to unsettle the visitors until Patrick Kluivert races through, from what looks to be an almost comically offside position, to put Barcelona 2–0 ahead. The crowd, who had been roaring the Athletic players on to what seemed like an inevitable equaliser, was stunned into silence.

Despite the linesman having flagged for offside, the referee chooses to overrule him and allow the Dutch striker to run on unchallenged. Orange peel and bottles rain down from the stands 'Referee, you're a Spaniard!' shouts the man behind me. I don't think it was a compliment. At half-time the referee and linesmen are escorted from the pitch by the Basque police in their bright red shirts and berets.

When Barça keeper Ruud Hesp clatters local hero Julen Guerrero outside the penalty area just after half-time, supporters all around the stadium produce handkerchiefs and wave them in the air, a gesture borrowed from bullfighting to request a kill. On this occasion a yellow card has to suffice. The whistling reaches deafening proportions. This is one brave referee. Ten minutes from time Luis Figo adds a third goal and the Athletic fans are stunned into silence. Goatskin bags of coarse red wine are passed around, their contents squirted down throats which not too much earlier were encouraging the home side to a famous victory. Cocu adds a fourth just before the end to compound the home fans' misery. Fans all around me throw their hands up in despair, whilst the Barcelona supporters tucked away in the corner dance with delight and display a huge Catalan flag.

At the final whistle the Barça players and supporters celebrate their first domestic away win for two months. Disconsolate Athletic fans leave quietly and melt away into the streets. 'The result was incredible,' says a stunned Mikel afterwards. 'We had a weak defence tonight anyway, but their first two goals were down to elementary mistakes.' As we speak, Howard Kendall walks past: the former

Athletic manager is back in town to watch his former club in action.

'Kendall was always well-liked here,' says Mikel. 'He left many friends behind when he left Bilbao and often returns. I'll never forget his final press conference. He had tears in his eyes and said that after managing Athletic, any other club would be second best.' I didn't like to tell him that Everton and Manchester City fans have heard similar tearful platitudes.

Bilbao is a compact city hemmed in by steep hills, making most of it walkable. As the crowd disperses I head for Casco Viejo, the old part of town which provides a contrast to the classical lines of the more modern parts of the city. It's a labyrinthine hotch-potch of identical dark, narrow streets where it is almost impossible not to become lost. Fortunately there are plenty of bars in which to prepare another attempt at negotiating the maze of lanes.

This is where Bilbao began in the Middle Ages and the street plan has changed little. Nowadays it's where most of the city's young people congregate to drink long into the early hours. Tonight, on the ubiquitous television in every bar, they have been watching the highlights of the match that ends Athletic's European hopes for this season. It's now time to drown a few sorrows and attempt to work out how the team managed to lose, by four goals, a match they had controlled for long periods.

Meanwhile the rest of Spain awaits the result of its general election. The lack of interest here is almost total. Many locals speak of Spain as if it were a foreign country. The only election posters visible are those put up by the political wing of ETA urging people to abstain from voting: one version shows a Euskadi shirt and a Spanish national shirt side by side, and asks the voter to make their choice.

Tonight aside, the city has a vibrant feel. A city that grew rapidly during the industrial revolution thanks to its rich sources of minerals and industrious locals, Bilbao was until recently an ugly, grimy, graffiti-smeared city with little appeal. A concentrated clean-up operation has revealed its beautiful architecture and plazas that were once litter-strewn and boarded-up are now brimming with flowerbeds. The new metro system, designed by Norman Foster, crisscrosses the city beneath its pavements, passengers emerging to street level from snail-shaped clear domes. And a skeletal new footbridge across the river is lit from underfoot at night, a space-age accompaniment to the centrepiece of the new Bilbao – the Guggenheim Museum.

Earlier that day I am receiving a guided tour of the new Bilbao, a four-hour slog around the streets in the company of the clean-cut, earnest tour guide Mikel, a serious and knowledgeable young man. What Mikel doesn't know about Bilbao architecture isn't worth knowing; and he is justifiably proud of his city.

I learn that the Guggenheim's titanium plates were just two millimetres thick and that they would never oxidise. I discover just when, how and of what the Guggenheim was built. The Guggenheim has come to represent the regeneration of Bilbao, its walkway curving out over the river – once an unpleasant brown fizzing mess of pollutants but now a clean, living waterway again.

Our aching feet arrive at the Iglesia de San Anton, a formidable riverside church on the fringes of the old part of Bilbao. Before Mikel can launch into another monologue involving the gothic and groynes, I nod across the river and ask, 'What's over there?' On the other bank, in contrast to the cleanliness we've seen so far, the buildings are still grime-darkened, with shutters hanging loosely from windows. From many balconies hang white banners with red and black lettering.

Mikel stiffens. 'You mustn't go there, it's not safe,' he says, nervously.

'What do you mean?' I ask.

'It's full of immigrants. Immigrants and drug addicts,' he replies and launches pointedly into the history of the church in front of us.

Later that night I return to cross the bridge and plunge into Bilbao La Vieja, the hotbed of crime from which Mikel warned me away, clutching the address of a friend of a friend. Long, dark cobbled streets lead uphill into the darkness, crowded in by the tall, gloomy buildings looming over our heads. I hope Mikel is wrong. I am soon lost, so I stop a passer-by and ask him if he speaks Spanish.

(A strange question to ask in Spain, but the right question to ask in this part of Bilbao. Indeed, the only time squeaky-clean Mikel's mask had slipped throughout the tour was when we stopped at a bar tinged with the smell of stale marijuana smoke and strong coffee. 'Although it was banned in schools,' he said with a conspiratorial smile, 'when the government officials weren't there, our teachers would give lessons in Euskara'.)

Luckily for me the man in the street does speak Spanish and I am able to track down Ana. A former language teacher turned interior designer, in her fashionable clothes Ana doesn't quite fit in with the drug-addled immigrants at whose hand Mikel seemed certain I would come to a sticky end. Indeed, despite its run-down appearance there is a multicultural vibrance in Bilbao La Vieja – a positive sense of community echoed earlier at the San Mamés.

Warmed by strong Cuban rum, we leave Ana's apartment in the early hours of the morning for a tour of the area. From her window hangs one of the banners I'd seen earlier which call for the transfer of Basque political prisoners to prisons nearer their homeland and families.

We explore the streets, the cobbles shiny from the brief shower of rain that had freshened the balmy evening. As we round corners, hollow-eyed girls with sallow cheeks lurk in shadowy doorways. Members of the Guardia Civil, the military police, stand conspicuously at a crossroads. The embodiment of Spanish rule, the Guardia Civil is not popular in the Basque Country and has been a prime target for ETA. Hence earlier in the day, when I had strolled inadvertently into a military installation across town, I was ushered out politely but firmly by a young soldier with a gun and frightened eyes. Only some fast-talking prevented valuable camera equipment being confiscated.

Ducking into a bar with its shutter half closed, we find it is run by Moroccans of Ana's acquaintance. 'Don't call them Moroccan, though,' she whispers over the top of her beer. 'They come from a part of Morocco that wants to be independent.' This national determinism lark is catching.

Curious to find out more about Bilbao La Vieja and the regeneration of Bilbao as a whole, I ask Ana what provoked the clean-up.

'After the state-sponsored industrial conversion plan succeeded only in closing down many of its industries, the Basque government is trying to give the region a bit of a boost,' she explains. 'They are trying to create jobs and boost income by making the city attractive to tourists and "professional tourists" – conventions, company meetings and so on.'

Indeed my hotel in the centre of Bilbao is packed with business people wearing expensive suits. They are in town for a huge trade fair. In the tourist office the previous day I had heard that there were only 11 vacant hotel beds left in the whole of the city.

'That's all very well,' Ana continues, 'but it tends to overlook aspects of the city which need urgent attention, such as better transport and cleaner streets in areas like this. It's easy to criticise, but the plan has brought in a lot of income to Bilbao and created jobs, although I think the extra employment is a little precarious.

'You said that the tour guide told you to avoid Bilbao La Vieja because it was full of drug addicts and immigrants. There are drug users here, but that's because it's one of the main areas for selling drugs in the whole of Vizcaya. This is in fact one of the safest areas in Bilbao, as borne out by police reports. Yet still people avoid this area because they think it's dangerous. Why should the fact that immigrants live here be a reason for avoiding the area?

'Although racism does exist in Bilbao I'm not sure it's a big problem here. It's hard to say, because until recently there were not many people of other ethnic origins in the city. In the past it is gypsies who have been the victims of racism, but now that more people have come over from Africa it's they who tend to suffer – not just here, but in all the major cities.

'I am involved with an anti-racist organisation here and can tell you that people feel rejected because the government and media always link immigrants to crime and prostitution. Most of the complaints we receive are against the police, the laws and the press.'

Support for independence is strong in Bilbao La Vieja. Cynics may suggest that this is why the region, which sprang up a century ago as a home for the workers labouring at the now long-exhausted iron mines in the surrounding hills, was three years ago the target of substantial investment. The EU-sponsored regeneration project appears to have had little visible effect; but Ana says that whenever pro-independence murals and graffiti go up, where before they would stay up for weeks or months, they are now removed within 24 hours.

It may still be one of the poorer parts of Bilbao, but Mikel's horror appears misplaced. Bilbao La Vieja is hard up but happy, a welcoming ramshackle alternative to the stern architecture and financial bustle of the main part of town. As we walk back to Ana's apartment, the moonlight reflecting from the dark, rain-soaked cobbles looks just as beautiful as that bouncing around the titanium shell of the Guggenheim.

Returning to my hotel, I learned that Jose Maria Aznar's Popular Party had won a clear majority in the election to bring to an end the coalition of the previous four years. It was the first time a right-wing party had won a clear election victory since the death of Franco. The left had gambled on an across-the-board coalition of hard left to centre-left which had backfired spectacularly. Voters in the Basque provinces had turned out in roughly the same numbers as usual, and those that did backed Aznar. The government interpreted this as a resounding defeat for ETA which had ended an 18-month ceasefire a few months earlier with a resumption of its car-bombing campaign.

As the next day drew to a close, I took the funicular railway up the hillside. Looking down through the haze as the sun set over Bilbao, I watched car headlights disappear over the bridge and into the Guggenheim complex. Sitting there then, it was hard to imagine that the gallery sits on the birthplace of football in Bilbao. Beyond the

Guggenheim, the white arch of the San Mamés became gradually invisible as night fell and the bright lights swallowed up the darkening buildings of the city.

There is a Basque saying: *Izena duen guzia omen da.* 'That which has a name exists.'

Having a football team can help, too.

9.

IRELAND: ACROSS THE GREAT DIVIDE

The best view of Derry City's Brandywell stadium is from the raised banks of the cemetery across the road. When the sun is out and you are looking from between the Celtic crosses and obelisks, the pitch looks lush and green, the red seats look bright and the word 'Brandywell' is picked out amongst them in white. Away to the left across the rooftops of the Bogside the old walled city of Derry rises from the rows of closely-knit terraced houses atop neatly manicured grassy slopes. In the background the River Foyle glistens in the sunshine. Out of sight on the other side of the river, and the other side of the walled city, is the Waterside.

Derry, as the city has been officially known since 1984, is divided. Not divided to the extent of total ghettoisation – but, broadly speaking, the river separates the Protestant and Roman Catholic communities. Given that the population of the city consists of 70 per cent Catholics and 30 per cent Protestants (exactly the opposite of the composition of Belfast), the Foyle does not represent an exclusive division. Being in the minority, the Protestant population does have a close-knit feel, even to the extent of kerbstones, lampposts and bus shelters in the Protestant districts being painted red, white and blue to mark out their territory.

Looking across the city, it's hard to imagine that the Bogside was until as recently as 30 years ago virtually a slum, with housing and sanitation facilities dating back in some cases to the eighteenth century. The area and the city have undergone massive changes in the intervening period and there is a feeling of regeneration wherever you go in Derry.

Unfortunately for Derry City, though, the graveyard vista could prove to be an appropriate one. Playing in a foreign country in the most economically impaired part of the city, the club have fought and overcome insurmountable odds in the past. That they have survived into the new millennium is miracle enough. But the financial problems that have been part of daily life almost throughout the whole of their history look set to overcome the famous old club.

Descending from the cemetery, I pay my entrance money and take my place on the crowded terraces. An enthusiastic sun-drenched crowd watches a great game of football with plenty of goals and goalmouth action that at its conclusion sends the gathered throng happily into the nearby pubs to discuss the match. Unfortunately for Derry City, this is Gaelic football and the home side has just comprehensively defeated their visitors from Fermanagh on the Celtic Park ground next to City's stadium.

And here lies the incongruity of Derry City's situation. Although, through their history, they have attracted players and supporters from both sides of the community – unionist and nationalist, Protestant and Catholic – Derry City Football Club's location in the heart of the Catholic Bogside and Creggan districts has always left them associated with that side of the community. Yet next door the Gaelic Athletic Association (GAA, a sporting body closely identified with Irish nationalism to such an extent that members of the British security forces are barred from playing in any match under its jurisdiction) loftily refuses to acknowledge football, dismissing it as the 'garrison game' introduced by the occupying British forces.

In the city the GAA games attract bigger crowds than Derry City football matches. However, football is by far the most popular sport: everywhere you go in the city children chase footballs around the streets, parks and wasteland. Unfortunately for the football club, most of them wear the shirts of Manchester United, Liverpool or Glasgow Celtic and prefer to watch their football on the television rather than at the Brandywell. Indeed, because of the hurling and Gaelic football double-header I have witnessed that sunny Sunday afternoon, the football club was obliged to move their Eircom League of Ireland fixture with Sligo Rovers to the previous evening.

On a freezing night, a loyal band of around 2,000 watched City's hopes of a place in Europe fizzle out during a frustrating 0–0 draw with their relegation-threatened opponents. Derry, in their red and white stripes, dominated a poor but stoutly resolute Sligo side. The stadium, which doubles as a greyhound track, was sparsely populated, but the loyal group of fans kept up a constant barrage of noise and encouragement until long after the match had finished. The ground looked shabby around the edges. Dozens of carrier bags fluttered noisily in the chill wind, caught on the barbed wire surrounding the Brandywell's perimeter wall. It was a scene to be found week in, week out in the lower divisions of the English league: knots of spectators, clad in red-and-white scarves, clumped on the terraces sipping steaming tea from styrofoam cups, linking their fingers around them to keep warm. Lottery ticket-sellers moved amongst them while a crackling Tannoy played scratchy records and boomed out the team changes. Noisy encouragement was mixed with caustic sarcasm and an opposition player became the target of loud booing for a misdemeanour committed in a previous match. On the face of it, all very normal.

In such humble environs it is hard to perceive that Derry City are a unique case in European football – that, because of their location, the troubled history of their city and homeland, and the vagaries of sport in Northern Ireland, the club play across the border in the Republic. They are the only club in Europe to compete outside their home political jurisdiction. A combination of huge expenses, falling attendances and the proliferation of English Premiership matches available on television is conspiring to drive out of existence a club which negotiated their way through the Troubles (even when they were literally on their doorstep), lay dormant for a dozen years and relaunched themselves in groundbreaking fashion. If ever anyone claims that football and politics don't mix, a quick recap of the Derry City story will soon put them right.

Football in Ireland has long been viewed as the secondary sport in the country behind the Gaelic games. Perhaps inevitably, the game's roots lie in the north where British influence was always strongest. Derry City were formed in 1928 and soon became a major force to rival Linfield and the now defunct Belfast Celtic. Linfield, from Windsor Park in the heart of the protestant area of Belfast, have long been identified as a Protestant and unionist club, whilst Belfast Celtic were a fiercely nationalist outfit. Derry at the time fell somewhere between the two – in more than one sense, for in the 1930s Derry finished as runners-up on four consecutive occasions.

Matches between Linfield and Belfast Celtic were always blighted by violence. Celtic even withdrew from the Irish League twice, between 1915 and 1918, and 1920 and 1924, due to the prevailing political climate. On Boxing Day 1948 Belfast Celtic travelled to Windsor Park for a match against Linfield and drew 1–1. However, as the final whistle blew the Linfield supporters swarmed onto the pitch and attacked the Belfast players. Jimmy Jones had his leg broken so badly that he never played again. Within four days Belfast Celtic had withdrawn from the league and folded.

Meanwhile Derry City continued with a board of directors split evenly between Protestant and Catholic members and a policy of signing players from both sides of the divide. Fans were drawn both from the Catholic Bogside and the Protestant Waterside.

However, as the civil rights movement in the city gathered strength, City found themselves at the epicentre of British and Irish politics. The Bogside in the late 1960s was an area of extreme poverty. The unionist government in power at Stormont Castle at the time was heavily biased towards the Protestant population. Protestants were given first refusal for many jobs and important posts in the public sector, whilst gerrymandering ensured that they stayed in power. And enfranchisement was given only to householders, which meant that in Catholic areas especially, where households tended to encompass large families, only a minority of the actual population had the vote.

In order to combat these injustices the Northern Ireland Civil Rights Association was founded in 1967, with cross-community backing. Resisting the influence of staunch republicans, the NICRA organised its first march in the city in October 1968. It was banned by the government and only 400 turned out. Gathering on the banks of the Foyle, the small march crossed Craigavon Bridge and exchanged insults with the RUC gathered at the other end. A bout of pushing and shoving led to a police baton-charge against the marchers, who fled into the city centre and the Bogside, where minor rioting took place. Derry had played Coleraine that day: it was their lowest crowd of the season. The link between the club's fortunes and the politics of Northern Ireland was forged.

A month later 15,000 people turned out in Derry and many more did likewise in cities across the province. The tactic seemed to work. The Stormont government introduced some reforms and promised more, but its heavy-handed repression of similar marches caused the Catholic community to lose faith in the state.

By early 1969 the mood in the Bogside was one of impending anarchy. Unemployment was high, conditions were appalling and the disaffected youth's hostility to the regime was increasing. In April a group of 200 civil rights demonstrators staged a sit-down protest in the city centre. They were attacked by extremist unionists and forced back into the Bogside by the RUC. When the demonstrators fought back in greater numbers, the RUC used water cannon and armoured vehicles in an attempt to disperse the rioters and were in turn pelted with bricks and stones from the top of the Rossville flats at the entrance to the Bogside near the city walls. Over 160 people were injured – half of them police officers – and one civilian died after being beaten by the police.

Ominously, the marching season was approaching. Every July the Protestant Orange Order marches to commemorate the victory of William of Orange over the Catholic James II at the Battle of the Boyne in 1690. A month later the Apprentice Boys march around the walls of Derry to commemorate the siege of the city in 1689, when 13 of the city apprentices closed the gates in the city walls to repel James's army. That seven-month siege is the longest in the history of the British Isles and forms a major landmark in Protestant history. Derry's walls, 17 feet thick and a mile in circumference, resound each year to the Protestant pipe bands as the Apprentice Boys remember the occasion. In the late 1960s houses in the Bogside went right up what are now grassy slopes, almost to the walls themselves. The march was a major flashpoint.

In August 1969 a crowd of 15,000 Apprentice Boys marched around the walls singing the Protestant anthem 'The Sash My Father Wore'. The riots that followed lasted two days. Eventually the Catholics, who regarded the march as a provocative gesture, were forced back into the Bogside and repelled the police who attempted to follow them with bricks and petrol bombs. Barricades went up and, controversially, the British sent in the troops (who have remained in the province ever since). Home rule was suspended.

Against this background Derry City attempted to play football. The 1969–70 season saw many games at the Brandywell – situated deep in the Bogside – postponed or moved to Coleraine over thirty miles away. City's match with Ards three days before the Apprentice Boys march proved to be their last at the Brandywell for two months. Their match at Linfield was marred by violence and the scheduled home match never took place. The following season was a little more peaceful, but matches deemed to be 'high risk' were played at Coleraine. However, in November 1970, Derry were due to visit Linfield's Windsor Park. Understandably, given the prevailing climate and the fact that Windsor Park was in the centre of Belfast's Protestant district, City refused to travel, fearing for their safety.

The Irish Football Association (IFA) said they understood the club's reasons, but awarded Linfield the points and fined Derry £300. However, when Protestant clubs refused to visit the Brandywell they were not fined; nor were City awarded the points. Derry managed to reach the 1971 Irish Cup final, having beaten Linfield at a neutral venue in the semi-final (the aftermath of which was blighted by fighting between rival supporters). In the final Derry were due to meet Distillery, but at Linfield's Windsor Park. Only a couple of hundred Derry fans made the trip and City lost 3–0.

Meanwhile in the Bogside the riots worsened. The Irish Republican Army (IRA) was waging a guerrilla war against the

TOP: RAPID DECLINE: DESPERATE DEFENDING
FOR THE AUSTRIAN ARISTOCRATS.

ABOVE: INTER THE NEXT ROUND: MARIAN LALIK'S WONDERGOAL
BEATS RAPID KEEPER LADISLAV MAIER.

INSET: SAYING IT LOUD, THE PAŠIENSKY SCOREBOARD SHOUTS
THE GOOD NEWS FOR SLOVAKIA.

TOP: BAGUETTING
THERE EARLY: PARC
LESCURE, BORDEAUX.

RIGHT: BASQUEING IN
GLORY: SAN MAMES
STADIUM, HOME OF
ATHLETIC BILBAO.

LEFT: WILL THE REAL JULEN GUERRERO PLEASE STAND UP?

BELOW: THE MAN HIMSELF GOES CLOSE AGAINST BARCELONA.

TOP: NOT BERET IMPRESSED: ONE ATHLETIC FAN RESISTS
THE WARES OF THE STREET TRADERS.

ABOVE: ATHLETIC BILBAO, PRIDE OF A NATION.

TOP: GRAVE EXPECTATIONS: DERRY CITY'S BRANDYWELL
STADIUM, SEEN FROM ABOVE.

ABOVE: SUPPORT AND BRANDYWELL: A GOALKEEPER'S
EYE VIEW OF DERRY CITY.

TOP: LOYAL SUPPORTERS: MUNICIPAL FOOTBALL PITCH BEYOND
PAINTED KERBSTONES IN THE PROTESTANT WATERSIDE AREA OF DERRY.

ABOVE: SARAJEVO GRAVESTONES LEADING
UP TO THE KOŠEVO STADIUM.

TOP: THE 'DIVINE PONYTAIL', ROBERTO BAGGIO, ON
HIS BACKSIDE IN THE NAME OF PEACE, SARAJEVO.

ABOVE: FJORD ESCORT: TROMSØ IL AND FRIENDS
PREPARE TO TAKE THE FIELD.

TOP: FLYING THE FLAG AT THE NORTHERNMOST CLUB IN THE WORLD.

ABOVE: NORTHERN EXPOSURE: POLAR MOUNTAINS AS SEEN FROM TROMSØ'S ALFHEIM STADIUM.

British forces and in an attempt to root out IRA members, the government introduced internment, whereby the police and army could detain people without trial. In July and August 1971 the army rounded up over 450 people for questioning. Predictably, this led to an increase in rioting throughout Northern Ireland. The Bogside became 'Free Derry', a no-go area for the security forces. The narrow streets and tall apartment blocks made the area unsafe for the army and police, and the famous 'You Are Now Entering Free Derry' slogan went up on the end of a row of terraced houses to mark the boundary.

Derry's first match of the 1971–72 season, against Crusaders, was postponed because of the barricades. However, that day a civil rights rally at the Brandywell attracted 7,000 people – enough in the eyes of the IFA to condemn the club as a subversive influence. The Association's attitude to the club had already been demonstrated in their response to the Windsor Park situation.

The IF A has always been associated with unionism, seeing itself as an independent association like those in Scotland and Wales but remaining loyal to Britain. The fact that Derry's stadium had hosted the rally identified the club as a threat to the union and turned the IFA irrevocably against the club; it turned supporters of other Northern Irish clubs, with one or two exceptions, against them as well.

Eventually a match took place against Cliftonville, one of the very few Catholic-associated clubs in the Northern Irish game, but only 200 fans turned out where attendances before the Troubles had been as high as 5,000. In September a young girl was run over and killed by an army landrover and the rioting reached an unprecedented scale around the Brandywell. At one point shots were fired from inside the ground at the army (who returned fire), another example in the football authorities' eyes that the club was inextricably linked with nationalist violence.

The following month the Ballymena United team bus picked its way gingerly through the barricades to the Brandywell. As the game commenced, a fresh bout of rioting erupted and the match took place against a background noise of breaking glass, chanting and the zing of plastic bullets. Suddenly a group of youths ran into the ground, pushed the Ballymena team coach out of the gates and set it ablaze. The match finished with the visitors taking the points, having won 1–0.

It was the last time the Brandywell would stage an Irish League match. For the IFA and the security forces, the Ballymena incident was the last straw. City were banned indefinitely from staging matches at the Brandywell

Derry were forced to adopt Coleraine as their home stadium.

Inevitably attendances plummeted, in some cases to as low as a hundred, and the club faced ruin. A few months later, in January 1972, British troops opened fire on a peaceful civil rights march in the Bogside and 13 civilians were killed on Bloody Sunday. The hostility of the Catholic population to the British forces was sealed.

For the 1972–73 season the security forces gave Derry City clearance to return to the Brandywell. They staged a friendly against Finn Harps, a club from just over the border in Donegal, and greyhound meetings had started again at the ground. However, the club were thwarted by the IFA's refusal to let them return to their home stadium. City knew that unless they returned to the Bogside the club would die. Two home matches early in the season never took place. The dispute went on until Derry issued a threat: unless their match with Portadown on 14 October 1972 went ahead at the Brandywell, they would resign from the league. Even Portadown had informed the league that they were prepared to play at the Brandywell; but the IFA, backed by a narrow majority of IFA clubs, was adamant that the Brandywell would not stage league football. So Derry City quit: the only Northern Irish club ever to reach the second round of the European Cup vanished from the football map.

As the years went by, the Brandywell continued to be used for greyhound racing. However Derry City survived virtually in name only, as a junior team and a social club.

Meanwhile the Bogside has changed beyond recognition. The appalling housing has been removed and smart, clean public housing erected in its place. The Free Derry wall no longer stands at the end of a narrow street. The wall itself still stands but that's all it is – a wall in the middle of a new traffic-flow development.

As I stand nearby, close to the Bloody Sunday memorial, a simple grey obelisk in the heart of the Bogside commemorating the 13 Derry citizens killed in 1972, a small boy passes from behind me. No more than eight years old, he walks briskly with a slight skip in his step past the monument towards the houses beyond. Behind his back he clutches a small bunch of white flowers. He barely seems to notice the memorial, in front of which a single candle flickers inside a jam jar. All he's concerned with is the person for whom he's picked these pure white blooms. They could be for a sweetheart, they could be for his mother; whoever they are for, this juxtaposition of troubled history and excited optimism seems appropriate to the modern city of Derry.

For many people, the names Derry and Northern Ireland still

conjure up grainy television images of soldiers on the streets, petrol bomb-lobbing youths, armoured vehicles and palls of smoke. Yet if you visit the city now, those images might as well be of somewhere a thousand miles away. The tribulations of the football club, with plastic bullets whizzing around during matches, and gunmen holing-up inside, seem unreal today. The dichotomy between popular conceptions of the south and north of Ireland is striking: pints of Guinness versus Martin McGuinness, bodhrans versus bullets. It's a perception that today is increasingly inaccurate and unfair, especially as Derry itself is virtually on the border of the Republic. Indeed, such has been the recent growth of the city (it has multiplied in size sixfold since the '60s) that the suburbs are now nudging the Donegal border.

Derry must be one of the fastest-changing cities in the world. The Bloody Sunday Inquiry, in progress at the city's impressive gothic Guildhall, has had to produce a computer generated 'virtual Bogside' to recreate the area as it was then, as even the street plan has changed beyond recognition. Derry children, generations of whom now have no first-hand memories of the Troubles, study those times as part of their history GCSE. That's not to say that the people want to forget what happened, the search for the truth about Bloody Sunday has been unflinching, but Derry is also developing as a cosmopolitan city relatively free of sectarian trouble.

Nearly half the population is under the age of 25, giving much of the Derry a youthful vibrancy. Bars and cafés are springing up everywhere to provide a lively nightlife and the city's first purpose-built theatre is nearing completion. It's extraordinary to think that a town that produced such literary luminaries as Seamus Heaney and Brian Friel is yet to have its own theatre, but there it is, visible through the scaffolding and sandwiched between two new shopping-centres.

A visit to the city's Workhouse Museum in the Waterside area is a sobering experience. Whole families were divided by gender and set to work, seeing their loved ones once a week at church on a Sunday morning. Startlingly, these Dickensian practices continued until as recently as 1947.

The heart of Derry is within the city walls. As I look between the ramparts across the Bogside, the sun breaks through the scudding cloud, sending a pool of light across the city that scampers over the hills and into Donegal. Impossible to miss from the walls are the vast murals that adorn the sides of buildings in both the Protestant and Catholic areas. Incredible works of art, these enormous paintings are an extraordinary sight commemorating the major events and organisations of the Troubles from the point of view of the people. The Bogside murals are the work of a group of three men known as the Bogside Artists and commemorate, on a vast scale, images of the city's turbulent past.

'In the last six years or so Derry has progressed gradually like someone nudging himself from sleep to wakefulness,' says William Kelly. A graduate of the National College of Art and Design in Dublin, Kelly is one of the Bogside Artists along with his brother, Tom, and Kevin Hasson. 'There is a new optimism abroad brought about mainly by jobs coming into the city and the gradual erasure of the forces of oppression within and without. Things really began to improve when soldiers could no longer be seen on the streets, proving that their mere presence was provocative and antagonistic to Catholics.

'The world has moved on and politicians have finally understood and are running to get on board. The prosperity in the South dubbed the "Celtic Tiger" has also served to whet their appetite for change and prosperity in view of the fact that the old bedrocks of the linen and clothing industries are no longer capable of sustaining the population. The recent order for Harland and Wolff to make four new ships at a cost of £300 million has been the best news all year.'

Walking within the old city, watching shoppers darting through revolving doors and people enjoying lunch in the city's growing number of restaurants, it's hard to appreciate that there is barely a building here that was not damaged during the Troubles. The religious divide is still tangible, but not as insurmountable as it once seemed. A less insular outlook brought about by improved communications and self-esteem has given the city a confident, less divided air.

'There is a change of atmosphere,' says Kelly. 'Protestants and Catholics are beginning to talk to each other again. The Bogside Artists have in fact recently completed a project with Protestant artists from the Waterside area of the city. Not so long ago that would have been unthinkable and impossible.

'The positive feeling is hard to define,' he continues, as I look out from the walls to one of his murals commemorating the civil rights marches – a two-storey high representation of a young woman with a megaphone. 'I wouldn't take it at face value because Derry people are not hard to please. A sunny day here can lift everybody's spirits just as a miserable day can bring us all down. The young people who have no memory of the Troubles had their parents' neuroses and fears dumped on them. Street-fighting among the disenchanted youth here is still a big problem at the weekends. Many young people here are out of work or holding down badly paid jobs. But one feels a gradual awareness developing of a social life that still has the Christian values of concern and succour at its base. Our world becomes more human as a result. In that respect we are getting back to where we were before all hell broke loose.'

The Bogside Artists form just part of a burgeoning arts scene in the city. Currently four more murals are planned and their work has recently toured Australia. 'The new murals will form a unique site,' says Kelly, 'an entire street given over to art, a people's gallery – the "Bogside Modern" if you like. The Bogside Artists have recorded their times in a way that even the most colour-blind misinformed stranger could understand.'

Leaving the walls and passing through the city gates, I happen upon a red shopfront bearing the legend Planet Soccer. The window display mixes Derry City souvenirs with those of Celtic and the Republic of Ireland. As I enter, a boy in front has just asked the man behind the counter if he has any Derry City mugs. 'What, you mean the eleven on the pitch or something to drink your tea out of?' he replies.

'I'm allowed to say that, I'm the goalkeeping coach,' he tells me with a wink. I have happened upon the shop of Eddie Mahon, one of the men responsible for reviving Derry City from its Troubles-induced dormancy. Now grey-haired, with twinkling eyes and a twitching moustache, Mahon signed for the club in 1963 and went on to win an Irish Cup-winner's medal the following year and a League Championship the year after that. He was club captain when the decision was taken to withdraw from the Irish League. Twelve years later Mahon and his associates decided the time was right to revive senior football in the city.

Every season after 1972 City reapplied to the Irish League; every season the application was rejected on security grounds. In the spring of 1984 a new board attempted to find a suitable location for a new stadium. Two possible sites were identified on the Bogside and three on the Waterside. All were rejected by the security forces. In desperation the city council turned to the then Northern Ireland Secretary Jim Prior, but he claimed he was unable to interfere in RUC matters.

'In 1984 three other ex-players and I decided it was time for senior football to return to Derry,' says Mahon. 'It was obviously out of the question to play in Northern Ireland, so we made an application to the Football Association of Ireland.'

It had been an idea first aired soon after the withdrawal from the Irish League, but given little credence. There had never been a case of a club playing its matches in a foreign league. One stumbling block to the application was that the FAI could not consider the bid without City being released by the IFA. In addition, smaller clubs in the Republic might have been put out if Derry were seen to jump the queue straight into the top flight.

However, plans were already afoot to restructure the League of Ireland for the start of the 1985–86 season, circumventing that problem. Once the IFA released the club, the FAI accepted City's application and they took their place in the league's new ten-club second division. Senior football had returned to Northern Ireland's second city.

'When the club came back to football there was a great deal of euphoria,' recalls Mahon. 'That coupled with the fact that we had players from Brazil, South Africa, France and Scotland gave the whole thing an unreal atmosphere and brought the crowds out in their thousands.'

In September 1985 Derry City, featuring former Manchester City player Dennis Tueart in the side, took the field for their first competitive home match at the Brandywell since the burning of the Ballymena bus. The veteran midfielder inspired the home side to a 3–1 win over Dublin side Home Farm in front of an ecstatic Brandywell crowd of over 7,000. Within two seasons City had won promotion and in 1988–89 they achieved a League and Cup double which led to the visit of Portuguese giants Benfica in the European Cup the following season.

Inevitable decline set in, however. The novelty slowly wore off and City went into financial decline. The league was won again in 1997 but team boss Felix Healy warned that the party was over for the club: the financial stresses of playing across the border, the competition from televised football and the stale nature of Irish League football were taking their toll. The club was forced to cut wages drastically and release non-local players in an effort to reduce outgoings. The year after their 1997 title, Derry avoided a relegation play-off by a single point. Since then they have hovered in the middle of the table.

In April 2000 Derry chairman Kevin Friel – who was tragically killed in a road accident in Donegal three months later – revealed that the club's financial situation was growing steadily worse. Without a social club the football club relies on gate receipts for the majority of its income, and £2,000 every other week is not enough to run a top-flight outfit.

'For Derry City to survive, the business community and local supporters must return to the Brandywell,' said Friel to the *Derry Journal*. 'People have a choice: come to support us or stay away. But if they continue to stay away, there will be no senior club in this city. I can't put it any simpler than that – our situation is serious.

'Current board members are not well-to-do people,' he continued. 'As much as I would be delighted to act as guarantor for a loan I can't. Banks demand security for a loan and I could not and would not do that on my family, and I wouldn't expect any of my colleagues on the board to do so either.'

In early 2000, however, as the Northern Irish Assembly gathered at Stormont and old foes shared the political chamber, Derry City received planning permission for a new £750,000 stand. The nature of the modern game being what it is, it will contain more corporate facilities than seats, but when the ground is not in use these lounges will become the base for Derry City's new community scheme. In an attempt to bring young players through, City have created an independent Lottery-supported trust whereby young players will spend time working in the community when not training or playing. Their wages for community work will come from the trust – in effect meaning Derry will have full-time players to whom they pay part-time wages, the shortfall coming from the community trust. The scheme also aims to raise awareness of the club in the city, and to double the club's current average gate of around 1,500 within the next couple of years.

———————————

However, on that freezing evening against Sligo, such grandiose plans seem a long way off. You know you're at a club with financial problems when they announce the gate receipts over the Tannoy at half-time instead of the crowd figure. When that figure raises the loudest applause of the night, things must be bad.

The result effectively denies Derry a crack at Europe. At the end of the game, long-standing Derry fan Niall Conway is sanguine about the situation facing the club.

'Qualification for Europe would be such a morale booster for everyone here,' he says with an air of disappointment. 'Financially it wouldn't bring a huge payday to the club, as the days of drawing any big European names are over. Yet it would put into perspective what the club has managed to do this season on a tight budget. If nothing else, playing in Europe is good PR for the club, something we could do with at the moment.'

Derry's crowds may not be what they once were, but the band that do turn up give the team an extraordinary backing. If only a few more would turn out and show similar loyalty to their city's football club.

'Yes, the fans – and I mean the true fans, the hard core that turn up week in, week out – have been magnificent. The level of noise has increased recently, almost in defiance of the armchair supporter at home in front of Sky Sports. We all need to get behind the club, both vocally and financially, and ensure that it has a future.

'I think that a town the size of Derry with its long footballing tradition deserves a senior club without a doubt. The problem of attracting people to the games isn't unique to Derry City, it's a story which is repeated all across Ireland. The local game is in decline, unable to compete with the English and Scottish football on the television.'

I ask him whether the club draws its support from both sides of the community, or whether part of the problem may be that the club is still carrying its image as a Catholic outfit.

'Derry's support would be mainly but not exclusively Catholic. From its inception the club has been a cross-community one, although the demographics of the city dictate that the support is predominantly from one section of the community. The "garrison game" mentality has never been that strong in Derry – it's been traditionally a footballing town. There is still a lot of interest in the club in the area. For example, everyone seems to have an opinion on what is wrong with the club and what should be done to fix it. I run the Derry City website and there is a really strong feeling for the club amongst the expat community. I just wish it could be matched by those closer to home.

'It's hard to define exactly what has caused the decline in support. The level of support was bound to decrease after the first few seasons. That's only natural, as the novelty was bound to wear off, but no one expected it to be as bad as this. The increase in coverage of football from across the water must be a major factor. For most people the thought of watching your local team from a cold terrace comes a poor second to sitting in a warm pub with a beer watching Sky's slick coverage. As the English Premiership has gone from strength to strength the smaller clubs have suffered.

'If we can get this new stand built and the new community scheme up and running then I think we could have a bright future. Ultimately, though, I think that the creation of an all-Ireland league is what's needed to secure the future of many clubs north and south.'

Declining attendances when the game in Europe is booming are one indication that Ireland is clearly too small to sustain two federations and two league competitions. With the popularity of English football and the Old Firm in Scotland, and the ease with which Irish football fans can travel to games in England and Scotland or watch matches on television, the game north and south of the border is slowly but surely dying on its feet. Even with crowds of 2,000 and falling, Derry City are still one of the best supported clubs on the whole island. Clearly the game needs a shot in the arm and an all-Ireland league could provide it.

'An all-Ireland league would benefit not just Derry City but every senior club on this island,' says Conway. 'The media interest generated by such a move, in addition to the commercial sponsorship that would follow, would revive the game at local level. I just hope the people within both associations have the vision to see the potential of the idea and the courage to implement it.

'Security is obviously an issue and I do fear that it could attract an element of support from both sides who go to games for the wrong reasons. This is something that has to be addressed. Segregation would have to be improved, along with stewarding and policing, but it's not an insurmountable problem.'

Relations between the IFA and the FAI have thawed in recent years as the political climate has done likewise. In February 2000, Ards' chairman Norman Carmichael proposed a 'Super Eight' championship involving the top four clubs in each association to run alongside the individual leagues. A prize fund of £500,000 was mooted which, when divided among the eight clubs, would still represent more than most of them would take through the gate over an entire season. The Eircom League in the Republic backed the idea with enthusiasm, as did many of the northern clubs; the IFA, however, essentially refused even to entertain the idea.

Ireland needs a united league. And Derry City needs it fast. As this book went to press the club appealed for £60,000 just to keep the club in business until the start of the 2000–01 season and a fund-raising event was being organised in, of all places, New York. As Niall Conway pointed out, there seems to be more feeling for the club from its diaspora than from its own city.

An all-Ireland league could be the key to jolting the comatose body of Irish domestic football back to life. Maybe then promising players might stick around, instead of jetting off to England and Scotland at the first opportunity. After all, if every other sport can present a united front, what's to stop football? Derry's revival has coincided with the growth of a new feeling in the city itself. The last bomb to explode in Derry went off in 1984 – the year the club made its application to the FAI – and there is surely the potential in the city for the club to thrive.

However, the football-watching populace needs to be weaned off the televised game and encouraged back to the Brandywell. The key to that lies with a successful team and to build a successful team you need money. Unless the Irish game snaps out of its stupor, Derry's whirling spiral of problems could see the end of the famous old club. I think back to the small boy passing the Bloody Sunday memorial with the bunch of white flowers behind his back. If the club can harness that hope and optimism, it might just survive. Certainly the players, officials and the supporters who do turn up lack nothing in an enthusiasm that characterises the city of Derry today.

As the floodlights go out and the advertisement hoardings are carried into the club's Portakabin office, I leave the Brandywell and head into town. Live music thumps out of the bars and clubs, a music scene that has produced artists as varied as The Undertones and Dana. I arrive at a busy and popular pizza restaurant recommended to me by locals. It's full, but they tell me that if I go to the pub next door they'll come and fetch me when there's a table free. Oh, and I might want to get a bottle of wine while I'm out.

As I await the call, I reflect over a pint of the black stuff on how unfair the popular perception of Derry is. From the cultural regeneration of the city to its proximity to the tranquil Donegal countryside, Derry does not deserve to retain its war-torn image. There's a thriving football club waiting to happen here, if only the city would sit up and take notice.

Before long the waitress retrieves me and seats me near the window. She produces a lighter and the single candle on the table flickers into life alongside a vase of white flowers.

10.

BOSNIA-HERZEGOVINA: FOOTBALL FOR PEACE

I had arrived in Sarajevo without knowing what to expect. The Bosnian war which had finished five years earlier had left me with images of shoppers sprinting across open ground between shattered buildings to avoid snipers . . . A hard-bitten, cynical people, I thought, numbed by the three-year siege which claimed the lives of over 10,000 of their fellow *Sarajlijle* between 1992 and 1995.

I certainly didn't expect the conglomeration of Turkish, Austro-Hungarian and Italian cultures that I found there, nor a chic, friendly, cosmopolitan people happy to pass hours over strong coffee and ice-cream in the pavement cafés that spill on to every street.

One permanent reminder of the siege can be seen on the road to Sarajevo's Koševo stadium. The stadium looms ahead as you approach from the city centre alongside a tightly packed cemetery stretching for hundreds of yards with rows and rows of obelisk gravestones packed in tightly like some morbid crop awaiting harvest. If ever there was a venue ideal for an initiative called 'Football For Peace' then the Koševo is it.

At the end of April 2000 a FIFA World Stars XI arrived in Sarajevo to play the Bosnia-Herzegovina national team in a fundraising match for one of FIFA's chosen charities, SOS Children's Villages (which opens orphanages in war-affected cities). Originally scheduled for a year earlier, the match had been postponed due to the NATO bombing campaign against Belgrade. This time the match appeared to coincide with a major breakthrough for Bosnian football and the closing of ethnic divides in the region.

On a list of successful international peace-brokers, FIFA probably wouldn't rank too highly. Some way above the Continuity IRA, yes, but probably several places behind even Geri Halliwell's contribution to world peace, which appears to consist of bursting into tears at various political hotspots. Yet after a meeting at FIFA's HQ on the shores of Lake Geneva early in 2000, it was announced that a newly ratified Bosnia-Herzegovina Football Association had been all but rubber-stamped. Hardly earth-shattering news on the face of it; but beneath the surface of what appeared to be little more than the minor bureaucratic machinations of a national federation, it seemed that FIFA had achieved what world leaders could not – bringing together peacefully the divided ethnic factions of Bosnia and brokering an agreement between them all.

Since the end of the war in Bosnia, the nation has remained divided between its Serb, Croat and Muslim communities. Ethnic displacement and migration have left Bosnia divided broadly between the Bosnian Muslims (or Bosniaks) and Croats in the west, and the Republika Srpska bordering Yugoslavia to the east and south where the Bosnian Serbs, who have a slight majority in the population, have settled. Taking their lead from Belgrade rather than the capital Sarajevo, the Serbian area is almost a different country. Taxi drivers from Sarajevo, which sits close to the unofficial border with the Serbian area, will take you only to within a couple of hundred yards of the beginnings of the Republika Srpska. The memories of a horrific war are still fresh in the mind of a divided populace and this is even reflected in Bosnian football.

The game in Bosnia has been similarly split since FIFA membership was ratified in 1995. Although FIFA recognises the Sarajevo-based federation NSBIH as the governing body which selects the national team, this federation broadly has only the Bosniak clubs and players under its jurisdiction. The Croats have a separate federation, the NSHB. Meanwhile, up in Banja Luka, the Bosnian Serbs have the FSRS. Each has its own league and cup competition and, initially, each refused to play off against leading clubs from the other leagues to decide who would progress into European competition as the Bosnian representative.

Not only was FIFA keen to see a unified game, but a multi-ethnic structure was also stipulated by the Dayton Accord which fixed the uneasy peace in the region in 1995. But in spite of this, the 1995–96 domestic campaign – the first following the end of the war – remained split along ethnic lines. As a result UEFA had no option but to refuse Bosnian clubs admission to European competition for the following season. The national team was permitted to enter the qualifying round for the 1998 World Cup, however, provided that 'home' matches were played on neutral territory.

Drawn in a group with Italy, Croatia, Slovenia and Greece,

Bosnia's first home fixture, a 4–1 defeat to the Croats, was staged in Bologna. By April 1997 the Bosnians had beaten Italy in a charity match in Sarajevo and picked up their first World Cup points with a 2–1 win in Slovenia. UEFA had also relented and permitted the Bosnians to stage their first competitive match in Sarajevo. Greece provided the opposition; but despite a capacity crowd turning out in torrential rain, the Greeks left with the points thanks to a solitary goal.

Increased efforts at unification, particularly by the Muslim and Croat federations, resulted in UEFA permitting Bosnian clubs' entry into European competition after the three factions agreed to play off at the end of the 1996–97 season. However, in a dispute over venues for the matches, the Serbs pulled out and two extra Bosniak teams filled their places. Both Sarajevo clubs – FK Sarajevo and Zeljeznicar – contested the final, the latter clinching the championship with a last-minute winner in front of 35,000 at the Koševo.

The national team was improving dramatically, meanwhile. Bosnia inflicted Denmark's only defeat of the 1998 World Cup qualifying campaign with a convincing 3–0 win in Sarajevo; and they completed the double over a Slovenia side which was to go on to great things in the next European Championships.

Although Zeljeznicar put up a strong performance against Kilmarnock, both they and FK Sarajevo were knocked out of the UEFA Cup at the first attempt. The lack of further progress on the unification front also prompted the governing body to exclude Bosnian clubs from European competitions until play-offs, at the very least, could be held among the three ethnic federations to determine which clubs could qualify.

With the splintered leagues attracting tiny crowds, the federations knew that they had to come to some sort of compromise – otherwise the game in Bosnia-Herzegovina would be in danger of collapsing altogether. Bosnia is barely large enough to sustain one league, let alone three. But football had been hugely important for morale during the Bosnian war. In the three years that Sarajevo was under siege, for example, FK Sarajevo played a number of friendlies against UN peacekeepers, and occasionally escaped from the city via a two-kilometre tunnel to play against teams abroad. Nine Sarajevo players were killed during the siege, either by snipers whilst out on training runs or in mortar attacks. An excellent performance against Parma, where Sarajevo lost narrowly 3–2, led to the Italian club offering some of the Sarajevo players a crack at Serie A. They refused, preferring to take their chances with their team-mates and fellow citizens in beleaguered Sarajevo. Parma then offered to buy the whole squad, missing the point with the emphasis of a Chris Waddle penalty.

Ironically it is a connection with those giants of commercialism at Old Trafford which is helping to keep FK Sarajevo alive. Manchester United beat the Bosnians on the way to their 1968 European Cup triumph (drawing 0–0 in Sarajevo and squeezing through 2–1 at Old Trafford) and invited officials of the club to Manchester in 1997. A tour of the Umbro factory resulted in a sponsorship deal that finances a 600-strong football academy in the Bosnian capital.

Even after the war, there was little thawing in ethnic relations until football stepped in. In November 1999 a coachload of 30 Bosniak children arrived in Srebrenica, the scene in 1993 of the worst civilian massacre since the Second World War. Nobody will ever know exactly how many of this town's Bosniaks died at the hands of Bosnian Serb troops – some estimate as many as 7,000 – while the UN stood by, powerless. But six years on, the Muslims returned for the first time. To play football. In an exercise designed to foster relations between the ethnic groups the UN arranged for football pitches to be marked out on the very spot where families had been separated and the men were marched off into the hills never to return. Several matches took place over a weekend between Serb and Muslim youths and relations were reported to have been friendly. Sadik Vilic, the coach of the young Muslim players said, 'It's difficult for me. In these hills I lost 90 per cent of the ones I love. But here, the children have made the first step.'

That first step probably didn't lead directly to the announcement three months later that a unified Bosnian League and a new unified football federation would be in place for the start of the 2000–01 season. Nevertheless it certainly showed that, even in this most ethnically divided nation, football has the potential to break down barriers previously regarded as insurmountable.

All sides had agreed the text of the statute that was announced. Play-offs would finally take place among all three factions to determine European entrants at the end of 1999–2000; and a new unified league structure would be in place for the following season. By the middle of March the format was within a month of completion. Eight clubs from each of the three federations would play off for the one Champions League, two UEFA Cup, and one Intertoto Cup places. The visit to Sarajevo by the FIFA World Stars and FIFA president Sepp Blatter was intended to be a celebration of the breakthrough, a symbol of Bosnia's unconditional acceptance into the international football fold.

But just a week before Blatter and his cohorts arrived, the Bosnian Serb clubs announced their withdrawal from the new set-up. They claimed they had not been part of the consultation process that had determined the format of the play-offs – a hollow claim on the face of it, since they had been willing signatories to the statutes. As the end of the season approached, the play-offs were scheduled to proceed without the Serb clubs and the new unified competition looked set to commence without the Serbian contingent. The plan for Blatter's visit had included a trip to Banja Luka, the 'capital' of the Republika Srpska region. This part of his visit was promptly cancelled.

Therefore the Bosnia-Herzegovina team that opposed the World Stars was not the multi-ethnic outfit FIFA had been expecting to find in Sarajevo.

Sitting at the bottom of a valley, Sarajevo is a narrow, elongated conurbation surrounded by steep, greenery-smothered hills. Hemmed in north and south, the city spreads east–west almost in tribute to the conglomeration of eastern and western cultures which have met here since ancient times. In the far distance are the snow-capped mountains that characterise the Bosnian landscape, but which look a little out of place in the sun-baked surroundings. Although it's only spring, the temperature is already creeping up towards the thirties.

My hotel is on a hillside to the east, overlooking the city. Koševo is in the north-west and I make my way to the match on foot at sunset, a westerly journey which, as it happens, follows the historical development of Sarajevo. As the sun goes down, the muezzins begin their calls to evening prayer from the sheaf of minarets that rise above the city's mosques. It's an eerie but soothing sound, amplified and echoed across the city as the sky turns deep orange.

Walking alongside the Miljacka river, a surprisingly timid waterway whose progress is aided by the steps cut into the river-bed to help it along, I pass the National Library – originally the city hall. It's an ornate, beautiful Ottoman building overlooking the river, but one that took a battering during the recent conflict. In fact, mortars first rained down upon it exactly 100 years to the day after its construction had begun. Burnt pages from the library's million books floated down on the city for hours afterwards. The building is little more than a shell today, but an EU-sponsored reconstruction programme is under way: every now and again a workman appears at one of the glassless windows to tip a barrowload of dust and debris into skips below.

Passing along the river, I arrive at 'Princip's Corner', the spot where Archduke Franz-Ferdinand and his wife Sofia met their premature ends in 1914 at the hands of the Bosnian Serb assassin

Gavrilo Princip (the event that triggered the First World War). A representation of the assassin's footprints used to be etched into the pavement on the spot from where he fired, but as the Serbs pounded the city from the hills during the recent siege, the largely Muslim Sarajevan population broke up this poignant symbol of Serb nationalism.

The footprints will be replaced, though, a cheerful young man tells me at the tourist office. 'Under communism, Princip was a hero,' he says, for the young Serb had struck a vital blow against imperialism; 'but after that people here were not so happy.'

Communism under Tito, whose name still adorns Sarajevo's main street, helped to preserve an uneasy peace in the region by assigning different priorities to the population. Yugoslavia was formed after the First World War from the independent kingdom of Serbia and parts of the old Austro-Hungarian Empire. Its ruler Alexander I set up a pro-Serb royal dictatorship to maintain control of the volatile region. His son Peter II succeeded Alexander following his father's assassination in 1934 and the region was invaded by the Germans in 1941.

Yugoslav partisans under the command of their communist leader Tito came to power after the German defeat, and after the war Tito announced the founding of the Socialist Federal Republic of Yugoslavia. Following the communist leader's death in 1980, the six federations of Serbia, Slovenia, Croatia, Bosnia-Herzegovina, Montenegro and Macedonia gradually devolved from the central government, rejecting communist ideas and practices. Slovenia, Macedonia and Croatia seceded from the federation altogether in 1991, with Bosnia consequently declaring independence in 1992. However, the Bosnian nation's intricate ethnic mix led to the bitter war that followed. The Croats and Bosniaks were in favour of independence, but the Serbs were keen to see Bosnia part of a Greater Serbia. All three sides coveted Sarajevo – hence the city's place at the very centre of the war.

From Princip's Corner I pause at the riverside Stari Grad café for a revitalising local beer and to watch the world go by. Literally. Sarajevo has a burgeoning international population boosted by aid workers, United Nations officials and the international peacekeeping force that observes the city's slow but sure regeneration. White four-wheel-drive UN vehicles mingle unobtrusively with civilian traffic, while groups of soldiers saunter through the streets with pistols on their belts and instamatic cameras in their hands.

The current international flavour of the populace is perhaps appropriate: Sarajevo has long held a reputation for the tolerance and harmony of its multicultural life, a factor in its importance to all sides during the conflict. Situated on the crossroads of the main routes from Asia Minor to central Europe, the city has always been a cultural melting-pot. The catholic cathedral, central mosque, Serbian Orthodox church and synagogue all stand in close proximity, something of which Sarajevo is still proud.

Draining my glass, I plunge into the old town, an exciting mixture of colourful sights and exotic smells. It's here that the 400-year influence of Turkish Ottoman rule, which ended in the nineteenth century, can clearly be seen. Indeed for most of the Ottoman period, this region was the largest commercial centre in the Balkans. The narrow streets are lined with low-roofed dark wooden shops – selling brass and bronze ornaments and richly decorated Turkish-style rugs – and cafés where locals drink Turkish coffee from traditional brass dzezdvas.

From a souvenir shop I purchase a T-shirt with a spoof representation of the Coca-Cola logo. 'Enjoy Sara-jevo', it says, a tongue-in-cheek image devised by Trio, a group of young local artists. Anywhere else it might have seemed tacky but here, somehow, it doesn't.

Ferhadija, the main pedestrian thoroughfare, throngs with people at all hours of the day. The shops give way from the small, heavy-lidded bronze emporia to larger establishments with familiar names and logos in the windows. The architecture melts from Ottoman into Hapsburg, the legacy of Bosnia's short period of Austro-Hungarian rule. In one square a large group of men pores over a giant chess set in the cool sunset-streaked shade of a clump of trees. The café tables nearby are packed with a mixture of fashionable young people, fearsomely hairstyled middle-aged Bosnians, old men in berets and camouflage-clad soldiers.

Despite the city's cosmopolitan appearance there is barely a building in Sarajevo not pockmarked by shrapnel, whilst the pavements and roads are strewn with 'Sarajevo roses', star-shaped gashes in the asphalt where shells and mortars landed.

As I progress further west the buildings become more modern, more reminiscent of the soulless architecture of the former eastern bloc. Just before the junction with the road that leads to the stadium there is a pleasant park area. Smartly dressed young women sit on benches chatting, people gabble into mobile phones among the trees and children drive electric cars around a fountain. It's a scene to be found in most European cities, but the incongruous aspect of this view is the two dozen or so gravestones that stick out of the neatly manicured grass. During the siege every spare piece of land was pressed necessarily into cemetery service.

Heading further west, the devastation becomes more apparent.

The main road, which leads out to the airport, became known as 'sniper's alley' during the conflict. It was once the most dangerous stretch of tarmac in the world. The stark, wide thoroughfare houses; the yellow modernist monstrosity of the rebuilt Holiday Inn, where journalists were holed up during the siege and from whose roof Bosnian Serb snipers shot dead 12 peaceful civil rights demonstrators to launch the conflict in earnest eight years earlier; shot-out office buildings and apartment blocks, some little more than concrete skeletons – all make the old quarter seem suddenly very far away. Looking at the war-ravaged view in front of me, I find it hard to imagine that this whole region was once, not so very long ago, a single country represented on the football field by a single team.

Things had looked good for Yugoslav football in the 1980s. In the 1987 World Youth Cup, the Yugoslavs outclassed all the opposition to win the tournament almost at a canter. Youngsters such as Zvonimir Boban, Robert Prosinecki, Robert Jarni, Igor Stimac and Davor Šuker looked to have the successful future of Balkan football firmly in their teenage grasp. Rarely had a crop of such talented youngsters emerged at once under the flag of one nation.

Yet within a couple of years, events commenced to splinter that nation into several pieces and bring open, bloody and vicious warfare to Europe.

Most, if not all, historians and journalists overlook the match between Dinamo Zagreb and Red Star Belgrade in May 1990 when they examine the events that led to the actual outbreak of war. But many within the old Yugoslavia point to that game as the catalyst for the open conflict that followed.

The rise to power of Slobodan Milošević and his promotion of Serb nationalism ahead of Yugoslav unity caused a heightening of ethnic tension at the turn of the 1990s. Matches between Dinamo, a staunchly Croat club from the Croat capital, and the Serbian- (and Milošević-) backed Red Star had seen outbreaks of ethnic violence on the terraces throughout the 1980s. Things were coming to a head in 1990 when the match in Zagreb took place. Horrendous violence occurred between Dinamo's *ultras*, the Bad Blue Boys, and Red Star's Delije. As tensions were mounting in the region the BBB hooligans had already commenced self-styled military training and the fighting in the ground was vicious. This was no prearranged 'off' between a couple of rival club firms: this was the real thing. Centuries of rivalry and discontent were coming to a head and Dinamo's football ground turned into the battlefield that triggered things on a far wider scale.

Dinamo's Zvonimir Boban was seen to aim a flying kick at the head of a Serb policeman, later arguing that he had been defending himself and a group of young Dinamo fans from a formidable beating at the hands of the police. This wasn't Dinamo versus Red Star any more, it was Croatia against Serbia. Many recall this day as the moment the realisation dawned that the old Yugoslavia really was dead.

The leader of the Red Star *ultras* at the time was a patisserie owner named Zeljko Rážnétović. He would in the ensuing years become better known by his nickname of Arkan, the alleged mastermind behind the paramilitary Serbian Tigers' brutal ethnic cleansing programmes that characterised the Balkan conflict. Wanted by the UN on a number of war-crimes charges at the time of his assassination in a Belgrade hotel early in 2000, by the turn of the 1990s Arkan already had a substantial international reputation thanks to his connection with several bank robberies in western Europe. He is also reputed to have broken out of a significant selection of European jails in his pre-war gangster career.

Once the war started in earnest, Arkan and the hard core of the Red Star hooligans became the notorious Tigers. Many of those responsible for the chilling rounds of ethnic cleansing on both sides in Bosnia and Croatia had been involved in the fighting in Zagreb that afternoon. On the other side, the Bad Blue Boys and Hajduk Split's hooligan faction, the Torcida, were among the first to sign up for military duty on the Croatian side, forming their own paramilitary units.

Red Star Belgrade defeated Marseille in the 1991 European Cup Final where, despite having played some beautiful football in the previous rounds, they played for penalties (their success was met with widespread derision). At their first game in Yugoslavia after the final, Arkan appeared on the pitch as part of the celebrations, back from duties in Croatia for some R&R. His growing international notoriety had made him a folk hero amongst the Serbs, who were being fed increasingly paranoid propaganda by the Milošević regime. While Red Star's players paraded the European Cup around their stadium, Arkan danced behind them waving a road sign 'liberated' from a 'cleansed' Croat village – to a huge ovation.

Arkan's efforts to work his way into the Red Star hierarchy were thwarted, however. Keen to establish himself in the game, he instead turned his attention to one of Belgrade's smaller clubs, FK Obilić. Taking its name from one of Serbia's folk heroes, Miloš Obilić – who had killed the Turkish sultan Murad I at the battle of Kosovo Polje in 1389 – the club, under Arkan's patronage, soon rose from the lower ranks to become one of the strongest teams in the modern

Yugoslavia. A little like Barnet walking away with the Premiership.

Many opposing teams complained (quietly) that Arkan had advised them that, should they beat Obilić, members of their squad would be on the receiving end of what he called 'knee surgery'. Arkan's wife Ceca, a leading proponent of a Serbian brand of music called turbofolk, is officially listed as president of the club, and indeed it was she who accompanied the team on their Champions League travels to IBV in Iceland and Bayern Munich in Germany in 1998. Arkan was reported to be 'away on business' for both matches. Perhaps the fact that he would have been arrested as soon as he set foot outside Yugoslavia and dispatched to the Hague on war crimes charges also influenced his decision not to travel. Fortunately for some, Bayern won the two-legged encounter.

In 1997, two years after the end of the war, Dinamo Zagreb – under their new name of Croatia Zagreb – were drawn against Partizan Belgrade in a Champions League qualifying tie. It was the first time Serbs and Croats had been drawn together in a sporting fixture since the outbreak of hostilities. The first leg, in Belgrade, saw a relentless outpouring of hatred from the terraces. Despite being the better side Croatia, obviously terrified, missed numerous chances and lost the match 1–0. Later Newcastle United's Silvio Maric, who played for Croatia Zagreb that night, said, 'I was scared that we wouldn't get out of the stadium alive if we'd won. I'm not saying we deliberately missed the goal, but it was very hard to shoot in the knowledge of what might happen if we scored.' The Croats returned the abuse in the second leg, and their side swept to a 5–0 win over an equally terrified Partizan. Zagreb's main square was filled with people celebrating as if they'd won a war.

The moment everyone had been dreading occurred when Croatia and Yugoslavia were drawn together in the Euro 2000 qualifying groups, playing each other home and away. (Just to add to the fun another former Yugoslav republic, Macedonia, came out of the hat as well.) The original schedule was disrupted by NATO action over Kosovo; the two sides finally met in August 1999 in Belgrade. Despite ticket prices equivalent to a week's wages, the match was a 50,000 sell-out almost as soon as tickets went on sale.

Perhaps predictably, the match finished goalless. Predrag Mijatovic hit the post for the home side in the first minute, with Davor Šuker also striking the woodwork for Croatia twenty minutes later. When Yugoslav defender Sinisa Mihajlović's header looped towards his own goal ten minutes before the interval, he could have been forgiven for thinking of Andres Escobar. To his immense relief, the ball hit the bar and was cleared, sparing the hapless defender the ignominy of putting Croatia ahead with a perhaps unique football version of 'friendly fire'.

Early in the second half, the floodlights went out for 40 minutes, allowing the crowd to indulge in some anti-Milošević songs. A tear-gas canister was launched, but reports conflict as to whether it came from the police into the crowd or vice versa. Once the game restarted, it petered out into an unspectacular draw and thankfully, without too much trouble. The ban on away supporters appeared to have succeeded, although the BBB had been expected to show up in some shape or form.

Arkan was assassinated in the lobby of a Belgrade hotel in February 2000. Unsurprisingly, Obilić's title challenge faded instantly.

Back in Sarajevo I return to the park-cum-cemetery and join the crowds heading up Koševo Street to the stadium, which was constructed to house the opening ceremony of the 1984 Winter Olympics. Inside, a crowd of around 25,000 has gathered. A large military contingent is present in the crowd, with peacekeeping troops from the US and France making their presence known by draping flags across the seats in front of them. Given the huge, bowl-like arena, it doesn't take long for a Mexican wave to start. The World Stars are an eclectic bunch. Coached by Carlos Alberto Parreira and captained by Dunga, the squad has a strong Brazilian contingent in Aldair, Augusto Cesar and Sonny Anderson. Ronaldo was due to appear, but a month earlier had suffered a recurrence of the knee injury that threatens to curtail his career. Bernard Lama, Victor Onopko, Taribo West, Abedi Pelé, Mustapha Hadji and Roberto Baggio all warm up together before the match, an impressive selection of international talent. At the pitchside smiling for the cameras, are Blatter and Michel Platini – the latter looking as ever, with tie at half-mast, stubbly chin and mop of unruly black hair, like a tipsy uncle at a wedding.

The teams arrive on the pitch, each player hand-in-hand with a child from the Sarajevo orphanage. Perhaps unsurprisingly, the match itself is a disappointment. The Bosnians are the livelier of the two sides, with Elvir Bolić seeing a steepling header come back off the bar and a later shot from the edge of the area spectacularly pushed away by Lama. Most of the players, many at a crucial stage in their domestic season, are understandably more concerned with avoiding injury than winning the game. Baggio looks most interested out of the FIFA side, buzzing between the towering Bosnian defenders, his thickening waistline calling to mind a tugboat chugging between two ocean liners. Twenty substitutions do little to help the game as a spectacle. It is settled a few minutes before the end when Abedi Pelé is bundled over in the penalty area, Baggio doing the necessary from the spot.

But this occasion was never really about the match itself. As Jusuf Pusina of the Bosnian federation wrote in the programme:

> The children of Sarajevo experienced vast horrors during the four years of aggression. Many of them were killed whilst actually playing football under conditions the world today finds hard to understand. A great amount of football talent vanished because they never had the chance to kick a ball around. To stage this Football For Peace event will send a message to the world. Let the children of all continents live in peace so that they can play football regardless of where they are.

I join the crowds walking back to the centre of Sarajevo in search of a drink and duck into a bar that apparently was once called the Internet Café. It was a bar with no connection at all to the information superhighway, and the owners presumably became so fed up with spotty backpackers asking to check their hotmail accounts that they've renamed it simply 'The Bar'. Now their only problem might come from itinerant lawyers wanting to discuss the finer points of local corporate law.

The Bar is a simply furnished underground establishment dispensing cocktails, local beer, Budweiser and, bizarrely, Kilkenny Irish Beer. In one dark recess is a stage, one of the few live music venues in Sarajevo if you discount the restaurants with resident bands who all sound like eastern European entries to the Eurovision Song Contest.

Like its beer, The Bar has an international flavour and the conversations among the groups of young friends around the candlelit wooden tables seem to be taking place almost exclusively in heavily accented English. Laughter punctuates the curious soundtrack of UB40's greatest hits, which seems to be on a permanent loop from the speakers. Young faces glow in the candlelight, cocktails go back and forth on trays, friends greet each other warmly and I am bathed in Sarajevo *bonhomie*.

The bar is in a cellar, the sort of place in which many of the city's inhabitants spent much of the war. Over a Sarajevsko Pivo I wonder how the Muslim/Croat Bosnian national team will fare in international competition, and what will become of football in the alienated Republika Srpska. The Bosnian Euro 2000 qualifying campaign was steady and unspectacular, but with a wider array of talent prepared to pull on the shirt, perhaps the future is brighter for Bosnian football. Certainly, being admitted into European club competition can only benefit the game in the country, and it may persuade top players to stay at home rather than seek their fortune in the German and Turkish leagues. The achievements of Slovenia will have given heart to the Bosnians: teams visiting Sarajevo will not arrive to find an easy three points waiting there.

Ascending the wooden stairs as the evening becomes the early hours, I emerge into the street and flag down a taxi. Every other vehicle in Sarajevo is a cab: taxi-driving's a lucrative occupation in a city filled with foreigners on expenses. My head lolls against the window and I feel a warm glow of affection for this unique city. And as we glide through the darkness, the obelisk gravestones in the park shine blue-white in the moonlight.

11.

GERMANY: THE BUNDESLIGA IS UPSIDE DOWN

Munich, home of football, beer-halls, improbably large *wurst* and *lederhosen*. Crimes against the humble trouser notwithstanding, is there any city in Germany with a finer footballing pedigree? The Bavarian capital is home to Bayern Munich, sixteen times German champions, ten times German Cup winners and three times European Cup winners. Bayern's history is littered with great names, from Muller to Matthäus, Breitner to Beckenbauer, and they have fans all over the world.

Their city rivals, TSV 1860, have also been regular competitors on the European stage. And Die Löwen, despite having played second fiddle to Bayern for the past 30 years or so, have had their moments too: in the past few seasons have frequently demonstrated the potential to eclipse their glamorous cohabitants at the Olympic Stadium on the domestic front.

And of course there's SpVgg Unterhaching.

OK, so their only previous claim to fame is being the club whose name sounds the most like a sneeze, but this tiny outfit from the Munich suburbs have astounded even themselves by reaching the Bundesliga for the first time. Perhaps even more remarkably, these minnows have made themselves relatively comfortable in the top flight, in spite of a minuscule ground capacity by Bundesliga standards and a team of journeymen whose star is a little-known Albanian striker with a name that contains an inordinate amount of double consonants.

Whilst Bayern and TSV 1860 have been amassing silverware, supporters and not a little cash over the years, Unterhaching have spent their trophy-free history happily chugging along in the lower leagues. As recently as 1994 they were facing Bayern's and 1860's reserve teams in the Regionalliga Süd as well as the might of teams such as Borussia Fulda and TSF Ditzingen. They have warmly welcomed cast-offs from the big two into their squad, as well as cheerily waving off their own hot prospects as they headed for the

152

Olympic Stadium with an eager smile on the face and a Bayern or 1860 contract sticking out of the pocket.

Until 1999, Unterhaching's crowds in their 11,000-capacity Sportparkstadion had rarely exceeded 3,000 At the end of the 1998–99 season TSV 1860 averaged 32,000 and Bayern 56,000. Unterhaching's promotion-winning campaign in the Zweite Liga, in which they earned the right to play against their city companions, attracted an average attendance of 3,700. The previous season they had narrowly avoided relegation back to the Regionalliga on crowds of 2,500 and had not noticeably strengthened their squad. So when they began to string some handy results together at the start of the 1998–99 season, most pundits who concerned themselves with Zweite Liga matters waited patiently for Haching's inevitable slide down the table.

Somehow, though, despite their limited talent and resources, Haching finished the season in second place. Only relegated Wattenscheid boasted a lower average attendance than promoted Haching's. It was a remarkable rise for a club where football is not even the main sport. Like many lower-division clubs in Germany, Unterhaching is an umbrella for a number of sports, the reason why the club's crest is dominated by a four-man bobsleigh. Many expected this to be an appropriate analogy for the velocity with which Haching would plummet from the Bundesliga; but the little club soon proved that they were made of stronger stuff.

Their football wasn't pretty but it worked. Although they scored only 47 goals in their 34 league matches during their promotion season, Haching conceded only 30 – the best defensive record in the division and a record bettered only by champions Bayern in the Bundesliga. Haching's success under coach Lorenz-Günther Köstner was based on the grinding-out of 1–0 wins, and they were virtually invincible on their home turf.

Early in their first-ever Bundesliga season Unterhaching staked their claim on 15th place, one above the relegation places, and set about making sure they stayed there. At the end of August they played their first Munich derby (apart from matches against their neighbours' reserves) when the little club headed across town to the Olympic Stadium to face Bayern. A crowd of 63,000 packed into the ground, more than had watched Haching at home in the previous two seasons put together. A superb performance between the sticks by goalkeeper Jurgen Wittmann restricted Bayern to a narrow 1–0 victory and Haching left the field to a standing ovation. A few weeks later it was a similar story against 1860, but again Haching lost by the odd goal after their Albanian striker Anton Rraklli missed a penalty.

As the season progressed, the upstarts picked up points against luminaries such as Borussia Dortmund and Werder Bremen. A home defeat to Bayern was Haching's first loss at the Sportparkstadion for almost a year and a half.

As the end of the campaign drew nearer, the minnows were able to look down from the lofty heights of tenth place at clubs of more opulent means such as Borussia Dortmund, Eintracht Frankfurt and Schalke 04. But it was on the last day of the season that Unterhaching made their greatest contribution to the Bundesliga.

It was a remarkable final day. The title race had been between Bayern and Bayer Leverkusen for most of the campaign and, going into the last round of matches, Leverkusen appeared to hold the advantage. Three points clear at the top and beaten only twice all season, they needed only to avoid defeat at Unterhaching to clinch their first-ever title. Haching had battled hard against the odds to keep their place in the top flight, when most pundits had predicted a swift return to the Zweite Liga, and they were now comfortably placed above the drop zone. In terms of their own position Unterhaching had nothing to play for.

Across the city in the Olympic Stadium, Bayern's task looked slightly less straightforward. With a better goal difference than Leverkusen, Bayern had to win against Werder Bremen and hope for a miracle at Unterhaching. Although Werder sat one place below the UEFA Cup places, their defeat to Bayern in the German Cup Final had secured them a place in the tournament as Bayern were certain of a Champions League place. However, Werder would have been thinking back to the climax of the 1985–86 season when they needed just a point on the last day to take the title ahead of Bayern. A defeat of 2–0 in Stuttgart, coupled with Bayern's 6–0 win over Borussia Mönchengladbach, snatched the championship from the Bremen club.

When Bayer Leverkusen coach Christoph Daum had brought in a motivational guru to gee up his players the previous season, people sniggered. When the players revealed the guru had had them walking across broken glass, the rest of the league fell about laughing. Bayern Munich's general manager Uli Hoeneß found it so hilarious he put forward the assertion that 'Leverkusen will not overtake us in 100 years'. So when Leverkusen beat TSV Munich 1860 in April to go two points clear of Bayern – who could only draw 1–1 at Vfl Wolfsburg (coached by Wolfgang Wolf, would you believe?) – no one could confirm sightings of a grim-faced Hoeneß heading for the Bayern training ground clutching a big bag of milk bottles.

Whatever the reason behind the Ruhr club's elevation, Hoeneß and Bayern should have seen it coming. Leverkusen had finished in the top three in each of the previous three seasons, even reaching the quarter-finals of the Champions League in 1998. It had been a remarkable transformation since the arrival of the former Besiktas coach Christoph Daum in 1996.

Having helped the club avoid relegation by a matter of minutes that summer, Daum brought in two Brazilians – Paulo Sergio and Jorginho – and introduced a fluid 3–5–2 formation. Playing some beautiful football, Leverkusen astounded the nation by finishing as runners-up in 1997. The most obvious beneficiary of the Daum revolution was veteran striker Ulf Kirsten, who finished as the Bundesliga's leading scorer, a feat he repeated the following season when Leverkusen finished third. Kirsten, reaching the end of his career, became the first player since Karl-Heinz Rumenigge in 1981 to finish as Germany's leading scorer two seasons running.

In 1999 Leverkusen finished again in second place to earn another crack at the Champions League. Drawn in a tough group, Bayer notched two notable draws with Lazio, a win in Slovenia against Maribor and a draw and a defeat against Dynamo Kyiv. If it weren't for a frustrating 0–0 draw with the Slovenians in the final game, Leverkusen would have been surprise qualifiers for the second group stage.

In fact, failure to progress may have worked to their advantage. Bayern's continued participation in the Champions League and the German Cup had left them with a crowded schedule. Leverkusen, free of other commitments, seemed to go from strength to strength, their fluid attacking style manifesting itself most ominously at struggling Ulm in March. Their astonishing 9–1 victory was a club record and sent warning signals to Bavaria that Leverkusen meant business. They appeared to be hitting their best form at exactly the right time.

Ironically, Daum is a Bayern fan. He had said earlier in the season that he hoped Bayern would win the Champions League, but leave the domestic title to Leverkusen. Despite the lead his side held going into the last few matches, he knew that Bayern were an experienced team. 'It's going to be exciting,' he told reporters after a victory over 1860; 'we may be ahead but they've been there before. Even their cleaning lady has won ten titles.'

But Leverkusen had in their ranks one of the highest-rated players in the Bundesliga, the Brazilian midfielder Emerson. Widely tipped to depart for Serie A during the winter break (indeed, no German sports bulletin was complete without an item speculating on the latest European giant preparing a bid), the player described by Bayer skipper Jens Nowotny as 'the best midfield player in the world' had pledged his future to Leverkusen at least until the end of the season.

Two matches, one city, one title. Leverkusen had the easier task on paper, but had reckoned without Bavarian pride. The southern province has always felt a sense of 'otherness' from the rest of Germany, of which it comprises one fifth. There has always been a rivalry between the industrial northwest – where Leverkusen grew from a chemical works team – and the more rural south. Unterhaching have always enjoyed good relations with their big brothers at Bayern and 1860 and their journeymen players would have liked nothing more than to help bring the title back to Bavaria.

The settings could not have been more different. Leverkusen and Unterhaching stepped out on to the Sportparkstadion turf in front of a capacity crowd of just 11,000. Meanwhile across the city, 63,000 crammed into the Olympic Stadium to roar Bayern on to victory against Bremen. They're a funny lot, the people who watch Unterhaching. The small crowds that gathered to watch them in the lower leagues were generally made up of Bayern and 1860 fans watching a bit of football whilst their team played away. Hence Haching's attendances were affected more by how well or otherwise the big two were doing, than by their own exploits on the pitch. It was safe to say that on that Saturday afternoon in mid-May, the crowd were rooting for both Haching and Bayern.

Playing with three strikers, Bayern tore into Werder from the kick-off at the Olympic Stadium. With just two minutes played, Markus Babbel's cross was met by the towering figure of Carsten Jancker, whose thumping header flew past Rost in the Bremen goal. Ten minutes later Jancker's head was again on the end of a cross, this time from Paulo Sergio (signed from Leverkusen the previous summer) and before Werder could realise what had hit them, the Brazilian himself cleverly flicked a third goal from a Mehmet Scholl pass. With just a quarter of an hour played, the match was over thanks to an astonishing, relentless onslaught from Bayern.

Meanwhile, over at the Sportparkstadion, Leverkusen had suddenly assumed the mantle of a rabbit caught in the headlights of a Bayern steamroller. Unterhaching's uncompromising man-to-man marking was harassing the nervous visitors who created openings but fell victim either to unforced errors or found Haching keeper Gerhard Tremmel in the way. Meanwhile every Bayern goal was greeted with a roar from the Unterhaching fans and it became obvious to Christoph Daum's side that the onus was on them. It's a strange experience seeing a football ground erupt with joy when nothing is happening on the field. Rarely has an Unterhaching throw-in been greeted with such rapture as when one coincided with news of Bayern's third goal. Leverkusen, used to grander arenas than this, looked bewildered by their surroundings.

When they trotted out of the clubhouse behind the goal, along the dark metal mesh tunnel and into the cramped, low-rise arena, Leverkusen must have thought they'd turned up at the wrong place. The Sportparkstadion is reminiscent of a Football Conference ground owned by an ambitious, upwardly mobile club from a home counties market town. They might only have been a couple of miles from the Olympic Stadium, but Leverkusen must have felt they were in some parallel football universe. Haching's zigzag-roofed main stand, the open concrete seating opposite and the temporary seating behind one goal are all squeezed right up to the edge of the pitch: a player on the wing can feel the breath of the crowd on the back of his neck. Every Unterhaching tackle was cheered. Every pass received a roar of encouragement.

Nevertheless, although Bayern were winning convincingly, a draw was still good enough for Leverkusen. But disaster struck for the visitors on 20 minutes. As news of Bayern's third goal spread around the tiny stadium, Leverkusen midfielder Michael Ballack diverted the ball past his own goalkeeper to give Unterhaching the lead. The ground erupted. It's an old cliché, but there really was a cup-tie atmosphere in the Sportparkstadion. It was like a Ryman League side taking the lead against a Premier League team.

Back at the Olympic Stadium, the news of Unterhaching's goal lifted the hitherto muted atmosphere. Werder Bremen pulled a goal back, but by the interval the Bundesliga advantage had passed to Bayern. A long hard season looked set to be decided by that frantic opening 20 minutes of football in two Munich suburbs.

As the second half got underway Bayern had run out of steam, exhausted by their relentless opening half hour. Across town Leverkusen forced no less than ten corners but couldn't find the net. Every Haching clearance was cheered to the skies. Every time a corner swung in and Tremmel's gloved hands emerged from the pack to claim the ball, the collective expulsion of breath nearly blew the dugouts away. Just 21 years old, Tremmel had begun the season as Haching's third-choice goalkeeper, playing in the amateur leagues, but injuries had thrust him into the Bundesliga spotlight. He was coping like a seasoned international.

A couple of swift counter-attacks from the home side sounded warning bells for Leverkusen, whose attacks were becoming more and more desperate. With 20 minutes left the championship was decided for sure. Markus Oberleitner – who had grown up next door to the former Bayern player Paul Breitner, learning his skills as a child on the German international's living-room carpet by taking on Breitner's young daughter – ran through to score the second and decisive goal for Unterhaching. The roof nearly came off the stand. Maybe it hadn't been so zigzagged before the game.

At the final whistle the Haching players and crowd celebrated as if they had won the huge silver Bundesliga plate themselves. Shell-shocked Leverkusen players fell to the turf. All they'd had to do was avoid defeat, something they'd done in all but two of their previous 33 Bundesliga games on bigger stages than this – but they'd been overwhelmed by the pressure of the occasion and the terrier-like determination of the tiny club from the Munich suburbs. Christoph Daum's moustache drooped further than ever before.

'Tiefe Depression bei Bayer, totale Euphorie in München,' said *Kicker* magazine a few days later. No translation needed. 'This was our Barcelona,' said Leverkusen's General Manager Reiner Calmund, in reference to Bayern's defeat from the jaws of victory in the previous year's Champions League Final. The club had blown their best chance of winning their first-ever domestic title and they remain the only club in Europe to have won a European trophy but not their domestic championship. They drowned their sorrows in the knowledge that hangovers wouldn't worry them too much: their backers, the huge Bayer chemical company, developed the aspirin.

Munich's main square soon filled with jubilant fans. Bayern scarves and flags mixed with Unterhaching ones. Unterhaching's players mixed with Bayern's at the championship celebration This was a victory for Bavaria.

While a small team from the south celebrated their unlikely role at the heart of the championship, in the northwest the previous day one of the giants they had replaced had been preparing one last charge at a swift return to the top flight.

Borussia Mönchengladbach have fallen on hard times. If Leverkusen had wished the 1999–2000 season could have ended a week earlier, then Gladbach may wish that football had ended around the mid-1980s. During the 1970s the club, from an oft-overlooked small town in the industrial northwest that is rarely mentioned in guidebooks, had been one of the dominant forces of European football. The Bökelberg faithful saw five Bundesliga titles, two UEFA Cups and two German Cups waggled at them from the pitch by the men in green-and-white in the space of ten years. Berti Vogts spent his entire playing career there; Allan Simonsen became European Footballer of the Year whilst wearing Gladbach colours; Gunter Netzer bulged the Bökelberg nets on countless occasions; and Lothar Matthäus took the first steps of his long career in Mönchengladbach.

Bayern Munich and Gladbach were the two great rivals of the

German game during the '70s. It seems hard to believe now, but the great Bayern and West Germany goalkeeper Sepp Maier used to complain that Borussia received all the attention from the media and public ahead of Bayern. But this weekend in May 2000 demonstrated how the game in Germany had changed since then. Bayern clinched the title in the modern Olympic Stadium in front of 63,000 to earn their third title in four years, confirm their status as 'FC Hollywood' and start celebrations among the members of their 1,250 supporters' clubs worldwide. Meanwhile their old rivals, Borussia Mönchengladbach, were preparing to take on struggling FSV Mainz 05 in the hope of keeping up with the promotion pack in the Zweite Liga at the friendly, atmospheric but hopelessly outdated Bökelberg stadium. Whilst Bayern had that season faced the likes of Real Madrid in the Champions League, Borussia's fixture list contained names such as Greuther Fürth and Rot-Weiss Oberhausen.

The decline has been slow and steady, but one that was perhaps even inevitable in the modern climate. In the heady days of the '70s, Gladbach's team contained a core of local players, many of whom stayed for a long time. As well as Vogts's distinguished long service, Jupp Heynckes and Gunter Netzer spent the best years of their careers in white, green and black. Today, the youngsters depart for more lucrative pastures almost as soon as they pull on a pair of boots. Lothar Matthäus moved on to Bayern. Steffen Effenberg also started here before going on to greater things with Bayern, whilst Germany's great young hope of Euro 2000, Sebastien Deisler, also came through the ranks at the Bökelberg before departing at 18.

Well behind in the financial stakes, Gladbach look condemned to also-ran status. Promoted to the Bundesliga in 1965, they set about winning friends and a few matches with their fluid, exciting attacking style. In their début Bundesliga season Gladbach scored 70 goals, the joint-highest total. The following year they topped that figure by seven, including a 10–0 stuffing of Borussia Neuenkirchen on the way. In the summer of 1968, Gladbach coach Hennes Weisweiler spent a German record DM225,000 on striker Horst Köppel. Köppel only scored five times that season, but it didn't matter. The team were top scorers again, finishing in third place. It was almost Total Football: everyone chipped in with the goals and the crowds loved it.

The dawn of the '70s saw the beginning of Gladbach's golden years. Weisweiler, coach since 1964 and the man behind the club's rise from regional football to the top of the European game, realised that for all their goalscoring exploits his side desperately needed shoring up at the back. Luggi Müller was signed in a Nuremberg car park after a match and Klaus-Dieter Sieloff arrived from VfB Stuttgart. It worked. A mid-season unbeaten run of 11 matches in 1969–70 saw

Gladbach go top for the first time in their history following a 1–0 win in Cologne. And top they stayed. In the last game but one of the season, Gladbach needed only to beat Hamburg to clinch the title. With half an hour left the Bökelberg side were 4–0 up and the terraces were jumping. However, Gladbach somehow managed to concede three goals – provoking Weisweiler to arrive in the penalty-area puce with rage to berate his defenders. Fortunately for Gladbach and Weisweiler's blood pressure, the home side held on to carry off their first major honour.

The following season saw one of the Bundesliga's more extraordinary incidents. Battling with Bayern for the 1971 title, Gladbach were being held to a frustrating draw by Werder Bremen in April. With two minutes remaining, Gladbach striker Herbert Lauman launched himself at a cross with Werder's keeper Günter Bernard. The keeper touched the ball over, but both players crashed into the post, shearing it off at the bottom. As the players picked themselves gingerly from the wrecked goal, the referee summoned the groundsman to repair the damage ready for the last two minutes. Gladbach, realising they'd have more chance of winning a rearranged match, decided that the match should be abandoned and left the field. Unfortunately the Bundesliga saw it differently and awarded the points to Bremen.

As the last game of the season approached, Gladbach's walkout looked like it might prove costly. Their old foes Bayern led by one goal on goal difference; so Gladbach had to rely on Duisburg to beat the Munich side, or else win by two more goals than Bayern did. Gladbach beat Eintracht Frankfurt 4–1, but Bayern crashed to a 2–0 defeat in Duisburg to hand another title to the Bökelberg side.

In 1973 Mönchengladbach reached their first European final. Having beaten Aberdeen, Hvidovre, FC Cologne, Kaiserslautern and Twente Enschede *en route*, Gladbach faced Liverpool in a two-legged UEFA Cup Final. The first leg at Anfield was a disaster. Two early goals from Kevin Keegan caught the Germans before they could settle and when Larry Lloyd added a third on the hour, it looked all over for Gladbach. However, roared on by a capacity crowd at the Bökelberg, Jupp Heynckes gave the home side an early lead. When he added a second, five minutes before the interval, a surprise looked suddenly possible. But Liverpool resisted everything the Germans could muster in the second half, to prevent a Gladbach equaliser and carry off the trophy.

That season also saw the departure of Netzer for Real Madrid. The gifted playmaker had not always seen eye to eye with Weisweiler, and when the coach left Netzer out of that season's German Cup Final following the death of the player's father and the announcement of the Real deal, Netzer was not happy. At half-time, with the scores level, Weisweiler wanted to bring on Netzer but he refused to go on. When the match went to extra-time and Weisweiler made it clear that he wanted to make a substitution, suddenly Netzer's tracksuit was off and he was striding onto the field. With his first touch he scored the winner and bade farewell to the Bökelberg faithful.

In 1975 Gladbach again reached the UEFA Cup Final. There they faced Twente Enschede again – the team they had beaten in the semi-final two years earlier. Since then, diminutive striker Allan Simonsen had been plucked from Danish amateur football and was proving to be a shrewd acquisition. Despite drawing the home leg of the final 0–0, Gladbach travelled to Holland and produced a remarkable performance to win 5–1. Simonsen and Heynckes had given the Germans a two-goal advantage in the first ten minutes, and when Heynckes added two more early in the second half Gladbach were assured of their first European title. Although the home side pulled a goal back, three minutes from time, Simonsen added the fifth from the penalty spot. It had been a brilliant performance, exemplifying all that was good about Gladbach's attacking style, a philosophy which had also brought them another Bundesliga title that season. The team Weisweiler had patiently been building for over a decade was reaching its brilliant peak.

Shortly after the match in Enschede, however, the visionary coach stunned the players – and German football as a whole – when he announced that he was moving on to take over at Barcelona. His replacement was Udo Lattek, a former Bayern coach whose philosophy was based more on defence than the freescoring attacking that was bringing so much success to the northwest corner of Germany. It was a curious appointment and not popular with the players, but despite the change in style Gladbach again won the league in 1976.

The long-serving core of the team was beginning to age, however. Vogts and Heynckes were struggling with injuries and the goals were not coming as thick and fast as before.

Despite their advancing years, the Gladbach team progressed to the 1977 European Cup Final, where they met Liverpool again. Simonsen, voted European Footballer of the Year that season, equalised Terry McDermott's opener in Rome's Olympic Stadium, but Liverpool came back to win 3–1. That night proved to be the beginning of the end of Gladbach's glory years.

In 1977–78 the club went into the last league game level on points with local rivals Cologne (now managed by their old master, Weisweiler) but with a goal difference inferior by ten goals. So, if Cologne won 1–0, Gladbach needed to win by 12 goals to snatch the title from them. An impossible task, it seemed. However, opponents Borussia Dortmund, long-standing rivals of Cologne and with nothing to play for themselves, fielded a reserve team. Incredibly, Gladbach rattled in 12 goals without reply. Meanwhile, however, Cologne had won 5–0 to take the championship by four goals.

As the decade closed, Gladbach began to fade. Their 1979 UEFA Cup win over Red Star Belgrade was to be their last major honour to date. The following season they lost the UEFA Cup Final on away goals to Eintracht Frankfurt in a tournament which saw all four semi-final places occupied by German clubs.

From there it was steady decline. In 1984 Gladbach finished third in the league, but level on points with champions Stuttgart and runners-up Hamburg, and they lost the Cup Final to Bayern on penalties. In 1986 they managed to lose a 5–1 first-leg advantage to Real Madrid in the UEFA Cup third round, although they did reach the semi-final the following season. But as the 1990s progressed, the club from the town of just 400,000 inhabitants found it hard to keep up as the big city clubs hogged the honeypot. Football was gradually overtaking Borussia Mönchengladbach.

Despite the constant stream of local talent leaving the Bökelberg for lucrative contracts elsewhere, Gladbach managed to stay near the top of the table as the '90s progressed. A German Cup win in 1995 was a brief highlight but in 1998, a year after Gladbach had beaten Arsenal in both legs of a first-round UEFA Cup tie, the club only avoided relegation by goal difference, having won their last two matches. That late-season rally just delayed the inevitable. In 1999 Borussia Mönchengladbach were relegated by a mile. Winning just four games all season, they trailed safety by 16 points at the end of the campaign and their 34-year run in the top flight came to a humiliating and undignified end. In the space of seven days at the end of October, Gladbach lost 8–2 at home to Leverkusen and were hammered 7–1 at Wolfsburg. It was a week that spelled the end of coach Friedel Rausch's reign; but even then everybody knew that Gladbach were destined for the Zweite Liga. Dishevelled, dispirited and devoid of inspiration, the club awaited the inevitable.

And just when it seemed things couldn't get any worse, Gladbach lost their first five games of the 1999–2000 season. Four league defeats left them stranded at the bottom of the Zweite Liga and talk of relegation to the Regionalliga began in hushed whispers. A defeat on penalties to little SC Verl of the Regionalliga West-Südwest in the German Cup completed Gladbach's disastrous start to the campaign. After a spineless 3–0 defeat at Karlsruhe in September, coach and former player Rainer Bonhof resigned.

Just 12,251 had watched Gladbach's opening home match (a 2–0 defeat to Chemnitzer), the club's worst home league gate in many years. However a 2–0 win, thanks to a superb second-half performance at St Pauli, put a more positive slant on their next home game: the derby against long-term rivals FC Cologne, who had also fallen on hard times. The Bökelberg was packed to its 34,000 capacity to see Gladbach notch their first home win of the season by three goals to one. This proved to be the turning-point and new trainer Hans Meyer commenced guiding the club through the mire at the bottom towards the top half of the table.

A home defeat by Bochum in early November was followed by a 19-match unbeaten run which carried the club to the fringes of the promotion race. The goals of lumbering striker Arie Van Lent, plus the brilliance of midfielder Marcel Ketelaer, had given Gladbach supporters hope of returning to the Bundesliga at the first attempt – something beyond their wildest imagination during the opening weeks of the season. It was always an outside possibility, but it was still a possibility.

With two games remaining, lowly Mainz 05 arrive in town on a wet Saturday afternoon. Aside from Cologne, who have led the division for almost the entire season, Gladbach are the best-supported team in the Zweite Liga, attracting an average crowd of nearly 23,000 to the Bökelberg. The suburban residential streets among which the ground is set throng with fans long before the game. A visit to Gladbach is a little like stepping back to the glory days of Simonsen, Netzer and Vogts. Well, off the pitch anyway. The fans queuing at the ticket kiosks are mainly clad in leather, topped with cut-off denim jackets. On the back of the denim jackets are sewn as many patches and badges as the owner can manage. Knotted to each wrist is at least one scarf. The mullet hairstyle is the *coiffure de rigeur*, and most of these are complemented with a droopy moustache.

Inside, the ground consists of three sides of steep terracing. The fact that it only costs a fiver to stand on the terraces increases the feeling that you're in a time warp. I buy my *wurst* and take my position amongst what appears to be the crowd at a '70s heavy rock festival.

Loud rock music thunders out of the speakers and the packed crowd jumps along in time on the *Nordtribune*, where the most vociferous fans congregate. I soon realise that they are singing along and that the thumping rock tunes have been written specifically for Borussia. The rain fails to dampen their enthuisiasm. A man with a microphone interrupts the proceedings to read out the teams. As in

Austria, he gives only the first names: the crowd shout back the surname. 'Danke,' says the man with the microphone as he finishes reading the substitutes. 'Bitte,' reply 26,000 people.

Eventually a man with a mullet squelches on to the pitch with a guitar and proceeds to sing another bombastic heavy rock tribute to the Gladbach team. Unfortunately for him, his performance is overshadowed mid-song when the visiting Mainz fans unfurl a huge banner the size of the entire away terrace celebrating the friendship between the two sets of fans. Caught up in the *bonhomie*, I have already purchased a scarf which bears Borussia's black-and-green on one half and Mainz's red-and-white on the other, the two designs being joined by a handshake and the words *Im Freundschaft*, 'In Friendship'. Almost 26,000 people applaud the banner; the rest are temporarily under canvas. Borussia's fans answer by holding up squares of green paper and bouncing up and down. This makes the north terrace look like a well-kept lawn undulating due to a horrendous mole problem.

The man with guitar finishes his song with a thundering climax, raises a clenched fist in the air and bows his head in readiness for the applause. Unfortunately the crowd's attention is still on the vast banner wafting at them from the other end of the stadium and the singer squelches back from whence he came. He passes a man dressed as a horse in full Borussia kit going the other way, who cavorts around on the soggy turf to more Gladbach-inspired heavy rock.

Despite the importance of the game to Borussia and in spite of the wet weather, the atmosphere is festive and friendly. Even when Mainz midfielder Robert Ratkowski is sent off after 12 minutes for his second bookable offence, he's given a rousing ovation as he trudges past the Nordtribune to the dressing-room. You'd be forgiven for deducing from the party atmosphere that Gladbach were already up, rather than chasing a slim chance of promotion. Against ten men it's all Borussia until just before the half-hour mark when Mainz break away and score. The Bökelberg falls briefly silent – this wasn't supposed to happen. Disbelieving Mainz fans jump up and down at the far end and the banner is unfurled again. Rumblings of discontent are heard beneath the singing, especially when Gladbach's Brazilian midfielder Chiquinho accelerates down the left and crosses, only to find that not a single white shirt has managed to reach the penalty area. However just before half-time, midfielder Marcel Ketelaer breaks through, takes the ball around the goalkeeper and slots it into the empty net.

Ketelaer is by far the best player on the field, a class above the rest. 'He'll be handy to have if you go up,' I say to my neighbour.

'Not really,' he replies, 'he's already signed for Hamburg.' The polarised nature of the modern game just gets worse for smaller clubs. Describing Gladbach as one of the smaller clubs in German football seems a little incongruous, but the former European giants look destined to be at best a lower middling Bundesliga team, or, more likely, a yo-yo club between the top two divisions. Unless some serious funding can be found, not least for a modern stadium, Gladbach's glory days will never come close to being repeated.

A minute after the interval, Chiquinho eases the tension by smashing in Gladbach's second via the underside of the crossbar. And within 30 seconds, Ketelaer has netted the third from close range. Just after the hour it's 4–1, thanks to a contender for the worst goal ever scored: Ketelaer crosses from the right; Nico Frommer turns the ball against the post; Gladbach's leading scorer, arboreal Dutchman Arie van Lent, slips as he goes for the rebound three yards out, succeeding only in heading the ball back against the post; as he falls, the rebound hits him on the hip and rolls gently over the line.

Van Lent scores a fifth from the penalty spot with 20 minutes remaining. Then, on 75 minutes, Marcel Witeczek wraps up the scoring after Ketelaer has once again bamboozled the Mainz defence, this time down the left. The 6–1 scoreline has boosted Gladbach's goal difference in their quest for promotion and recalls – however briefly – the joyous abandon of the Bökelberg in the '70s.

Exactly 25 years earlier, to the day, Gladbach had gone on a similar goal rampage: the 5–1 mauling of Enschede in the second leg of the 1975 UEFA Cup Final. The club's impressive programme for the Mainz game devoted several pages to commemorating that anniversary. Indeed, the centre pages were given over to a pull-out poster of beaming skipper Berti Vogts lifting the trophy high above his head. Suddenly it all seemed a very, very long time ago.

Other results had not gone Gladbach's way and promotion was by now unlikely. The following week the team went into the last game knowing that they'd have win and rely on other results to go up. True to their unpredictable nature, having looked awesome against Mainz, Gladbach fell to the occasion and lost 2–0 at Nuremberg. This left Energie Cottbus in third place to join VfL Bochum and FC Cologne in the Bundesliga.

On 8 August 2000 Borussia Mönchengladbach celebrated their centenary. The Mainz programme invited fans to pick their team of the century from a list including Berti Vogts, Rainer Bonhof, Stefan Effenberg, Lothar Matthäus, Günter Netzer, Uli Stieleke, Jupp Heynckes, Frank Mill and Allan Simonsen. Some the game's most famous names have worn Gladbach colours, but history counts for nothing now. That Borussia Mönchengladbach can be struggling in a German game at its lowest ebb for decades does not bode well for the future of football in the town.

Meanwhile Unterhaching continue to be the exception that proves the rule. Perhaps the key to Gladbach's survival at the top lies somewhere between the two clubs.

12.

HUNGARY AND ROMANIA: THE POISONING OF THE GAME

On 30 January 2000, over 100 tonnes of dangerous chemicals leaked from a commercial lake at a gold-processing plant and into the river Maros at Baia Mare, northern Romania. The leak contained enough cyanide, if taken in tablet form, to kill a billion people. In addition to the cyanide, lead and other heavy metals poured into the river from the half-Romanian, half-Australian-owned Aurul plant. So poisonous was the water in the breached lake that birds dropped dead just as a result of flying over it.

Within days the spill had crept into the river Tisza and on into Hungary, eventually making its way through Yugoslavia and into the Black Sea. Nearly all the fish in the river were killed, and in some places dead fish created a silvery carpet as they lay motionless on the surface of the filthy water, passing through towns at an appropriately funereal pace.

All along the river people mourned the death of their waterway. At Szeged, a town in southern Hungary that straddles the Tisza in the heart of the Great Plain, a black flag flew over the town hall. Townspeople dressed in funeral garb threw wreaths into the lifeless river as the glinting procession of dead fish passed under the town's bridge.

Szeged has known disaster before. In 1879 the river Tisza burst its banks and all but destroyed the town; but thanks to aid from foreign governments, whose capitals gave their names to the main boulevard which runs around the city, Szeged rose again. It's a town that relies on the fish from the river, which local legend says is 'two thirds water, one third fish'. *Szegedi halászlé*, a spicy fish soup is the town's speciality (for which it is internationally known) whilst *halapaprikás*, fish in a paprika sauce, is also popular. In January 2000 the town's fishermen had the easiest catch of their lives – hooking the dead, poisonous fish from the water and dumping them on to the city's rubbish tips.

Szeged, like Bratislava, is a city of two halves: the Tisza separates the elegant old town and the modern, industrial area of Újszeged. Usually it is a lively place. The university at Szeged is one of the most popular in Hungary and there is a vibrant student culture. But the poisoning of the Tisza destroyed a little piece of the city's soul. And, indirectly, it destroyed the city's only first-class football club.

The telephone just rings and rings at Szeged Labdarúgó Club. The 1999–2000 season had started brightly as the club embarked on its first campaign back in the top flight, having won promotion in 1999 after many years in the doldrums. However, the financial problems which cripple the game in most former eastern bloc countries soon took their toll and Szeged were left with only five registered players at the end of the winter break. The league had also imposed a transfer ban on the cash-strapped club, so they turned to the local authority for help. A loan of around a quarter of a million dollars was in the process of being arranged when the poisonous tide came fizzing out of Romania and choked the town's life-giving artery. The council was forced to direct the money intended for the football club into the emergency clean-up operation and Szeged LC disappeared quietly from Hungarian football.

They were lying seventeenth out of eighteen at the winter break, and their results were expunged. Szeged had never really set the Hungarian game alight – they lost the only cup final they ever reached 5–1 (in 1930) and their highest finish in the league was third (in 1941) – and they had existed in a number of different incarnations. But one of Hungary's major towns is now without a senior football club. As the Hungarian federation removed Szeged's results from the table and the league got under way again, it was as if football in the city of Szeged had never existed.

Three weeks after the leak, Australia were due to visit Budapest for an international friendly. The Hungarians blamed the Australian company Esmeralda Exploration – co-owner of the Baia Mare plant – for the leak. and the company's conduct after the problem came to light could have been better. At first they denied that any spillage had taken place and accounted for the thousands upon thousands of dead fish in the Tisza by proffering the bizarre theory that the water was too cold for them. They were also accused of putting lives at risk by not warning Hungary and Romania of the danger sooner.

Shortly after the news came to light, a jar of pickled herrings was lobbed symbolically through the window of the Australian embassy in the Hungarian capital Budapest. Against this background the Socceroos arrived in the country. There couldn't possibly have been a worse time for the Australian team to play in Budapest. A larger crowd than usual of around 14,000 turned out and some kind of protest was expected: Hungary's national team had not come within a country mile of qualifying for the European Championships and Australia were hardly crowd-pulling material. Attendances for even major Hungarian internationals rarely top 20,000 these days. Major league fixtures rarely attract more than 5,000 spectators even in the capital.

The Australian team, including Mark Bosnich, Mark Viduka and Harry Kewell, had been warned that protests might be aimed at them in Ferencváros's Üllöi Út stadium, but no one was quite sure what form they would take. Security was doubled in and around the ground as a precaution. Banners were unfurled bearing messages such as 'FISH HOLOCAUST' and 'IN MEMORIAM TISZA'.

The visitors soon went a goal up. The match appeared to be passing off without incident until the Australians' second goal, quarter of an hour from the end. It was then that a dead fish landed just inside the touchline. And another. Then another. Within minutes dozens of fish lay lifeless on the Budapest turf, some weighing in at over two pounds. Mark Bosnich tactfully tossed behind the touchline some of the scaly specimens that had come to rest in his area. Other fish remained on the pitch until the end of the match. The Australians added a third goal in the last minute and departed the field quickly. Aside from the protests, the 3–0 reverse to the Australians was the latest humiliation to a once-proud football nation. This latest football disaster served to underscore the crisis facing the game in central and eastern Europe.

The poisonous fluid that seeped through Romania and into Hungary was a fitting allegory for the game in both countries. Corruption, match-fixing and ineffectual administration make a damaging triumvirate in many central and eastern European nations, but Hungary is worse hit than most. Not helped by a national team that is currently at its lowest ebb, having once dominated the world game, Hungarian football is in poor shape. And after their embarrassing 12–1 World Cup aggregate qualifying defeat to Yugoslavia in 1997, the fans' one consoling thought was that at least things couldn't get any worse. *Could they?*

The date of 29 October 1997 will live long in the memory of Hungarian football fans. They had scraped into the World Cup play-offs thanks to a bizarre own-goal in the last minute of their final group match in Finland. The Finns needed to win, to snatch second place from the Hungarians and earn a play-off place. Anything but defeat would do for Hungary. On a rainy night in Helsinki the Finns scored the goal they needed just after the hour when Antti Sumiala met a corner at the far post.

Hungary seemed out of sorts and never seriously threatened to score the goal they needed. But in the final minute, defender Vilmos Sebök prodded the ball towards the goal-line. Finnish defender Sami Mahlio attempted to clear the ball, but succeeded only in launching it straight at the backside of goalkeeper Teuvo Moilanen. Agonisingly for the Fins the ball rolled gently over the line and Hungary were through.

However, with only ten minutes of the first leg against Yugoslavia played on that fateful day, Hungary were already beaten – their hopes of qualifying for the finals of a major tournament for the first time since 1986 extinguished by three goals from Branko Brnovic, Miroslav Djukic and Dejan Savicevic. The Nepstadion faithful saw their pitiful team ship another two goals before the break; and two more by the time an hour had been played. Fortunately for the home side the Yugoslavs eased off, even allowing Hungary a late consolation from Béla Illés. The 7–1 scoreline was the exact reverse of that meted out to England on the same pitch by Puskas' and Czibor's Golden Team in 1954 following the famous 6–3 win at Wembley a few months previously. A perfect demonstration of the depths to which Hungarian football had plummeted over the previous 40 years.

The return leg in Belgrade was a formality and Yugoslavia strolled to a 5–0 win. But it was during that first ten minutes in Budapest that the hopes of Hungarian football had been well and truly shredded. The looks of, first, bewilderment and then resignation on the faces of the Hungarian players made those ten minutes the perfect portrait of contemporary Hungarian football. After this humiliation the government forcibly changed the set-up of the Hungarian FA, the Magyar Labdárúgo Szövetség, by forcing the incumbent regime to resign. So dire was the state of the game in Hungary.

Early signs were good, but within six months the Hungarian Minister for Sport and Youth, Tamás Deutsch, had suspended the new president of the Federation, Anton Kovács, on the grounds of financial mismanagement. FIFA stepped in and threatened to suspend Hungary from international competition unless the situation were resolved satisfactorily. FIFA, being of course more important than a national government, told Deutsch that they would only recognise an administration elected according to their statutes: the government-imposed replacement did not conform to this practice.

As a result of this farce, Hungary's joint bid with Austria to host the 2004 European Championships lay as dead in the water as the fish of the Tisza. The 'Danube Games' might have provided a much-needed fillip to the game in both countries, but the tournament went instead to Portugal. Unsurprisingly, the Hungarian national team missed out on qualifying for Euro 2000; and World Cup 2002 already looks beyond Hungary, who have been drawn in a group with Italy and Romania.

As the Hungarian national team plumbed new depths, things were as bad on the domestic front. Violence and racism in grounds, combined with some poor-quality football, was leading to dwindling attendances. In a vicious circle, clubs found that they could barely afford to pay the players. Not surprisingly, the pick of the crop headed for Austria and Germany in search of better football and the guarantee of a regular pay packet.

The examples of Hungarian football's cash crisis are numerous. In May 1999, someone issued a bomb hoax to the stadium of Dunakeszi while their match against Palotás was in progress. The hoaxer had to phone the spoof warning to the factory next door, as the club's telephone had been cut off. Meanwhile, Stadler FC went out of business. Their owner, Józéf Stadler (who modestly gave the club his name), was sentenced to nine years' imprisonment for tax evasion in April 1998. Although the club made it to the end of the season, they were wound up as soon as it closed. But they were not paddling alone in the financial mire: most clubs in Hungary are heavily in debt.

As the game rotted like the fish on Szeged's rubbish dumps, the problems increased with the passing of each month. Whilst Szeged's misfortunes led to the club folding during the 1999–2000 winter break, Gázszer – lying fifth in the championship – were taken over by second-divison Pecs-Mecsek as the former club caved-in to its huge financial problems. In turn, Pecs sold their right to a second-division place to a club from lower down the leagues. Gázszer took on the Pecs name and most of their playing squad, in an extraordinary move whereby a second-division club had effectively purchased a first-division place in mid-season.

The Hungarian FA, under new boss Imre Bozóky, claimed that it could do nothing to prevent Pecs' extraordinary mid-season coup. However, a new league structure is due to be introduced for the 2000–01 season, which is to include new legislation designed to prevent such bizarre events as the Pecs takeover.

The cumbersome 18-team top flight will be cut to 16: the top 14 from the first division and two promoted clubs. For the first half of the season clubs will compete in two eight-team groups. After the winter break the top six from each group will contest the championship. It's a complicated new format, but at the moment anything seems better than the turgid set-up that has preceded it.

Tweaking the league format will not solve Hungary's problems, however. There are not just financial issues blighting the game. Violence and racism are also rife. In March 2000 a referee was badly injured by objects thrown from the crowd when he sent off three Újpesti players in the space of two minutes during a match with Dunaferr. Zoltan Szlezak went off for a second bookable offence; two minutes later Zoltan Tamasi was dismissed for a bad tackle; he was followed immediately by Balazs Kovács for protesting too vehemently. Újpesti coach Péter Várhidi was then ordered to the dressing-room – the last straw for the home fans. A hail of missiles injured the referee and one of his assistants and the match was abandoned with just 44 minutes played. The league responded by closing Újpesti's Megyeri stadium for two months, fining them heavily and awarding Dunaferr the points.

The Újpesti fans failed to be deterred, however, as barely a month later were involved in serious violence during their Budapest derby at Ferencváros. Budapest derbies have a history of simmering violence. This is mainly due to the fact that Újpesti were, during communist times, the club of the Interior Ministry and the secret police. A crowd of 2,000 Újpesti fans descended upon Ferencváros' all-seater Üllöi Út stadium and despite the large police presence 50 people were injured in the fighting.

János Vaczai of the Ministry of Youth and Sports blamed the poor condition of Hungarian football for the increase in violence of recent seasons. 'The quality of the game has declined and so have attendances,' he said. 'Those that do attend have an apathy towards the game, whilst a significant minority go purely to cause trouble.' The last day of the 1998–99 season saw the match between Akaszto and Gázszer attract a 'crowd' of just 84, possibly an all-time low for a top-flight game in Europe.

The Ministry launched an initiative called 'Support Don't Fight' in an attempt to dissuade troublemakers from attending matches and encourage peaceable fans to return to Hungarian stadia. With the backing of giants such as Adidas and Hungarian boxer István Kovács, a huge PR campaign was launched in March 2000, three days before the Újpesti–Ferencváros confrontation. It's still early to gauge the effect of the campaign, but at least something is being done.

Racism is a further ugly blight on the Hungarian game. The prime targets are the country's significant gypsy and Jewish populations, who have long suffered prejudice and violence in the region. Since the collapse of communism in 1989, Hungary's Jews have enjoyed a cultural renaissance. With the repressive communist regime, gone people no longer feel afraid to be Jewish. Synagogues have reopened and there is even a Jewish cookery programme on television. Not bad for a minority of 100,000 out of a population of 10 million. However, with this revival has come a resurgence in anti-semitic feeling. Late in 1999 a Jewish cemetery in Budapest was desecrated with swastikas and attacks on Jews by skinheads are becoming less rare.

For the Hungarian Roma, who at 600,000 are Hungary's most sizeable minority, the problems go even deeper. For centuries central European Romanies have been the targets for abuse and prejudice. Not surprisingly, the modern gypsies have tended to stick together, making them a target for prejudice. But this prejudice goes beyond taunts and attacks, to discrimination in the employment market and denial of civil rights. Whilst the Hungarians' record is not as bad as the neighbouring Czech Republic and Slovakia, the European Union recently warned Hungary that their aspirations to EU membership were being hampered by their treatment of Hungarian gypsies. Progress has been made on both sides, with over 150 independent Romany cultural and civil organisations having sprung up since 1989; but on the terraces of the nation's football grounds anti-Roma songs are sung with feeling, and attacks on gypsies around football grounds have increased alarmingly in recent years. In March 2000 the Hungarian Foreign Ministry appealed for a crackdown on racist activity at football matches.

'The Foreign Ministry recommended in a letter to ministries affected to take strong measures against extremist phenomena conflicting with government policy and intentions,' said an official statement. 'These phenomena . . . have appeared recently at soccer matches in the form of racist slogans.'

The Foreign Minister, Zsolt Nemeth, had been alerted by the Israeli ambassador to a popular chant of 'The train is leaving for Auschwitz' – aimed particularly at supporters of MTK, a Budapest club formed by Jewish liberals in the nineteenth century which has always attracted a strong Jewish following. The club's president, Alfred Brüll, and many of its supporters were sent to their deaths in the concentration camps during the vicious flurry of anti-Semitism in Hungary in the closing stages of the Second World War. Envy also played a part: MTK are possibly the only top-flight club not to have financial worries, thanks to their owner, Gábor Várszsegi, being the richest man in Hungary.

As 1999–2000 closed it was still too early to judge how successful this crackdown initiative was likely to be. The penultimate round of matches saw Dunaferr's match with Diosgyör abandoned early in the second half when 40 fans invaded the pitch and began fighting.

Perhaps the combination of a positive public relations campaign and the restructuring of the league will provide a fillip to the game in Hungary. Dunaferr, a club from the very centre of the country, won the title from MTK in 2000. It was Dunaferr's first title in their 50-

year history. Like the Budapest club, they enjoy the backing of a major industrialist. And unless similar investment is ploughed into other Hungarian clubs, there will be many more Szegeds going to the wall.

Meanwhile in Romania, the source of the poisonous spillage, the game lurches from crisis to crisis in similar fashion to their neighbours. As with most of their surrounding nations the collapse of communism allowed the cream of Romania's talent to head west in search of riches unthinkable in their homeland. While the international adventures of Hagi, Popescu, Petrescu and (more recently) Ilie and Mutu have unquestionably helped the national team, domestic football in Romania is infested with the poison of corruption and the perils of financial hardship.

In April 2000, the entire playing staff of newly-promoted first-division side Extensiv Craiova went on strike in protest at having gone six months without being paid. The club had been due to leave for a friendly tournament in northern Italy with compatriots National Bucharest, Poland's Zaglebie Lublin and the Bulgarian club Liteks Lovech. However, the day before they were due to leave, the players announced that they would not be returning to the training ground until they had received what they were owed.

A few days later, Romania's former FIFA referee and domestic match assessor Adrian Porumboiu was dropped by the Federation of Romanian Football (FRF) for repeating certain allegations of bribery and match-fixing. He and a colleague had already been warned for airing these a few months earlier. Porumboiu voiced the opinion of many when he said that FRF president Mircea Sandu was allowing referees in the Romanian league to accept bribes from clubs in return for favourable decisions. 'Sandu knew all about the bribes right from the beginning,' alleged Porumboiu. 'He cannot say he knew nothing about it.'

Financial pressures and corruption have haunted the Romanian domestic game for a number of years. The success of the national team has always been greeted with joy by the football public – most notably after the victory over England in the last World Cup, their success at Euro 2000 and their first win over rivals Hungary for 63 years in the Euro 2000 qualifiers – but with most of the best Romanian players now based abroad, current attendances at domestic matches are woeful.

Whilst the top players can dream of riches outside Romania, the journeymen footballers find that football as a career is not proving to be a particularly lucrative option within their home nation. Last year the FRF was forced to cancel the playing contracts of a number of first- and second-division clubs simply because those clubs could not afford to pay them. The strike at Extensiv Craiova was inevitable and unlikely to be the last such action. No wonder promising young players pack their bags and head across the border at the first whiff of foreign interest.

Strict rules concerning sponsorship in Romania close off another potential avenue of income, leading to bizarre situations such as the goalkeeper who moved between two financially crippled second-division clubs for a fee of a lorry load of firewood. In 1998 one provincial club saw its star striker depart in return for two tonnes of meat. Second-division Olimpia Satu Mare received from their sponsors not a car for each of their players, nor expensive electrical equipment. Instead, the training ground took delivery of a pig and a calf, both of which were slaughtered and fed to the players at their training camp during the season's winter break.

While tales of such transactions can raise a chuckle in Britain, tragically even the tiniest cutting of financial corners can have devastating effects. During the opening match of the 1998–99 season, Astra Ploesti's Stefan Vrabioru collapsed on the Rapid Bucharest pitch. To save the equivalent of around £15, Rapid had not arranged to have an ambulance at the ground. Vrabioru died on his way to hospital amid oily rags and tools in the back of a battered transit van.

Perhaps unsurprisingly, given the financial rewards available in European competition, corruption in Romanian football is rife. Match-fixing is so common that unofficially it is virtually accepted as a part of the game. Few people dare to speak out, the exceptions being Porumboiu and Gheorghe Stefan, who resigned from the board of the FRF in December 1999 in protest at the 'hostile refereeing' received by his team (Ceahlul Piatra Neamt) in the two matches prior to the winter break.

One of the more notorious examples of this 'hostile refereeing' took place in a Bucharest derby match between giants Steaua and freshly promoted Rocar Bucharest in 1999. A goal up, Rocar had a perfectly good second goal disallowed, followed almost immediately by a blatantly offside Steaua equaliser. In the dying seconds Steaua were awarded a penalty so unjust that the 'sinned-against' striker was seen on the television footage to burst out laughing. Needless to say, the winner was dispatched from the spot.

The reputation of Romanian referees is now so bad that for the match between Dinamo Bucharest and Rapid Bucharest, which effectively would decide the destination of the championship that season, the authorities brought in a referee from Germany so as to avoid accusations of bribery and corruption. Rapid won 1–0 in a match unusual for the absence of controversy.

———————————

The situation in Romania today is typical of most of the former eastern bloc countries, where corruption and financial hardship threatens to widen the gap between east and west to insurmountable proportions. After all, it is only five years since Dynamo Kyiv, who have come closest to challenging western European dominance of the game in recent years, were suspended from the international game for attempting to bribe the referee of their European tie with Panathinaikos.

At the start of the 2000 Russian season, for example, things looked good on the surface when newly-installed Russian president Vladimir Putin watched Spartak Moscow open the defence of their Russian League title with a 3–1 win over Alania Vladikavkaz in front of 30,000 Muscovites. After a dismal 1999 – described by Russian Football Union president Vyacheslav Koloskov as a 'disaster for Russian football' – a thrilling game in front of a bumper crowd was a fitting dish to set before the country's new leader.

However, elsewhere in Europe's largest nation it became clear that the Russian game still faces some extraordinary problems. Across town the same day, Lokomotiv Moscow were due to take on rivals CSKA at the Lokomotiv Stadium. CSKA's preparations for the season had already been thrown into turmoil by the kidnapping of club president Oleg Dolmatov's wife, who has not been seen since February 2000.

Building work at the Lokomotiv ground had restricted the capacity to 10,000. However, in common with the corruption and black marketeering that blights the Russian game, thousands of counterfeit tickets in circulation led to a near riot at the ground as fans with legitimate tickets found their seats already occupied. Some heavy-handed policing led the *Moscow Sport-Express* to demand of clubs, 'Be Nice To Your Fans' on their front page the following day.

At least that game went ahead. Premier Division newcomers Anji Makhachkala were due to face Torpedo Moscow in the southern city of Astrakhan that day. However, the day before the match the Russian Football Union decided to call off the match amid security fears regarding the fighting in the breakaway republic of Chechnya (200 kilometres away).

'We weren't told until late on Friday that our match on Saturday was cancelled,' complained Torpedo president Vladimir Alyoshin. 'The club had to spend a lot of money on air fares and hotel bills and it's all been for nothing.'

This was not a promising opening to the season for Russian football. The Football Union had hoped that the new millennium would represent a fresh start for the ailing game, after failure to qualify for Euro 2000 and Russian clubs' early exit from the European competitions. Spartak's was seen as the biggest failure. The Moscow club, who have won seven of the last eight Russian championships, made no impression on the Champions League and then, given another chance in the UEFA Cup, fell at the first hurdle to Leeds United. Despite having their own centre of excellence and a formidable network of talent scouts, Spartak have failed to make any significant impression on the European game.

Coach Oleg Romantsev believes the war in Chechnya is partly to blame. 'Not a single world- or European-class player will come to a country where there is a war going on, no matter how much you pay them,' he said after Spartak's Champions League elimination was sealed by a 5–2 thrashing at Slavia Prague in September. 'It's clear that with the political situation in our country no one wants the top European clubs to come and play here. That is why they don't want us to advance to the final stages of the competitions.'

The precarious economic and political situation may well be deterring players from overseas, but some will point to threats to their own personal safety as reason enough to steer clear of Russia. The kidnapping of the unfortunate Mrs Dolmatov is well known; and 1999's leading goalscorer in Russian football, Oleg Veretennikov, had acid thrown at him and his two year-old daughter whilst out walking in a local park. Even the world figure-skating champion, Marina Batyrskaya, had her car blown up outside her Moscow apartment.

Despite the seemingly endless problems facing the Russian game, UEFA president Lennart Johanneson has given tacit backing to Russia's bid to host the European Championships in 2008. 'I have no doubt that Russia can host such an event, and it must go to eastern Europe,' he said in Moscow just before the start of the new season. 'Politics is something else and we're not involved with politics. Let the politicians deal with the Chechnya situation.'

It was a bizarre statement from the most powerful man in European football. In the former eastern bloc countries in central and eastern Europe, football and politics are almost inseparable. The demise of Szeged LC can be traced back to the easy profits desired by Esmeralda Exploration in Baia Mare. An impotent government, desperate to attract foreign investment, had problems enforcing safety regulations – already not as strict as in European Union countries – and the result was the cyanide spill that oozed through Romania and into Hungary.

Whilst the Champions League remains dominated by the richest western European clubs, and the major leagues continue to earn incredible sums from television rights, the gap in resources will continue to grow until the game in the centre and east of the continent is choked. The national federations must shoulder much of the blame, for their ineffectiveness at combating bribery and corruption is a major factor in the near-farcical condition of football in many countries, but European economics is a leading factor in the demise of the game in former communist nations.

Corruption appears to be endemic in all sectors of these nations' societies, but unless UEFA and national federations can arrest the increasing divide between western Europe and the rest, the future of the domestic game in Europe is in jeopardy.

There are signs of hope, however. In 1999 the Hungarian national youth team travelled to Wembley and beat their English counterparts 1–0: maybe not as earth-shattering a result as 1953, but an encouraging sign for this once-great football power to cling on to. Most worrying in the short term, though, was this: the 35,000 crowd watching that youth game in west London was over 5,000 more than the entire attendance put together for Premier Division matches played that day in Hungary.

Until someone takes a stand against corruption, violence and racism in former eastern bloc countries, then the deadly water that bubbled out of northern Romania that cold January morning won't be the only poison choking the life from Romanian and Hungarian communities.

13.

EUROPEAN CHAMPIONSHIPS: LOW COUNTRIES, HIGH IDEALS

In the early hours of an October morning in 1999 at Ljubljana airport, 3,000 people had gathered in the snow to welcome the conquering heroes of Slovenia back from their victorious Euro 2000 play-off encounter with Ukraine. Slovenia (population: 2 million) had just held Ukraine (population: 52 million) to a 1–1 draw in Kyiv, which, following their 2–1 victory in the first leg, was enough to earn them a place at the Euro 2000 table.

As the aircraft carrying the team emerged from a blizzard to touch down on Slovenian soil, the gathered throng reflected on their footballers' phenomenal achievement. The team had gained just a solitary point from their 1998 World Cup qualifying campaign and few had given them an earthly of qualifying for Euro 2000. However, the combination of a kindly draw and new boss Srecko Katanec's ability to turn a demoralised diaspora of foreign-based players into a hard-working attack-minded unit saw the Slovenes finish as group runners-up behind Norway.

Reaching the play-offs was seen as an achievement in itself by Slovenian sports fans, who are generally more concerned with skiing than football. So when the diminutive former Yugoslav republic was paired with mighty Ukraine, few were distracted enough from the piste reports to plan a Benelux expedition for the following summer.

With six minutes remaining of the first leg in Ljubljana, the Ukrainians looked to have secured a valuable 1–1 draw to take back to Kyiv as goalkeeper Aleksandr Shovkovsky trotted out towards the left touchline to take a free-kick. But he slipped slightly on the wet surface and his kick fell short, reaching Slovenia's Milenko Acimovic on the halfway line. Controlling the ball neatly on his thigh, Acimovic launched a speculative lob towards the visitors' goal.

High into the night sky it went, while Shovkovsky, suddenly leaden-footed, scampered back towards his undefended goal. The ball began its descent with the Ukrainian custodian still floundering across the sodden turf. The hapless keeper arrived too late, however, and Acimovic's punt dropped gently into the top corner ahead of his desperate and undignified lunge into the back of the net.

It was a goal of awesome impudence and one that gave the Slovenians genuine hope for the return leg. It will also give Shovkovsky anxiety dreams for the rest of his days.

Slovenia travelled to Kyiv in high spirits, but most pundits predicted Ukraine would overturn the deficit with relative ease; and when a Serhii Rebrov penalty cancelled out the Slovene lead midway through the first half, it looked as though the gallant minnows were on their way out. Ten minutes from time, however, a poorly taken Slovenian free-kick was hammered into the Ukraine wall. The ball squirted out to the left wing where Kaiserslautern's Miran Pavlin hit a 25-yard effort into the crowded penalty area. A slight deflection was enough to carry the ball past Shovkovsky and put little Slovenia into the Euro 2000 finals.

'This is phenomenal,' gasped coach Katanec, afterwards. 'We never even dared to dream of such a success.'

Football is still a relatively minor sport in Slovenia. Despite being the most economically advanced and 'westernised' of the former Yugoslav republics, Slovenia had watched Croatia, Yugoslavia and even Bosnia-Herzegovina make a bigger impression on the European game since independence in 1991. Until then.

Restricted by size and finance, the Slovenian FA hoped that qualification would inspire businesses to invest in the struggling domestic game, where attendances rarely topped 2,000. Such were the financial restrictions that the victorious players came home from Kyiv to a whopping £350-a-man qualification bonus.

'The Slovenians have demonstrated in this war of nerves that they are capable of being masters of their own fate. This is an historic moment for Slovenia.' Not the words of Srecko Katanec after the extraordinary 3–3 draw between Slovenia and Yugoslavia, but actually those of Janez Stanovik, President of Slovenia, in 1989 after a referendum in the republic came out in favour of independence from the Yugoslavs. And that set in motion the chain of events that led to Tuesday's match: within two years of that referendum Slovenia was independent, following a brief, half-hearted ten-day war with Yugoslavia, and in 1994 the tiny nation of just two million inhabitants played its first competitive international. Italy were the first visitors to Slovenia for a Euro 96 qualifier, escaping from Ljubljana with a 1–1 draw.

In the team that night was Srecko Katanec, an elegant attacking midfielder coming towards the end of an illustrious playing career. During spells with Olimpia Ljubljana, Dinamo Zagreb, Partizan

Belgrade, VfB Stuttgart and Sampdoria, the much-travelled Katanec amassed 31 caps for Yugoslavia and went on to play five times for Slovenia.

But it is in a coaching capacity that Katanec has become the toast of his homeland. Having managed Slovene club side HIT Gorica and the Slovene under-21 side, Katanec was not the most experienced coach in the world when he took over the senior squad after the disastrous 1998 World Cup qualifying campaign. Instilling an attacking philosophy borne out of his own adventurous combative playing style, as well as his willingness to give the magnificent Zlatko Zahovic his head rather than restricting him to a game plan, Katanec guided the Slovenes to second place in their Euro 2000 qualifying group.

Admittedly it wasn't the toughest of the groups, but their victory over Ukraine in the play-offs showed that Slovenia had resilience, intelligence and not a little ability. Milenko Acimovic's extraordinary 50-yard lob into the top corner to win the first leg in the closing minutes showed that Slovenia had flair to go with their organisation. Add a significant amount of national pride and you have the mixture that carried them into a three-goal lead against their former countrymen.

'We deserved to qualify,' said Katanec; 'we dared to be courageous throughout the campaign. If I've taught the boys anything at all it is that team spirit is vital and that we will achieve good results if we are good friends of the pitch and play from the heart on it.' Showing a commendable attitude, Katanec added: 'We will try to show character and try to score goals, but we are not afraid to lose 4–0 or 5–0.'

For a nation usually more concerned with winter sports than football, qualification sent the Slovenians into dreamland. Their allocation of 16,000 tickets for Euro 2000 was snapped up in no time, and by the time they played Norway in their final group game, 12,000 Slovenians were in town – whether they had tickets or not.

Always the most 'westernised' of the Yugoslav republics, Slovenia's population is renowned for its culture and intelligence. When striker Saso Udovic mentioned the word 'existential' in a pre-match interview, the BBC pundits were bemused and attempted to take the mickey, not realising that in doing so the joke was firmly on them. But the refreshingly open attitude of the Slovenian players and coaching staff was a welcome respite from the usual guarded clichés that characterise major tournaments. Their hotel and training camp was a virtual open house for Slovenians in the Low Countries.

For the Slovenians were there for more than football. 'After this a few more people will know about Slovenia,' said Udovic before the tournament. A major Slovene bugbear is that their nation is often confused with Slovakia – something John Motson managed to achieve within two minutes of beginning his commentary on the game with Yugoslavia.

To lose a 3–0 lead to ten men would have some coaches tearing their hair out. Not Katanec. 'I promised we would come here and play open football and we did,' he said after the game. 'We can be pleased with the point and proud of the performance.' He also paid tribute to Yugoslav coach Viktor Boskov, who was not only his manager for three years at Sampdoria but also his housemate. 'I literally shared the same roof as Boskov. He offered me his hospitality in Genoa and that's how I started my preparation for a career in coaching,' he revealed, sitting alongside his mentor.

Slovenia left an unforgettable mark on the tournament. Their flair, intelligence and pride has been reflected on and off the field. 'For those first 70 minutes we played some superb football,' said Udovic. 'I was proud to be Slovenian.' For – beneath the commercialism and sponsorship frenzy in which Euro 2000 is embroiled – isn't that what the tournament was all about?

It was an issue lost on the BBC's otherwise impressive Gary Lineker. 'Well,' he said sarcastically after the opening credits before Slovenia v. Yugoslavia, 'this is the one you've all been waiting for.' With a barely perceptible twitch of the eyebrow and the edges of a smile tugging at the corners of his mouth, Lineker condemned what he obviously considered to be two largely anonymous wholly uninteresting teams to mediocrity. A couple of days later, Lineker asked Johann Cruyff which teams had impressed him: Cruyff picked France, Portugal and . . . Slovenia.

Meanwhile, on ITV, the priorities of their coverage were made clear even before the first game. Gary Newbon asked a couple of bland questions of Sweden's Freddie Ljungberg, before diving in with what he really wanted to know. 'We've heard that you're not allowed to have sex during the tournament. Is that true?' With a weary smile Ljungberg deflected the question, preferring to talk about football. 'But is there a sex ban?' repeated Newbon. Again, Ljungberg moved the interview back to football. Newbon would not be deterred, however. Virtually drooling by now, he again asked, 'Is there a sex ban?'

An incredulous Ljungberg looked at Newbon's leering phizzog and replied, 'But our wives aren't even here, anyway.'

The anglocentricism of the television coverage was not as overt as usual, which was encouraging to see. There were no 'Skontons' for example. However, David Pleat announced that he was 'interested to see how Czechoslovakia will do'. He wasn't the only one, considering it hadn't existed for the previous seven years.

Terry Venables, talking about potential winners, said, 'No one's mentioned the Italians, and they will love that.' No one, that is, except the three Italian daily sports papers who devoted page after page every day to the rights, wrongs and rumours of Zoff's selection and tactics for weeks leading up to the tournament. What Terry meant was that no one in England had mentioned them, which is possibly not the yardstick the *azzurri* were using.

Naturally most of the attention was focused on England's group. Ten years ago England and Germany would almost certainly have been the two teams to qualify, but times have changed in Europe and the two former powers have now been left way behind.

'YOU ARE THE FOOTBALL BERKS OF EUROPE! GERMANY IS ASHAMED OF YOU!' was the *Bild* headline that greeted the disgraced German squad when they returned home following their spineless 3–0 defeat to a virtual Portuguese reserve team in Rotterdam. For the first time ever Germany, the reigning European champions, returned from the finals of a major tournament without having recorded a single victory.

'Bottom of the group! No victories! A pathetic goal!' were the facts laid out by the German red-top after Oliver Kahn's comedic blunder (which let in Portugal's second goal) had sealed Germany's fate at the De Kuip stadium.

'This is the low point of the last two years,' said the Bayern Munich goalkeeper afterwards, 'and we players are responsible. I am ashamed. We all are. Now there is no option but to build a new team.'

That night in Rotterdam will surely prove to be a watershed for German international football. Coach Erich Ribbeck tendered his inevitable resignation almost exactly two years after taking on the job. Never the first choice, following Berti Vogts resignation after the last World Cup, Ribbeck was the one unfortunate enough still to be standing when the Deutsche Fußball Bund (DFB) music stopped. Better-qualified names such as Jupp Heynckes, Paul Breitner, Ottmar Hitzfeld and Christophe Daum had either turned down the job or made themselves unavailable – realising the thankless nature of the task – before the German governing body approached the former Bayern Munich and Bayer Leverkusen boss.

That Ribbeck should shoulder the blame is unfair, for he inherited a dispirited, squabbling, ageing squad and had little young talent available around which to build a new team. He experimented with different players and tactics, but the shambolic state of German international football was there for all to see. Of the motley collection of veterans, journeymen and fresh-faced youngsters cobbled together for Euro 2000, only Kahn and Milan striker Oliver Bierhoff could be regarded as world class. The fact that Ribbeck was still required to build the team around a 39-year-old seeing out his career in American Major League Soccer sums up the dearth of talent at his disposal.

Germany were always on to a hiding in the Low Countries and Ribbeck knew it. 'It would be wrong to regard us as favourites,' he had said before the tournament. 'We will travel to the European Championships as outsiders behind several nations' – a remarkable statement for a German national coach and an indication of the rapid decline of the German team since they became European champions four years previously.

Midfielder Jens Jeremies went even further, following Germany's 2–1 defeat in a friendly against the Netherlands before the finals. 'Miserable' was how he described the squad. 'When you look at the national team over the past few years, when did they last offer an outstanding game?' he asked. 'Nothing has changed or improved. Maybe it would have been better if we had lost 5–0 to the Netherlands; that would have opened everybody's eyes to the situation in the national team.'

In their final warm-up match, Germany beat Liechtenstein 8–2. Not a bad result on paper. But five of the goals came in the last 15 minutes; and, with an hour gone, the part-timers from the tiny principality, who not too long ago lost 11–1 at home to Macedonia, were holding the European champions at 2–2.

Following Ribbeck's departure, the DFB will find it hard to deflect the anger of the German press and fans. Many critics argue that there are too many overseas players in the Bundesliga, suffocating the opportunities for young German talent to come through and shine. The production line of wonderful players that has kept Germany at the top of the world game appears to have spluttered to a halt. Cheap Scandinavian and eastern European imports litter the German league and there is little opportunity for home-grown talent to emerge. Only the performances of 20-year-old Hertha Berlin midfielder Sebastien Deisler during the tournament offer any hope for the immediate future of German international football.

'We need new men. Immediately. Because there is much to do. Very much,' concluded *Bild*, in a rare example of a tabloid newspaper mastering the understatement.

Group A showed perfectly how out of touch England and Germany have become. The vision and passing of the Portuguese and Romanians were quite some way ahead of anything their group opponents could produce. Even at 2–0 down against England the Portuguese calmly passed the ball around – has there ever been a tournament where the ball spent so long actually on the ground? – waiting for the openings they knew would surely come. Joao Pinto's equaliser shortly before half-time was the best example. England were chasing shadows, milling around like a primary-school team after a ball which was always just out of their reach. Even Romania, whose domestic game is in such as shambles that nearly all of the squad plays outside Romania, showed up England in the final group encounter. Although Romania's winner came from a penalty two minutes from time, the difference between the two sides was greater than the 3–2 scoreline suggested.

One of the few England players who looked capable of rising above the mediocrity was, before he was injured, Steve McManaman. Is it coincidence that he was the only member of the squad playing outside the English Premiership? Has the time come for English players to gain experience in Spain, Italy or France? Is it time for a non-English coach to inject new ideas into a tired national game? Or was the demolition of the English and German schools a blip, a tournament one-off?

The English press displayed a degree of humility, faced with such overwhelming evidence, but still displayed a modicum of the blinkered approach of the 1954 team that travelled to Budapest and were hammered 7–1. Michael Owen had a poor tournament, the weight of expectation hanging over him so heavily that it may be the reason why he hit the ground so often when anyone ventured near him. Luis Figo's opener for Portugal stemmed from England losing possession after an Owen dive near the left touchline. Another time, Owen launched himself two-footed at a Portuguese defender who, watching the ball, caught the England striker's heel as it hurtled past at thigh height. Clive Tyldesley somehow interpreted the challenge as a dreadful foul on the boy wonder.

Of the best teams in the group, Romania and Portugal couldn't have been better acquainted. They arrived at the finals from the same qualifying group, with the Romanians unbeaten at the top of Group Seven and Portugal qualifying as the best runners-up. Romania, in fact, inflicted Portugal's only qualifying defeat of the campaign, although the Euro 2004 hosts did need a frighteningly late equaliser to avoid defeat against Azerbaijan in Baku. Indeed, the Portuguese almost lost to what were effectively Azerbaijan reserves, as the national federation couldn't afford to bring home their players based abroad.

Quarter-finalists at Euro 96, Portugal had always promised much but failed consistently to deliver. Their squad has played some beautiful football over the past decade, earning them the sobriquet 'the Brazil of Europe', yet rarely had they looked like winning major honours until Euro 2000. Their midfield of Barcelona's Luis Figo, Fiorentina's Rui Costa, Paulo Sousa of Inter Milan and Lazio's Sergio

Conceicao is one of the most creative in the world. But the lack of a striker, to turn the midfield artistry consistently into goals, has meant that Portugal have not taken the place at the pinnacle of the European game as many had predicted they would do. For it was in 1989 and 1991 that the under-20 side, described as Portugal's 'golden generation', won the world championships with a team that included Figo, Costa, Sousa and Benfica's Joao Pinto.

For these players, Euro 2000 represented their last chance of success at anything approaching their peak; and with Benfica striker Nuno Gomes among younger players showing increasing promise and consistency, the incredible scenes of protest that greeted Abel Xavier's instinctive semi-final handball may be understandable. After all, as Rui Costa commented before the finals, 'You are not a golden generation if you don't win anything.'

Romania, meanwhile, had qualified only twice before – in 1984 and 1996 – and were eliminated at the group stage on both occasions. They had not even registered a victory in the finals and had but a solitary draw to their credit from both previous tournaments. The omens, this time, looked better. Their coach, 62-year-old Emeric Ienei, guided Steaua Bucharest to the 1986 European Cup and in a previous reign led Romania to the 1990 World Cup finals. Despite leading the team to undefeated triumph in the qualifiers, previous boss Victor Piturca was dismissed because of a poor relationship with the squad. Ienei was a surprise choice, but his popularity with the players is believed to have swung the appointment his way.

Although stars such as Galatasaray's Gheorghe Hagi and Gheorghe Popescu were reaching the end of their careers, Ienei pointed to the emergence of young players such as Laurentiu Rosu, Cristian Chivu, and striker Adrian Mutu as an indication that this blend of youth and experience could carry Romania to glory. 'It's right that we should want to cap so many successful years with a great performance,' he said, with Hagi adding: 'We have a lot of players who have been in the squad for ten years. Why shouldn't we think of ending our careers with glory?'

Hagi's career, unfortunately for him, ended with a red card and loud mutterings that the team did better without him. Romania certainly look set to be a strong force for some time to come despite Hagi's retirement. They are certainly better equipped than a Stoichkov-free Bulgaria.

Unusually, for the hyped finals of a major tournament, most of what emerged from Euro 2000 was positive. The football was fantastic, even the refereeing drew praise (apart from David Pleat's surreal comment that 'there'll be no chocolates in the referee's bedroom tonight' during one game, which, I presume, was meant to be some sort of criticism). France v. Holland in the group stage was as close to a perfect football match as you could get. And that was with France fielding a reserve team.

The humility and honesty displayed by Kevin Keegan after England's exit gives hope that Willy Meisl's gloomy, but largely vindicated, 1955 predictions might at last be coming to an end. England must look hard at its youth system. Slovakia have managed to strip their system down and start again and the Slovak under-21 team beat their English counterparts convincingly before Euro 2000.

If Euro 2000 proved anything, it was that the Charles Hughes school of football is now totally discredited. Norway tried it and came unstuck. France and Portugal were two teams that demonstrated some beautiful midfield and attacking play, yet their defences were also sound: between Steve McManaman's goal for England and the semi-final, Portugal went 392 minutes without conceding a goal, and that with a goalkeeper struggling for match fitness. France's back four of Lilian Thuram, Marcel Desailly, Laurenc Blanc and Bixente Lizarazu played together 26 times for their country and were never on the losing side. Enviable defensive records from committed attacking sides.

But we shouldn't forget the progress to the final of the Italians, who based their philosophy on defence and swift counter-attacking and came within seconds of the championship. Had Sylvain Wiltord not equalised in injury-time, perhaps the post-mortems and glowing tributes to beautiful football might have read differently. The battle between Dutch flair and a padlocked Italian defence in the semi-final was not thrilling, but it was certainly absorbing. Had Alessandro Del Piero not produced such a disappointing individual tournament, things might have been different for the Italians. And don't forget that they were also without Christian Vieri, one of the most potent attacking forces in the European game.

However, Italy didn't win, France did. The Italians aside, the defensive and unimaginitive teams went home early – Norway, England, Germany and the huffing, puffing co-hosts, Belgium. The passing teams, the ones with the flair, stayed in the tournament.

The only blight on Euro 2000 was the Charleroi violence. The tabloid press was quick to condemn it, but not to accept responsibility for fanning the flames of the warped nationalism behind much of the trouble. The press obsession with the Second World War has barely dimmed since the Euro 96 'Achtung Surrender' incident. Even *The Times*, on the day of the England–Germany match, noted that the match kick-off time was 1945, 'which has to be a good sign' (even though it was only 1945 in England: everywhere else in Europe was an hour ahead). After the tournament the announcement that Berlin's Olympic Stadium would stage the final of the 2006 World Cup produced the *Times* headline, 'HITLER'S STADIUM TO STAGE FINAL'.

Whatever the reasons behind the violence, I am certainly ill qualified to comment. I stopped going to England matches in 1989 after being jostled by those around me for not *sieg-heil*ing through the national anthem at an England–Poland World Cup qualifier and I find the ill-informed xenophobia from the minority that accompanies England matches hard to stomach. Thankfully the trouble didn't detract from what was a fantastic championship. But what puzzles me slightly is that the Germans and Dutch managed to prevent most of their hooligans from attending the championships *without* the added advantage of a dirty great expanse of water between their countries and the tournament.

Most fans, however, had a great time and enjoyed some memorable football. The slick passing, telepathic movement off the ball and vision of the French, Dutch Portuguese, Romanians – and even the Yugoslavs, who seemed to fare better with only ten men on the field – all combined to show that European football is currently leading the world. Slovenia again returned to Ljubljana airport to be greeted by jubilant crowds.

Dutch economists pleaded with their team not to win the trophy, for the sake of the economy, and Belgium's coach Robert Waseige urged his team 'not to be too Belgian' and relax too much. For an hour Slovenia could have beaten anyone in the world, but couldn't quite manage to beat the team they'd most like to, even with a three-goal headstart and a man advantage. Romania's victory over England, through which they progressed to the next stage of the competition, brought celebrating crowds on to the streets of Bucharest in numbers not seen since the end of the Ceaucescu regime. Filip de Wilde provided moments of high farce; Philip Neville a moment of tragedy.

It was all very European.

14.

NORWAY: NORTHERN LIGHTS

You can't go any further north in the world and watch top-flight football than Tromsø. Situated on an island off the Norwegian coast 250 miles above the Arctic Circle, Tromsø is as far north of its capital, Oslo, as Big Ben is of the Leaning Tower of Pisa.

Tromsø, the largest town north of the Arctic Circle, has many claims to northerliness. Its Catholic cathedral ministers to around 900 parishioners, spread far across the region, and is so short of flock that it had to import its bishop from Germany. But it is the northernmost cathedral in the world, standing as it does around 600 yards further north than its Lutheran counterpart. The Mack Brewery, which produces the region's refreshing yet expensive beer, and which is home (perhaps appropriately) to the British consulate, is the world's most northerly brewery. And the town's football team, Tromsø IL, is the northernmost first-class football club in the world.

It certainly feels like it. Walking from the harbour doesn't look far on the map but it's all uphill along a winding road lined with attractive, brightly painted wooden houses. By the time the floodlights and flagpoles hove into view at the summit, you almost know how Robert Falcon Scott felt when he found Roald Amundsen's Norwegian flag fluttering at the South Pole. Most of Amundsen's polar expeditions left from Tromsø, and it was from the harbour there that the Norwegian explorer departed for the North Pole in a flying-boat in 1928, in search of a lost Italian airship. He never returned. His formidably eyebrowed features peer out of at least two statues in the town and a whole floor of Tromsø's Polar Museum is dedicated to his exploits.

The floodlights at the Alfheim Stadium are largely redundant. Norwegian football is a summer pursuit and they know about summer in Tromsø: the sun comes up in mid-May and doesn't go down again until late July. It's certainly a strange feeling coming out of a bar at 3 a.m. into blazing sunshine.

So, despite the evening kick-off, the sun is still high in the sky over the Alfheim – the northernmost-possible point for my journey through European football and my last port of call. All I knew of Tromsø football before my arrival were the pictures that I'd seen of Chelsea's visit in the 1997 Cup-Winners' Cup, when the match had to be held up several times for volunteers to clear heavy snow from the lines. It was unfair, said Chelsea, who lost the match 3–2: the Norwegians were used to playing in such inclement conditions. Oh no they weren't – it was just that the UEFA competitions calendar makes no allowance for the long, dark, harsh north European winter.

I arrive at the Alfheim short of breath and in strong sunshine. 'Are you from Manchester?' asks the young man organising the press room with hopeful eyes. 'Oh,' he says crestfallen when I tell him between gasps that I'm not. 'My favourite team is Manchester United,' he says; 'I've loved them since I was . . . ' he holds his hand out flat about three feet above the ground.

The global marketing machine from Old Trafford has reached even here. Out of the window, I see a bus pull away from the ground with an advertisement for official Manchester United ice lollies on its rear end. I'm not sure if the sinister-looking specimens with wooden sticks up their posteriors are supposed to resemble any specific Manchester United players, but – put it this way, the back of a bus was an appropriate location for the gruesome phizzogs peering out from beneath the United crest.

'The best-supported team in Norway is Manchester United,' 28-year-old Eirik Johnsen had told me earlier in the day (which in the land of the midnight sun could have been any time in the previous 72 hours – you tend to lose all perception of time when the sun never sets). United shirts swing from hangers on stalls in the marketplace, alongside T-shirts of Ole Gunnar Solskjær. You've got to hand it to United's marketing machine: there's not even a McDonald's in Tromsø yet.

English football has been closely followed in Norway since the days of Stanley Matthews, even before the arrival of television coverage. Most English and Scottish clubs have supporters' clubs in Norway, and in the Tromsø match programme there is a large section on close-season to-ing and fro-ing in the English Premiership transfer market.

On the front cover of the programme is a plug for a raffle – first prize a trip to England, courtesy of the Norwegian airline Braathens. Presumably the rest of the plane would be taken up with footballers heading away from their native country, as has become customary for any Norwegian player with an ounce of talent.

Since Norway emerged on to the world scene by qualifying for the 1994 World Cup finals (their first major tournament since 1938), English Premiership and German Bundesliga clubs in particular have preyed on the Norwegian game for talent. English football lights up the television screen during those long dark winters, so Norwegian fans follow the game in England closely. Hence Eirik Johnsen's theory that Manchester United are the best-supported team in Norway. That signing of Ole Gunnar Solskjær was a shrewd move in both football and marketing terms.

'It's of course a problem for the Norwegian league that so many talented players leave the country,' journalist Kenneth Gabrielsen of the *Nordlys Bladet* newspaper tells me in the Alfheim press lounge over coffee and cake, 'but there are also benefits. The money is spent on bringing through new talent, who quite early get the chance at the first team. The money is often used building fields, improving facilities, developing young players and so on.

'There are always new talents. Here in Tromsø the club have created many attacking stars. We had Sigurd Rushfeldt – now at Racing Santander – and Tore André Flo here and when we lost them the club produced Ole Martin Arst who's now at Standard Liege and was top scorer in Belgium last year. When Arst left, Rune Lange came to the surface. And his replacement, Rune Johansen, has scored three goals in three matches.

'Not only does the money from the sales mean better conditions for the talents, it also enables the clubs to get players from other Scandinavian countries. Over the last years Norwegian clubs have bought quite a few players from Iceland and Sweden, and also some from Denmark and Finland. Here in Tromsø we have the Icelandic international Tryggvi Gudmundsson, the Finland international Marko Tuomela and the Finnish under-21 international Miika Koppinen. In a couple of weeks Tromsø should have a new player, when the Senegalese international Abdoulaye M'Baye joins the club as soon as he gets his work permit.

'Norwegian football has come a long way in the last ten years but, as the pessimist I am, I think we have come as far as we can,' Gabrielsen continues. 'There is a lot of potential in the national side, but with the defensive style of play the team can't develop. Rosenborg have not been as good this year as in earlier years. But they are constantly looking for new players, and we can only hope they can do well in the Champions League. They are the only Norwegian club I think can do well in Europe. Brann, Tromsø and a couple of others can beat many European sides, but they do not have the stability that Rosenborg have shown over the years. But as long as the national teams qualify for the championships, and Rosenborg play well in Europe, I think most Norwegians will be pleased with the way things are going.

'Of course, a lot of us were disappointed when Spain scored that last goal against Yugoslavia in Euro 2000. Now we know how Morocco felt when we beat Brazil in France '98.'

There is currently only one Norwegian club in a strong enough position to both attract and keep players, and that's Rosenborg of Trondheim. If ever there was an unsung team in the Champions League it has to be Rosenborg. Now in their tenth successive European season, the Norwegian club were rewarded for their tenacity by being allocated an automatic place in the group stages for 1999–2000 – an honour not bestowed even on the previous year's semi-finalists, Dynamo Kyiv. The ignominy of having to scrap for a place amongst the champions of Azerbaijan, Macedonia and Luxembourg was spared them, for a season at least.

Rosenborg's recent history is one of consistent success. As they commenced their 1999 Champions League campaign they were in the process of wrapping up their eighth championship in succession, adding the Norwegian Cup to their bulging trophy cabinet for good measure, and on the weekend of my visit to Norway had opened up a four-point lead at the top with 13 games played. Their average attendance of 13,000 may not look impressive from the outside, but in a league where the national average barely rises above 5,000 they are a considerable draw. Most importantly, Rosenborg have by far the best team in Scandinavia – achieving dominance through hard work, attacking football and a totemic coach.

When Nils Arne Eggen, a former Rosenborg player, arrived in Trondheim in 1990 to take over team affairs, he set about transforming a club that had already won four titles in six years. His was a long-term vision to turn Rosenborg into a far-reaching business, not just a football team. Off the field the club forged strong links with the local community and business world, and Eggen was determined to make the club a strong part of the community.

On the pitch he emphasised teamwork, discipline and fitness and soon displayed a rare talent for bringing the best out of his players. His motivational skills produced fantastic performances from players who found reserves of fitness and ability they didn't know they had. Eggen sealed his first championship title in 1992 and the trophy has not left the Lekvendal Stadion since.

Inevitably, foreign clubs came knocking at the door and an impressive list of Rosenborg alumni abroad includes Steffen Iversen, Vegard Heggem, Stig Inge Bjornebye, Øyvind Leonhardsen and Harald Brattbakk. Eggen, however, is critical of players who seek fame and fortune overseas and he claims that they would have been far better off staying in Trondheim. 'None of the players we have sold over the last five years have improved since they left us,' he commented.

The summer 1999 addition of Vålerenga's highly rated striker John Carew, for a club-record £2 million, also indicated that the money and status Rosenborg have earned through their European exploits is finally allowing them to buy players rather than seeing them disappear to the English and German leagues. However, Carew departed for Valencia after Euro 2000, and it will probably be a few more years yet before Rosenborg can think seriously of European glory. Nevertheless, with Nils Arne Eggen in charge it would be foolish to write them off. So highly respected is the Rosenborg coach that 50 Scandinavian coaches travelled to Trondheim recently to learn from his methods, whilst Norway's national coach Nils Johan Semb commented: 'I have learned a lot from him, and the national team has used important impulses from Rosenborg.'

The success of Norway's national team has been in inverse proportion to that of its domestic game, Rosenborg excepted. Renowned for their negative tactics, Norway were a huge disappointment at Euro 2000 thanks to the dull philosophy of Semb. Despite the presence of flair players such as Tore André Flo, Ole Gunnar Solskjær and the hirsute Panathinaikos midfielder Erik Mykland, Norway killed every game. Their reward for grinding out a stupefyingly dull goalless final group match with Slovenia was to find out that Spain had scored twice in injury-time to defeat Yugoslavia and qualify at Norway's expense. Heartbreaking though it was for the Norwegians, no one was sorry to see them leave a tournament blessed with beautiful football.

'I for one did not at all like what I saw of Norway in Euro 2000,' Kenneth tells me. 'They played much better in the game against Italy the week before. That was Norway as we like to see them. Unfortunately, the Norwegian team seems to have problems performing at their best in championships. In qualifying games and friendlies they often show a different side. But I hope that the likes of Flo, Solskjær and Iversen can guide us towards another era. An era where Norway can play in a bit more of an attacking style than they have done up until now.

'There is no doubt about it, Semb did wrong in Euro 2000 – Norway played too defensively, and the criticism from foreign countries is very understandable. In Norwegian club football the style and tactics we see from the national team are almost never used. Many teams play 4–5–1 or 4–3–3, but like Rosenborg, they like to keep the play in the opponents' half. They try to get towards the goal as soon as possible and they play the ball through the midfield. But of course different teams use different tactics and some teams –

among them Kjelsaas in the First Division – play an Egil Olsen kind of football.'

Olsen, the idiosyncratic coach known for his Marxism, his proficiency at poker and his wellingtons, emerged from the state-sponsored Elite Sport programme, which promoted success in Norwegian sport in the 1980s, often at the expense of style. Olsen instigated the route-one approach into the national team: his teams were not pretty but very effective. A spell at Vålerenga pushed the Oslo club into European competition and a narrow Cup Winners' Cup quarter-final defeat to Chelsea, but the club faded quickly when the coach left for his disastrous spell at Wimbledon.

Vålerenga's brief flirtation with Europe was a rare moment of recent football glory for the national capital, Oslo. Norwegian football is possibly the most evenly distributed in the world. Where the successful clubs in most European countries are generally concentrated in capital cities, or at least major conurbations, the vastness of Norway dilutes the focus of both population and football. However, Tromsø's location has not done the world's northernmost club many favours. A flurry of relative success occurred in the late '80s, when the club picked up a Norwegian Cup and runners-up and third places in the league, but other than that the club has only a 1996 Norwegian Cup win to show for its 80-year history. They are unquestionably a football outpost. Their only 'derby' is against Bodø/Glimt, from nearly 200 miles further south.

Kenneth Gabrielsen admits that Tromsø's relative lack of success is largely due to location, location, location. 'Being so far north causes some problems for the club,' he says, 'but 10–15 years ago the Skarphallen indoor facility was built and since then Tromsø have been able to train and play friendlies indoors during the winter. Before that, they had to train on snow in the winter. There are also problems getting the field at Alfheim ready for the first two or three games in the league. The Norwegian FA are planning to start the season in March rather than April in a couple of years, something which Tromsø are against. They do not think they can get the pitch ready that early. In 1997 we had over two metres of snow here in April. It's hard to attract players from southern Norway: often they don't want to come to Tromsø because of the snow and the fact that we don't see the sun for two months in the winter.'

Despite the lack of success, Tromsø is a friendly club to visit, even to the extent of passing litter bins along the rows of the stand at the end of the game for the punters to dispose of their rubbish. And the ground is a beautiful place to play football. A wooden grandstand stretches the length of one touchline, soon to be replaced by a new construction which will include the inevitable executive boxes.

'Tromsø plan to develop their stadium in many ways – among them building a new stand,' says Kenneth Gabrielsen. 'This will probably not mean room for more spectators, but an improvement of the facilities. In time, they hope to have an all-seated stadium.'

The final funds for the new stand had been secured the previous week when Tromsø sold their star striker Rune Lange to Trabzonspor in Turkey. A native of Tromsø, 23-year-old Lange is a proven goalscorer whose previous transfers had fallen through: one, allegedly, because the home-loving forward wanted to take his brother, who plays in Tromsø's defence, with him; another, apparently, because the prospective English Premiership club involved wouldn't import Lange's favourite chocolate spread.

Behind one goal is a clubhouse reminiscent of the cafés you often find in public parks. Behind the other, beyond a couple of houses with prime views from behind the goal, is a dramatic panorama of distant snow-sugared fjords across the Arctic Sea, where a thick band of mist forms a couple of hundred feet above the water, bisecting the mountains. The pitch looks in excellent condition – it should do, as £300,000 was spent on binding in plastic grass with the natural turf to help the pitch through the harsh realities of a Norwegian winter.

Eventually, both teams emerge from the clubhouse and await entry to the field. The Tromsø team-members each stand hand in hand with a youngster in full club kit and brandishing a club flag. Everyone in the ground has been handed a red card bearing the message, 'Say no to racism' which they brand as the teams entered the field. Rather unfortunate, then, that Roger Lange would be hauled over the coals by the Norwegian FA for racially abusing Vålerenga's Pascal Simpson during the game.

The attendance is a little over 2,600, easily the club's lowest of the season. Vålerenga are not the draw they once were, and only a clutch of away fans has made the thousand-mile trip from the capital. Perhaps, too, the live televised coverage of the women's international between Norway and the USA (two of the strongest nations in the women's game) has had a bearing on the attendance. Or perhaps the good weather has persuaded the townsfolk to stay at home and enjoy the sunshine.

The people of Tromsø certainly know how to enjoy themselves. I had arrived on the Friday before the Sunday match and investigated a bar close to my hotel, lured by the sound of live country-rock classics sung with a heavy Scandinavian twang (in more ways than one) wafting through the window. I entered to find the bar full of respectable-looking older people. I think I was probably the only person under 40 in the entire place.

I ordered a beer and handed over in return a sum that would have made a useful deposit on a house. I'd also asked for a mineral water (which I'd even looked up and pointed to in my Norwegian dictionary) but the woman serving kept producing a bottle of Coca-Cola – how's that for a triumph of globalisation?

I soon noticed that no one was really talking to each other. It's not as if the band were that loud ('cerntry rerrrrrrds, tek me herrrrrm, to derr plaaaaaace . . .'), but everyone was either sitting at a table saying nothing or standing around saying nothing. All seemed to be gazing vacantly into the middle-distance; it was like a scene from a '50s B movie where everyone had been reprogrammed by aliens except me. Then I noticed that a couple of people still vertical were swaying slightly and it dawned on me that everyone in the bar was absolutely paralytic. A man in his forties wearing a Manchester United baseball cap seated at a table nearby slid forward on his forearms until his chin rested on the table. Respectable-looking couples in their evening finery, groups of middle-aged men and women, family groups alike – all totally pie-eyed. It was 11.30 at night and the sun shone through the windows.

'Ah, well, it was Friday,' says Eirik the next day. 'In summer everyone finishes early on Friday and goes straight to the bar. Most of those people will have been there since about three o'clock. In Norway we tend to drink lots all at once.' Drink is heavily taxed at around 35 per cent in Norway and the real hard liquor has to be bought from strictly controlled state-owned outlets in an attempt to rein in the serious drinking that goes on. Maybe it's a Viking thing. However the drunks in Norway seem to be happy drunks. The Vålerenga supporters commenced drinking at 11 a.m. before a six o'clock kick-off, but remained in good spirits throughout (if you'll excuse the pun).

'When the sun doesn't go down you have to have a routine,' says Eirik, of life in the Arctic. 'We have to live by our watches. Luckily Tromsø is a lively town with a lot of students, so there's plenty going on. The population is around 60,000 of which about 9,000 are students.'

It turns out that the bar in which I'd encountered the living dead the previous evening is the venue for a popular television programme. 'Northern Norwegians are known for our humour,' says Eirik, 'so when they make comedy programmes they search out the local characters in that bar and stick them in front of the cameras.' Presumably after a lot of black coffee and face-slapping.

'It's a bit different in the winter to how it is now,' he continues.

'Two months of darkness can make you very depressed, so the council make sure there is plenty of entertainment laid on: theatre, cabaret, revues and so on, to keep people occupied. We have an international film festival that attracts around 3,000 people here every year.

'The city has grown from a small fishing village to the regional capital. When city status was granted in 1791, Tromsø had only 80 residents. Now we have the regional hospital, the university, over 18,000 bar and restaurant seats and 80 per cent of the population are employed in the service industries. We don't have to rely on fishing any more. Let's go in here . . .'

We dive into a bar decorated in the style of a railway station. 'The government won't build us a railway link because they say it's too expensive. We pay some of the highest taxes in Europe, so God knows where the money's going if they can't budget for something as important as a railway. In the end someone thought, if we can't have a railway we can at least have a station.'

We arrive at the bar-cum-ticket office in a station that is more chug-a-lug than chug-chug. Railway seats line up along the window, and at one end a fully fledged carriage serves as a snug. Posters of trains line the walls and every few minutes the jukebox cuts out and a Norwegian voice announces the arrivals and departures of trains that will never come and never go. It's an alcoholic trainspotter's wet dream but somehow it works and the bar is a popular haunt for Tromsø's party people.

It reaches three in the morning and I really should hit the hay. But because it's still daylight, ducking out now would feel almost like a cop out. Most of the bars are closing, anyway. As I gaze down the main street towards the mist-covered mountains in the distance, dozens of people stagger around in a scene played out every Friday night all over Europe. But here in the sunshine the uncoordinated lurching figures galumphing around the street in noisy packs look like something out of a Bosch painting. Seagulls swoop low along the street, picking up discarded chips and bits of kebab. A Dylanesque busker with impressive sideburns churns out another Byrds classic and I head for my bed to prepare for the game later that day.

Tromsø beer is certainly easy on the hangover – maybe it's the pure arctic water. I spend the next day strolling happily around the town and the harbour, whiling away the hours before my ascent to the game. At the Alfheim the match kicks off on the stroke of six. It's immediately obvious that the standard isn't great. Tromsø are halfway up the 12-team Tippeliga, Vålerenga sit near the bottom. Perhaps in an attempt to make up for the lack of quality, the Tannoy announcer interrupts the game at every opportunity to provide score updates from the other games and there are musical stings which greet every corner (something I hadn't come across since Wimbledon's bugle rallying calls at Selhurst Park). The peroxide blond Icelander Trggyi Gudmundsson catches the eye for the home side, his lightning raids down the left causing as many problems for the visitors' defence as the diving seabirds. Seven minutes before the break, however, Jan Eirik Ødegård capitalises on a terrible mix-up in the home defence to give the visitors the lead.

After half-time Tromsø look a bit livelier. Five minutes after the break the heir to Rune Lange's crown, Rune Johansen, scores his fourth in as many games with a tap in from a cross delivered from a suspiciously offside position. When, ten minutes later, a perfectly good Tromsø goal is ruled out for offside, one presumes that the linesman is what Ron Atkinson might describe as '15-all with himself now'.

The game peters out towards an inevitable draw and my European odyssey comes to an end with the final whistle. The players troop off, and the small crowd heads back downhill into town. Back in the press room I bump into Kenneth again. I comment that neither of the teams today look like troubling Norwegian trophy engravers in the near future. He shrugs and agrees.

'I don't think Tromsø can win the Norwegian league in the foreseeable future. They don't have the resources of Rosenborg, Molde and Brann. Tromsø is a club who depend on selling players, and therefore there is no basis on which to build a championship side. They have sold players like the attackers I mentioned before, central defender Steinar Nilsen and midfield general Bjørn Johansen. But the club work well with the other clubs in the area and I don't see them going down, either. A place in the middle of our top division is where I think we'll find Tromsø most years.'

I leave the Alfheim and head back to town. From this vantage point you can see the huge bridge which connects the island on which most of the city sits with the mainland. At the far end of the bridge is Tromsø's most famous landmark, the Arctic Cathedral. It's a modern building, constructed in the mid-'60s, and resembles a domestic iron on its end, or the prow of a ship jutting out of the ground. It's a little reminiscent of Sydney Opera House and apparently the architects of both buildings went to college together. Whether you're Norwegian or Australian tends to dictate your opinion on who copied whom.

The town is quiet tonight. The bars are nearly empty, but the busker is still doing his nasal thing. Down at the harbour I purchase some boiled fresh-caught shrimps from a recently arrived fishing boat and sit with my legs dangling over the edge of the quayside. The bridge is lit by the sun, the still water is a deep blue and the snow-sugared mountains rise darkly in the background. Seabirds caw overhead and the fishing boats bob in the harbour. Throwing the shrimp heads into the water where they are swooped upon by gulls, I reflect that it's almost time for me to head for home.

I've covered over 20,000 miles, chugging to and from these European countries. I've now reached the highest point in world football and everything – matches, tournaments, transfers, rule changes, campaigns to host major tournaments, everything – happens south of here. I've met players, club officials, journalists and supporters in different countries, each with different tales to tell and many shared experiences.

But wherever I've been, everyone has shared a love of the game of football: the rectangular field with a goal at each end and 22 players trying to put the ball into one of them. It's simple, easy to learn and it brings hope and pleasure to millions. From Barcelona to the Faroese Second Division, I've found the barely definable spirit of the game everywhere. I don't know for sure what it is. It may just be a sparkle in the eye when the conversation turns to the game, or that brief suspension of time and breath when a striker creates an opening and shoots. Whatever, it's something that can't be tagged with a price or smeared with sponsors' logos. And it's everywhere.

Some may hijack the game for financial gain, others may use it as a conduit for their own corruption, but underneath all that football is still there producing hope, anguish and joy to different communities and nations. People will still turn out up here to watch Tromsø, even though they realise there's little chance of them winning anything. The expressions of delight, frustration and hope on the faces of those 2,500 people at the northernmost ground in the world have been mirrored at every stadium I've been to over the last 18 months.

The Torino players of 1949 lost their lives in the name of football. So did the nine FK Sarajevo players killed on club duty during the Bosnian war. It's easy to lend too much *gravitas* to football, but as a vehicle of local and national pride it is almost unequalled. As someone disillusioned by the rampant commercialism that has taken over European football in recent years it's been encouraging for me to meet the Tomáš Králs, Paul Kriers, John Hansons and Lapo Novellinis of this continent. With people like that still holding the game dear, there is real hope for the future of football in Europe.

There is still much to be done – particularly in the eastern half of the continent – but spirit and passion for the game still burn even in the most difficult of circumstances. I hope I've demonstrated at least some of that, over the last 20,000 miles or so. European football is a rich, varied entity. It's one of the very few things that everyone on the continent has in common; the game generates the same passions, problems and pleasures wherever you go.

I hurl another shrimp's head out into the harbour. A gull swoops to snatch it from the water and flaps away. A plane leaving Tromsø airport heaves into the sky, ascending across the sun to who knows where, and a fishing boat chugs out to sea creating a gentle, widening wake in the water. The clock on the Domkirche chimes midnight and the town is quiet. The shadows may be lengthening, but there's still a long time until sunset.

FURTHER READING

EUROPEAN FOOTBALL

Armstrong, Gary and Giulianotti, Richard (eds), *Entering the Field: New Perspectives on World Football* (Berg, 1997)

Armstrong, Gary and Giulianotti, Richard (eds), *Football Cultures and Identities* (Macmillan, 1999)

Bailey, L.N. (ed.), *European Soccer* (Pelham, 1970)

Beccuti, Marina, *Il Grande Torino Calcio* CD-Rom (Wind Cloak, 1999)

Bent, Ian, McIlroy, Richard, Mousley, Kevin and Walsh, Peter, *Football Confidential* (BBC, 2000)

Brown, Adam (ed.), *Fanatics! Power, Identity and Fandom in Football* (Routledge, 1998)

Burns, Jimmy, *Barca: A People's Passion* (Bloomsbury, 1999)

Cresswell, Peterjon and Evans, Simon, *European Football: A Fan's Handbook* (Rough Guides, 1999)

Cronin, Mike, *Sport and Nationalism in Ireland* (Four Courts, 1999)

Dauncey, Hugh and Hare, Geoff (eds), *France and the 1998 World Cup: The National Impact of a Global Tournament* (Cass, 1999)

Downing, David, *Passovotchka: Moscow Dynamo in Britain 1945* (Bloomsbury, 1999)

Duke, Vic and Crolley, Liz, *Football, Nationality and the State* (Longman, 1996)

Edelman, Robert, *Serious Fun: A History of Spectator Sports in the USSR* (Oxford University Press, 1993)

Firmani, Eddie, *Football With The Millionaires*, (Sportsman's Book Club, 1960)

Giulianotti, Richard and Williams, John (eds), *Games Without Frontiers: Football, Identity and Modernity*, (Arena, 1994)

Glanville, Brian, *The Story of the World Cup* (Faber, 1993)

Guttmann, Allen, *Games and Empires: Modern Sports and Cultural Imperialism* (Columbia University Press, 1994)

Hammond, Mike (ed.), *European Football Yearbook* (Sports Projects Ltd, annual)

Hansen, Jóannes and Helmsdal, Finnur, *The Faroese National Team: Ten Years in International Football* (Forlagið Itróttarbøkur, 1999)

Helmsdal, Finnur, *Red, Blue and White: The Faroe Islands and the European Championships* (Forlagið Rangstøða, 1991)

Hocking, Ron and Radnedge, Keir, *Nations of Europe* [2 vols] (Articulate, 1993)

Holt, Richard, Mangan, J.A. and Lanfranchi, Pierre (eds), *European Heroes: Myth, Identity, Sport* (Cass, 1996)

Jeffery, Gordon, *European International Football* (Sportsman's Book Club, 1965)

Joy, Bernard, *Soccer Tactics* (Sportsman's Book Club, 1959)

Kuper, Simon, *Football Against The Enemy* (Phoenix, 1994)

Meisl, Willy, *Soccer Revolution*, (Sportsman's Book Club, 1956)

Murray, Bill, *The World's Game: A History of Soccer* (University of Illinois Press, 1996)

Perryman, Mark, *The Ingerland Factor: Home Truths From Football* (Mainstream, 1999)

Puskas, Ferenc, *Captain of Hungary* (Cassell, 1955)

Reid, Gerard, *Football and War* (Sigma, 2000)

Robinson, John, *The European Football Championships 1958–1996* (Soccer Book Publishing, 1996)

Rühn, Christov (ed.), *Le Foot: The Legends of French Football* (Abacus, 2000)

Ryan, Sean, *The Boys In Green: The FAI International Story* (Mainstream, 1999)

Sugden, John and Tomlinson, Alan, *FIFA and the Contest for World Football* (Polity, 1998)

Wagg, Stephen and Williams, John (eds), *British Football and Social Change: Getting Into Europe* (Leicester University Press, 1991)

Wangerin, Dave, *The Fussball Book: German Football Since the Bundesliga* (self-published, 1993)

Winner, David *Brilliant Orange: The Neurotic Genius of Dutch Football* (Bloomsbury, 2000)

EUROPEAN HISTORY, CULTURE AND TRAVEL

Anderson, Benedict, *Imagined Communities: Reflections on the Origin and Spread of Nationalism* (Verso, 1991)

Bew, Paul and Gillespie, Gordon, *The Northern Ireland Peace Process 1993–1996: A Chronology* (Serif, 1996)

Bew, Paul, Teague, Paul and Patterson, Henry, *Between War and Peace: The Political Future of Northern Ireland* (Lawrence & Wishart, 1997)

Brook-Shepherd, Gordon, *The Austrians: A Thousand-Year Odyssey* (HarperCollins, 1997)

FURTHER READING

Davies, Norman, *Europe: A History* (Pimlico, 1996)

Derry, T.K., *A History of Scandinavia: Norway, Sweden, Denmark, Finland and Iceland* (University of Minnesota Press, 1998)

Fraser, Nicholas, *Continental Drifts: Travels in the New Europe* (Vintage, 1998)

Garton Ash, Timothy *History of the Present: Essays, Sketches and Despatches from Europe in the 1990s* (Allen Lane, 1999)

Garton Ash, Timothy, *The Magic Lantern: The Revolution of 1989 Witnessed in Warsaw, Budapest, Berlin and Prague* (Vintage, 1993)

Garton Ash, Timothy, *The Uses of Adversity: Essays on the Fate of Central Europe* (Penguin, 1999)

Glenny, Misha, *The Fall of Yugoslavia* (Penguin, 1996)

Haines, Miranda (ed.), *The Traveller's Handbook* (Wexas, 1997)

Hobsbawm, Eric, *Nations and Nationalism Since 1780: Programme, Myth, Reality* (Cambridge University Press, 1990)

Hobsbawm, Eric, *On History* (Weidenfeld & Nicholson, 1997)

Hodgson, Geoffrey, *A New Grand Tour: How Europe's Great Cities made our World* (Penguin, 1995)

Honig, Jan Willem and Both, Norbert, *Srebrenica, Record of a War Crime* (Penguin, 1996)

Kaplan, Robert D., *The Ends of The Earth: A Journey at the Dawn of the Twenty-First Century* (Papermac, 1997)

Kennedy, Paul, *The Rise and Fall of the Great Powers* (Fontana, 1989)

Kurlansky, Mark, *The Basque History of the World* (Jonathan Cape, 1999)

Law, Jonathan (ed.), *European Culture: A Contemporary Companion* (Cassell, 1993)

Magris, Claudio, *Danube* (Collins Harvill, 1990)

Malcolm, Noel, *Bosnia: A Short History* (Macmillan, 1996)

Malcolm, Noel, *Kosovo: A Short History* (Macmillan, 1998)

Mazower, Mark, *Dark Continent: Europe's Twentieth Century* (Penguin, 1998)

Naughton, James (ed.), *Eastern and Central Europe: A Traveller's Literary Companion* (In Print Publishing, 1995)

Powell, F. York (trans.), *Færeyinga Saga* (Llanerch, 1995)

Reid, Anna, *Borderland: A Journey Through the History of Ukraine* (Phoenix, 1997)

Rohr, Bernd and Simon, Günter *Lexicon Fußball* (Leipzig, 1987)

Said, Edward, *Culture and Imperialism* (Vintage, 1994)

Smith, Anthony D., *National Identity* (Penguin, 1991)

Silber, Laura and Little, Allan, *The Death of Yugoslavia* (Penguin, 1996)

Vitaliev, Vitali, *Little is the Light: Nostalgic Travels in the Mini-States of*

Europe (Simon & Schuster, 1995)

Vulliamy, Ed, *Seasons In Hell: Understanding Bosnia's War* (Simon & Schuster, 1994)

Wolf, Eric R., *Europe and the People Without History* (University of California Press, 1990)

NEWSPAPERS AND MAGAZINES

Aux Armes!, *Bild*, BBC *Match of the Day*, *Corriere Dello Sport*, *Don Balon*, *Elfmeter*, *El Pais*, *Football Europe*, *Football Italia*, *Four Four Two*, *France Football*, *La Gazetta Dello Sport*, *Kicker*, *L'Equipe*, *Luxembourger Wort*, *Marca*, *Mundo Deportivo*, *Neue Kronen Zeitung*, *New Internationalist*, *Sosialurin*, *Sunday Herald*, *The European*, *The Slovak Spectator*, *Tuttosport*, *When Saturday Comes*, *World Soccer*.

INDEX

INDEX

PORTISHEAD
& AROUND
THROUGH TIME
Will Musgrave

AMBERLEY PUBLISHING

Aerial View of Portishead, 1970s

First published 2014

Amberley Publishing
The Hill, Stroud, Gloucestershire, GL5 4EP
www.amberley-books.com

Copyright © Will Musgrave, 2014

The right of Will Musgrave to be identified as the
Author of this work has been asserted in
accordance with the Copyrights, Designs and
Patents Act 1988.

ISBN 978 1 4456 2065 7 (print)
ISBN 978 1 4456 2072 5 (ebook)

British Library Cataloguing in Publication Data.
A catalogue record for this book is available from
the British Library.

Typesetting by Amberley Publishing.
Printed in the UK.

Introduction

Portishead, Pill and Long Ashton are to be found in the northern part of North Somerset. While the three places are different in nature, both geographically and historically, they have one thing in common: they share a close relationship with the city of Bristol. By the nineteenth century, much of Portishead was owned by the Bristol Corporation, Pill was reliant on the trading ships that visited its docks, and the land around Long Ashton was home to one of the city's wealthiest merchant families, the Smyths. But to view these three as merely dormitory towns or villages of Bristol is to underestimate them, and understate their individual characters. Rightly, all three are proud of their heritage. By dint of its size, Portishead has altered the most over the years, but Pill and Long Ashton have also undergone significant changes, not just in appearance but in the livelihoods of the inhabitants. Pill's two main functions, of piloting vessels along the River Avon and providing a ferry service, have disappeared, while Long Ashton is no longer simply an agricultural village that happened to be 2 miles from Bristol. By looking at these three closely located places through time, we can see that, although they are similar, they have adapted and changed in different ways. This is an ongoing process. The recent housing development boom has changed a significant part of Portishead, Pill now spreads from Ham Green to Easton-in-Gordano and Long Ashton residents are mainly commuters rather than farm labourers.

Standing on the shore of the Severn Estuary, close to the mouth of the River Avon, it is not surprising that the name Portishead means 'port at the head of the river'. Recorded in Domesday as Poresheve, a small village in the Portbury Hundred, it has been spelt in a variety of ways, including Portshead and Portshute, and is locally known as Posset. Although there is some archaeological evidence for activity in the prehistoric, Roman and Iron Age periods in the area, Portishead remained a fairly anonymous fishing village through the Middle Ages. Its secluded tributary provided good shelter for boats from the dangerous Severn waters (at about 15 metres, the estuary has the second highest tidal range in the world), and there are remains of iron boat mooring rings on the walls of the High Street from the pre-dock era. Portishead's strategic position was also recognised – its headland overlooks King Road (the stretch of water close to where the Avon and Severn meet) – and a fort was built on Battery Point. This was used during the English Civil War when the town supported the Royalists, before they surrendered to General Fairfax in 1645. Guns were later placed on the promontory during the Second World War. In the early seventeenth century, Bristol Corporation purchased the manors of North Weston and Portishead, and further properties were added to the city's property portfolio over the next two centuries. By the beginning of the nineteenth century, Bristol Corporation had begun to develop Portishead as a seaside resort and residential area for wealthy citizens. The artificial Marine Lake was dug out in 1910, and pleasure grounds laid out around its shores, with an esplanade running from Battery Point to Beach Road, in an attempt to draw visitors. But all these ambitious plans were only ever going to be partially successful – Portishead does not possess wide sandy beaches or an area close to the town centre suitable for promenading. In 1867, the new Great Western Railway, running from Bristol, started operating, providing the infrastructure for industry as well as tourism. A deepwater dock was built by the Bristol & Portishead Pier & Railway Co., to accommodate large cargo ships unable to easily access Bristol harbourside. Eventually the docks were taken over by the Port of Bristol Authority. Other industries grew up along the dockside. Two power stations graced Portishead's skyline for much of the twentieth century, as did a petroleum installation, a large mill and a nail factory stood nearby, and the Albright and Wilson chemical works left its indelible mark. During its life, the dock at Portishead had stiff competition with Avonmouth and Royal Portbury Dock and, when the power stations were decommissioned, it eventually closed in 1992. However, Portishead has risen ,phoenix-like, from the industrial ashes, and the dock area has been transformed into Port Marina. This housing development has created over 5,000 new homes in the past fifteen years, and will increase Portishead's population to an estimated 30,000 in the coming years.

Pill was originally called Crockerne Pill or 'pottery wharf', due to the large-scale pottery industry in Ham Green. The distinctive pottery, known as Ham Green ware, was produced between AD 1100 and 1250 and exported as far as Ireland, Spain and Portugal. The word 'pill' means a creek or pool, and it was around the small inlet on the River Avons's south bank that the village was built. Knowing the difficult waters of the Avon and Bristol Channel, Pill pilots were able to navigate cargo ships upriver to the Bristol dock. Their nickname of 'sharkers' arose from the competition between Portishead pilots (known as 'wreckers' for their reputedly dubious maritime practices). Sailors crossing the Doldrums dangled lumps of pork off the back of their boats to attract sharks, and there is a possible apocryphal story of Pill pilots ignoring larger, wealthier boats coming into port and heading instead to relieve smaller vessels of their forgotten shark bait (which was of more worth to them when times were hard). Besides the rowdy crews of pilots, Pill was home to rough gang of boat haulers, or 'Pill Hobblers' who dragged the laden ships up to Bristol either by hand or horse along the tow path or by rowing boat. It is not surprising that Pill, with its multitude of inns and hard-working men, had a reputation as a disreputable place.

Long Ashton can date its origins back to Saxon times, and the village is recorded in the Domesday Book as Estune, or 'the settlement by the ash tree'. Its full name does not appear until the nineteenth century and, although the 'Long' might refer to the de Lyon family who owned one of the manors from 1285, it is equally possible that is simply a good description of this unusually elongated settlement. In 1545, John Smyth bought the Ashton-Lyons manor, and successive generations of the family acquired more land in the neighbourhood, creating the Ashton Court Estate. The Smyth family was to play a major role in the life of Long Ashton for 400 years, before the city of Bristol became owners of the 860-acre property in 1959. During that time, farming was the main source of employment in Long Ashton and its market gardens were famous throughout Bristol. Mill work, stone quarrying, coal mining and the laundry industry also provided work, while the Ashton Court Estate employed its own labour force of groundsmen, gamekeepers, foresters, carpenters, painters and domestic servants. Many of these jobs have long since disappeared, but Long Ashton has remained prosperous, due to a combination of its charming character and the short commuting distance to Bristol.

View from Fore Hill, Early Nineteenth Century

This panorama looking across to the Severn Estuary clearly shows how rural the land was around the mouth of the pill, or small estuary, at the heart of Portishead. Although there is activity at sea (a steamboat can be seen ploughing its way across the waters, known as King Road), construction of the dock has yet to begin. The only buildings of note are St Peter's, the parish church, which dominates the scene and Courthouse Farm that can be spotted to the right. Housing developments and industry have drastically changed the landscape over the years, but there are still some unspoilt spots – on the side of Fore Hill is Lye's Orchard, where a number of ancient apple trees continue to flourish.

St Peter's Church and Court Farm, Mid-Nineteenth Century

Viewed here from Church Street South, the parish church and Court Farm (also known as Court House farmhouse and Tower House) are two of the oldest buildings in Portishead. The origins of St Peter's church can be dated back to Norman times, when a chapel stood in the spot (sadly the remains were lost in the nineteenth century). The church was built around 1320 in the Perpendicular Gothic style, and its bell tower was constructed in the fifteenth century. Court Farm dates from around the Tudor period: its distinctive hexagon tower was added by Edward Morgan, a Bristol merchant, during the Elizabethan era.

Court Farm, Church Street South, 1910

Once the manor house for this part of Portishead, Court Farm was purchased by the city of Bristol for £500 in 1619 during a period of land acquisition by the Corporation. The red-brick tower has large windows at the top, facing towards the waters of King Road and the Portishead Pill, which suggest that it was originally used as a lookout point for shipping. This beautiful Grade II listed building has managed to avoid the fate of the nearby rectory, which was demolished in the 1960s, and is now undergoing a period of interior alteration.

St Peter's Church, Early 1900s

Seen looking down Church Road North, St Peter's church has become a prominent landmark, and its four-stage tower, with its setback buttresses and pierced parapet, can be seen from most parts of the town. The church, which did not become known as St Peter's until the nineteenth century, was built in stages during the fourteenth and fifteenth centuries, and was altered in the 1800s. A clock was installed with faces on three sides of the bell tower, to commemorate Queen Victoria's Golden Jubilee in 1887. In the modern photograph, the old medieval village cross (Grade II listed) can be seen in front of the church; it was moved from its original location at the junction of Church Road South and Mill Street sometime during the early 1800s, during the enclosure of lands around Portishead.

Bird Tree Cottage, High Street, 1898

Sitting unobtrusively towards the southern end of the High Street is this mid-seventeenth century, Grade II listed cottage. The old photograph was taken just after the thatched roof was replaced by tiles, and the cottage had earned its new named thanks to its elaborate bird-shaped topiary.

The Anchor, Portishead.

The Anchor, High Street, Early 1900s

Known at the turn of the twentieth century as 'The Anchor', this inn (Portishead's oldest) has gone under a number of names in the past, including 'The Blew Anchor' and 'The Gordon Arms', and is currently called The Poacher. Today it is set back several metres from the High Street pavement, but in former times it would have looked out over the village green.

Portishead Co-Operative Society, High Street, Early 1900s

Standing outside the Co-operative Society are two horse-drawn delivery carts, and a hand cart being pushed by a young delivery boy. The society was formed in 1894 with thirty-five members and, by 1900, had taken over these premises in the High Street. It provided a range of services and goods – in the shop window are adverts for tea, cocoa and sugar. It is ironic that in this age of convenience shopping, many supermarkets are returning to a home delivery service. Fortunately, horse manure on the street (as seen in the old picture), which was a feature of the old delivery system, is no longer a problem.

Old Cottage, High Street, c. 1906

Sadly this cottage, which dated back to at least 1740, was pulled down in the 1930s to make way for a branch of the Westminster bank. In the latter part of the nineteenth century it was known as Tuck's Cottage, after its owner Stephen Tuck, a transport operator, who, among other things, ran a horse-drawn carriage service to Bristol. Sadly, after forty years in the business, Mr Tuck died in 1899 after being thrown from a fly carriage. Later the property became known as Gale's Cottage, before its demolition.

Tea shop, No. 76 High Street, Early 1900s

With no less than five signs in the windows advertising the fact that teas are available, it is clear what type of premises this was. Sadly many of the small, independent tea shops and coffee houses that used to populate the high street in English towns have given way to fast-food establishments. Charity shops, however, are prospering.

High Street, 1930s

The first noticeable difference between these two views, which look north up the High Street, is the lack of a wall on the left-hand side, and the broader pavement. The road itself is not significantly wider. On the left is a sign for Thomas Coles & Sons, a carriage company that operated a daily carrier service to Bristol in the pre-First World War years. Coles expanded his business after buying the late Mr Tuck's stock, and he later moved onto motor vehicles and opened a garage. On the right of the picture is the old Portishead post office. The colourful hanging basket and flower tubs brightening the modern photograph are thanks to the Portishead in Bloom initiative.

High Street, Early 1900s

Looking north up the High Street, from the Stoke Road junction, we can see that many of the buildings have retained their original shape. Today there are still a number of small outlets, but, unlike Bowen's the stationer on the right of the old picture, none of them have signs proclaiming to be 'The Noted House For Postcards and Writing Paper.' It appears shop awnings and gentlemen wearing hats were a much more common sight 100 years ago.

High Street, *c.* 1910

On the far right-hand side of the top photograph, the lady in the long, white dress is walking past the arched doorway of what was the National Provincial Bank of England. This impressive façade was erected when the bank moved into the premises in 1903. Today, the NatWest bank occupies the building, and a modern exterior has since replaced the classical design. Another replacement worth noting are the old gas street lamps, which have been removed and modern, utilitarian ones put in their place.

16

High Street, Postcard Dated 24 August 1921
This view is looking south towards St Peter's church (the bell tower can just be seen through the trees). As the population of Portishead continued to grow at the start of the twentieth century, the High Street also flourished. The buildings in the centre background were erected in 1903. Although cars were becoming a more regular sight, judging by the state of the road surface, horses were still the most common mode of transport.

A. T. Wilmott Butcher Shop, Nos 28–30 High Street, 1905

When Arthur Wilmott owned the butcher's shop, meat was truly fresh – behind the premises was an abattoir, which was accessed via the lane on the right of the photograph. Today the sheds still remain, though the current shop owner, Matt Westley, who took over in the premises in 1985, no longer has recourse to use them for their original purpose. Little of the original exterior of the shop remains; indeed the only visible remnant of Wilmott's butcher's is the stone on the ground, which can be seen through the back wheel of the young delivery boy's bicycle.

Peace Day Procession, High Street, 1919

The citizens of Portishead gathered together with demobilised military personnel and various local institutions for a Peace Day Procession through the town, on a rainy July day in 1919. Portishead played an active part in the First World War, and sixty-four servicemen lost their lives in the conflict. The photograph here is taken at the top of the High Street, looking back at the Methodist church (which had been in use since 1887), and the infant school on the right, which was built in 1840.

The White Lion, Wyndham Way, Early 1900s

The White Lion started life as a flour mill (unsurprisingly called the Old Mill) before being converted into a mill. It was initially powered by freshwater from the Portishead pill, or Yeo, which drained from the surrounding marshland into the estuary. It was converted into a tidal-powered mill in the eighteenth century (seawater could reach as far as the High Street at high tide), but drainage difficulties eventually brought operations to a halt. Looking back towards the top of the High Street, we can see the archway that allowed carriages, or flys, to carry passengers from the Weston, Clevedon & Portishead Light Railway station, on Wyndham Way, through to the centre of town. The White Lion is now a Grade II listed building.

Weston, Clevedon & Portishead Light Railway Terminus, *c.* 1910

Situated on Wyndham Way, the terminus was the end point of the Weston, Clevedon & Portishead Light Railway. This railway began operating in 1897 between Weston and Clevedon and, ten years later, the line was extended up to Portishead. It provided a simple, rather erratic, service which gradually declined in popularity with the advent of the car in the 1930s, and eventually ceased operations in 1940. The old terminus was a simple affair with just a timber waiting room, booking office and ladies' room. Today, with the boom in housing development, there is much interest in rebuilding a rail network link (the other rail line, the Great Western Railway, which connected Portishead with Bristol, fell victim to Dr Beeching's cuts in 1964).

Former United Reformed Church, Early 1900s

This former church, viewed from the corner of Cabstand and Battery Road, has undergone a number of name changes – it has been known as the Union church, Union chapel, Union Congregational church and United Reformed church. Congregational worship in Portishead increased in popularity in the nineteenth century, and plans for a suitably large church were made in 1875. The foundation stone was laid on 9 December of that year by Mr W. H. Wills. The cast-iron drinking fountain and the trough in the inset were erected in February 1907, with finance raised by the Fountain Committee. It proved to be a rather unpopular feature and raised complaints about its appearance (it was painted a rather gaudy mix of gold and green and had blue cups fastened to it), and its location. Shortly afterwards, it was moved to a spot beside the police station.

Battery Road, Early 1900s

This view of Battery Road is looking south-east, in the direction of the High Street. Built in the Gothic style at a cost of £3,344, the former United Reformed church dominates the end of the road (it was the largest church in Portishead). It was erected at an impressive speed of just sixteen months and held its first service on 24 April 1877. Dwindling congregational numbers in recent years meant the church could no longer afford the upkeep, and it was put up for sale. Developers bought the property in 2012, and it has now been converted into flats.

Royal Terrace, Eastwood Place, Early 1900s
This impressive row of six houses, on the corner of Leigh View Road, has been reduced in number in recent years. The terrace was built around 1880 and overlooked the Portishead Docks. Unfortunately, four of the properties were demolished in the 1960s, leaving just the two closest to Pier Road still standing.

Parish Wharf, c. 1910

Portishead Dock was created in the nineteenth century as a response to the neighbouring Avonmouth Dock, when there was competition to get cargo freight to and from Bristol and the West Country. The tidal waters of the inlet or pill were enclosed, and the dock was opened to shipping in 1879. Today, the scene has completely changed. In 1992, all port work ceased when the Port of Bristol Authority closed the dock and the area has since been transformed into a marina. The deepwater wharf is now home to around 250 pontoon berths, and housing developments have sprung up on either side of the old dock. If the workman, seen here loading coal into a cart on Parish Wharf, could have looked up and seen into the future, he would have dropped his shovel.

Portishead Dock, Early 1900s

This artistic photograph was taken at an early stage of the dock's development, when it just handled cargo ships and pleasure cruisers. By the 1920s, demand for electricity had increased significantly, and the first of Portishead's two power stations, 'A' Power Station, was commissioned in 1926, generating electricity from 1929. The coal-fed station was located beside the dock, so that supplies could be imported by boat from South Wales, and trains from east Somerset. Later, other industries changed the appearance of the dock – on the right-hand side of the modern photograph once stood Albright & Wilson's phosphorus works, which opened in 1951.

Portishead Dock, December 1908

The Port Marine development has altered the appearance and economy of Portishead. It has changed from being just a dormitory town for Bristol, to being a desirable and aspirational place to live. The development of the dock has created a vibrant community living in a variety of different types of accommodation. There are townhouses, flats and swish penthouse apartments. There is even an area designed to look like a Cornish fishing village, complete with narrow streets and different coloured houses (it was based on the seaside town of Polperro).

'A' Power Station, Portishead Dock, Late 1940s

When 'A' Power Station began generating in 1929, it was able to supply the demand for the whole of Bristol and much of Somerset; however, as the need for more power grew the station had to expand. Here we can see a new generator arriving in front of the station. The inset shows generators operating in the Turbine Hall. The photograph can be dated quite accurately, as the 107-metre chimney stack was covered in camouflage paint during the Second World War, and the No. 2 stack, which can be seen being built to the left, was completed in 1948. Today, residents could be forgiven for not being aware that there once were power stations standing on their carefully planned housing development.

Portishead Dock, 1950s

On the left-hand side of the picture above is 'B' Power Station. The relatively low output of 240 MW produced by 'A' Station, and the increased demand for electricity, meant a second plant was required and construction began in 1949. The new coal-fuelled station, with its two 117-metre stacks, was completed six years later, and a further 360 MW of electricity was now available. Eventually 'B' Station converted to oil in 1972, when the Somerset coal fields were closed.

Demolition of 'B' Power Station Stacks, Portishead Dock, 8 October 1992

The fate of 'A' Power Station was sealed when generating capacity at stations in Pembroke and Didcot increased to a significantly higher level than the old station could produce. It was closed in 1976, and its two stacks were demolished in the early 1980s. The oil crises of the 1970s meant that 'B' Power Station was also no longer viable, and it was closed in 1982. Ten years later, the two remaining power station stacks that had been such a part of the Portishead skyline were finally pulled down.

Entrance to Pier, Early 1900s

In 1839, Isambard Kingdom Brunel proposed building a pier at Portishead to enable transatlantic passengers to board his ship, *The Great Western*. The plans involved travellers staying at the Royal Hotel (which is located just to the left of the picture), and travelling by road across Portbury Marsh. Nothing came of this, but a small pier was built in 1849, and the Bristol & Portishead Pier & Railway Co. extended it further in 1870. Visitors, such as the ladies and gentlemen in the picture above, were able to disembark (a Campbell's steamer can be seen just leaving the pier) and travel into town via horse-drawn carriages that waited for them by the hotel.

Portishead Pier, Early 1900s

Unlike its neighbours, Weston-super-Mare and Clevedon, the pier at Portishead is not connected directly to the town centre, so it appears not to have attracted the promenading public (there are no amusement arcades or tearooms). However, it was a popular departure point for day-trippers who could take a paddle steamer across to South Wales, down to Ilfracombe in Devon, or up to Gloucester. Here we are looking out on the waters of King Road. The nautical training ship, BTS *Formidable*, lies at anchor just to the north of the pier. Today, concrete has replaced the old wooden parts of the pier.

The Beach and Pier, Early 1900s

Also known as Chesil Bay, the beach was popular with visitors as it was the nearest to the train stations and the pier. This scene of children paddling in the sea was taken at the northern end of the bay, where the rocky promontory protects the beach from the entrance to the dock. In the background is Portishead pier. The modern view is somewhat blighted by the industrial expanse of Avonmouth in the distance.

Chesil Rocks, Postcard Dated 12 July 1905
Located just below the Royal Hotel, access to Chesil beach was via a wooded path and a row of steps. Postcards, such as this by local photographer E. H. Wright, helped promote the idea of Portishead as a seaside resort. Its close proximity to Bristol, and good rail and charabanc access, helped boost tourism, but Portishead was always in stiff competition with other North Somerset coastal towns that could boast sandy beaches.

Chesil Beach, Postcard Dated 2 July 1917
This scene of a crowded Chesil beach is testament to its popularity at the beginning of the twentieth century. This was a time when societies, work clubs and religious groups in industrial towns and cities would organise annual days out, and travel out to the countryside and seaside resorts in convoys of charabancs (*inset*).

Chesil Beach, Postcard Dated 16 May 1923

This postcard cannot hide the rather rocky nature of the shoreline, but the protective curtain of trees does give the bay a pleasant sense of isolation – an escape from the grimy industrial world beyond. The rowing boat tethered at the top of the bay offered visitors the chance of an excursion out onto the estuary.

The Royal Hotel, Portishead Point, Mid-Nineteenth Century
Designed by the Bristol architect George Dymond, in a Gothic style and opened in 1830, the Royal Hotel was built by the Corporation of Bristol, then owners of much of the land in Portishead, as part of an initiative to promote tourism in the area. Although it is some distance from the High Street, the hotel is close to the pier, and was a short walk away from the Portishead Pier rail station; consequently it was popular with overnight travellers, as well as long-term guests.

Woodland Beauty, Early 1900s

The quaint, staged photograph above was taken in the managed stretch of woodland known as East Wood, which stretches from the Royal Hotel west to Battery Point. It was owned by the Corporation of Bristol and helped them sell the idea of Portishead as a place of bucolic charm, as well as a seaside resort.

38

Battery Point and Woodhill, 1850s

This engraving shows the view from Battery Point back towards the town, with its early Victorian houses. One of the early attractions to Portishead's seafront were the Baths and Reading Room on Woodlands Road (*inset*). Built in the 1830s, the Baths were described in a 1855 Portishead guidebook as possessing 'hot, cold and plunging baths, dressing rooms and saloons, with a singular contrivance by which the discoloured waters of the channel are converted, by filtration into a perfectly limpid element, without losing a grain of their saline impregnation.' Despite this hyperbole, the Baths were not a success and closed in the 1860s.

Open-Air Swimming Pool, 1968

Nestling just below Battery Point is Portishead's public open-air swimming pool, one of the few remaining in the country. Built by the local council in 1962, on the grounds of a miniature golf course, the pool is 33 metres long and once had three diving boards at the deep end. Today, health and safety concerns deemed the use of the boards as a potential danger and they, along with the ladders, have been removed.

Marine Lake and Woodhill Bay, 1910s

On the left-hand side of the old picture is Marine Lake, which was constructed by the Corporation of Bristol in 1910 in a further attempt to attract visitors to Portishead. It also provided employment for 200 Bristolians, who were brought in from Ashton Gate by train, to dig out the lake. They worked in two shifts, and the lake was filled in with water just 105 days after digging commenced. The modern photograph shows how housing has spread over Portishead Down during the past century.

Woodhill Bay and Battery Point, Postcard Dated 10 September 1908

This group of Edwardian ladies are showing an usually revealing amount of leg as they paddle in Woodhill Bay. In the modern photograph is the Battery Point lighthouse, which was erected in 1931. It was equipped with a fog bell, but this eventually became redundant. The old bell was moved to a spot at the end of Wyndham Way to commemorate Queen Elizabeth's Diamond Jubilee in 2012.

Young Ladies on Battery Point, Early 1900s

This photograph by E. H. Wright shows what fashionable young Edwardians wore to the seaside. As can also be seen in the postcard on the previous page, large hats and long white dresses were particularly popular. The top of the open-air swimming pool can be seen in the modern photograph.

Pleasure Ground and Battery Point, *c.* **1920s**

What constitutes a 'pleasure ground' has clearly changed over the years. However, it was a popular spot for people to sit and watch the shipping in the Bristol Channel. The bright paintwork of the open-air swimming pool certainly makes it stand out, while the long queue of people waiting to be admitted shows that the pool remains a popular attraction.

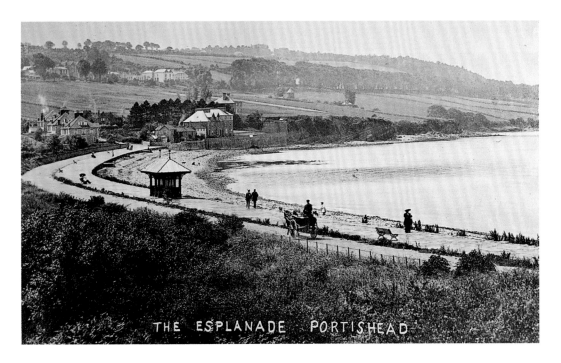

The Esplanade, Postcard Dated 3 August 1908

Plans to build a promenade between Battery Point and Beach Road were put forward in 1882, but were soon abandoned due to a lack of finance. Fortuitously, a great storm in the winter of 1883/84 deposited a large number of rocks and boulders along the proposed route, thus cutting down the construction costs. Eventually, the Esplanade was to cost £3,100 and, after numerous delays, was completed in July 1894. The shelter on the promenade was erected to commemorate Queen Victoria's Diamond Jubilee in 1897.

Esplanade and Battery Point, Early 1900s

The Esplanade is still popular with walkers, whatever the weather. The citizens of Portishead must have been grateful for the longevity of Queen Victoria's reign. Pressure had been growing in the 1880s to build the promenade in time for her Golden Jubilee, but delays meant that construction did not start until 1893, six years after that anniversary. However, the Esplanade was ready in time for her Diamond Jubilee four years later.

The Marine Lake, Portishead

Marine Lake, 1910s

As early as 1893, the city of Bristol Corporation had proposed building a freshwater lake on Rodmoor, an area of drained marshland behind the Esplanade, but a lack of funds prevented any progress. Eventually plans for the lake and surrounding pleasure grounds, designed by Peter Addie, were given the go ahead and the low-lying land was dug up at the start of 1910. The lake was filled on 11 May the same year. The picture above was taken from Battery Point shortly after completion.

Marine Lake, Early 1900s

The lake quickly became popular with local residents and visitors alike, who could spend a happy afternoon boating, relaxing in a deck chair or feeding the birds. A swan hut was built on the island in the middle of the lake, and the birds have continued to breed successfully over the years. In the old picture there is a sign advertising Portishead's annual flower show, which included a 'working bee tent'.

Marine Lake, Postcard Dated 3 August 1918

Judging by the amount of parasols in the postcard above, the photograph must have been taken on a sunny day. But no matter how warm the weather was, social etiquette dictated that ladies and gentlemen should be smartly dressed.

A Popular Corner, The Marine Lake, Postcard Dated 8 August 1931
By the 1930s, pedalos had joined rowing boats on the lake. Today, people still go sailing and rowing, and can rent pedalos in the southerly part of the lake, but the shallow water means swimming is not an option (unlike at the Marine Lake in nearby Clevedon).

Marine Lake, Postcard Dated 14 July 1922

The sight of bouncy castles in the picture below is a reminder that the area around the lake is more family-orientated than in the past (many of the old photographs have only adults in them). It is also obvious that dogs are unaware that the lake isn't for swimming.

Off For a Row, Marine Lake, Postcard Dated 13 September 1911
Today, dinghies with brightly coloured sails have replaced many of the old rowing boats. It is questionable whether rowing boats with quite so many passengers as those in the picture above, would be allowed out on to the lake now.

A Bit of the Marine Lake, Postcard Dated 22 February 1912

The boathouse at the southern end of the lake has been enlarged over the years. Originally, the little hut on the left of the old postcard simply sold tickets for boat hire, while today the premises are used for storage.

Marine Lake, Early 1900s

Here we are looking north up the western side of the lake towards Woodhill. In the distance can be seen the tennis courts, which were another part of the Corporation of Bristol's design to improve the leisure facilities of Portishead at the turn of the twentieth century.

Bridge Over Marine Lake, Postcard Dated 20 July 1927
This little bridge sits across the Marine Lake as it tapers out at its southern end. Children can be let loose in small pedalos without the danger of them drifting on to the main part of the lake.

Pleasure Grounds, Marine Lake, 1950s

Swans and children alike enjoy the public pleasure grounds by the Marine Lake. Laid out on the marshland of Rodmoor in 1910, with the help of the excavated remains of the lake, the grounds included tennis courts and a cricket pitch (Portishead Cricket Club pavilion can be seen in both pictures). Here we are looking towards Woodhill Road (the towers of 'A' Power Station can just be seen peering over the horizon on the left of the picture above).

Beach Villas and Esplanade, Early 1900s

This view is looking down Beach Road (West) and across Woodhill Bay to Battery Point. The Esplanade had only recently been completed, and the houses on the right are newly built. In the middle of the picture a lady is in conversation with a young porter.

Nore Road and Battery Point, *c.* **1900s**
It is possible to date this photograph to between 1894 and 1910, as the Esplanade across Woodhill Bay has been built, but the Marine Lake has yet to be dug. Taken near to the junction of Nore Road and Beach Hill, it shows how undeveloped this part of Portishead was. Fortunately, the modern allotments at the junction show Portishead has preserved some of its greenery. The houses in the foreground are mainly Victorian, though the third one from the right dates to the early 1830s.

Adelaide Terrace From Nore Road, Mid-Nineteenth Century

This panoramic view from Nore Road is of Adelaide Terrace and Woodhill. Below the houses are some of the stables fronting on to Battery Lane. Many houses on the terrace had wrought-iron balconies, but years of exposure to sea air led to widespread corrosion. The house sat among the trees, at the top of Woodhill, was called 'The Gnoll', and was demolished in 1985. At this time, Beach Road (West) had yet to be developed. Adelaide Terrace was once home to Caroline Boyle, a former lady-in-waiting to Queen Adelaide, consort of William IV.

The Beach and Battery Point from Nore Road, 1910s

The junction of Nore Road and Beach Hill offers a fine panorama across the Bristol Channel to South Wales. Looking straight ahead we can see the Marine Lake has been completed. On the right of the modern picture, a small, triangular traffic calming island can be seen at the top of the hill. It was built in 1900, and nicknamed 'Lorrimer's Park', after the chairman of the local district council. Originally it had an outer ring of chain-linked iron railings, and a park bench for passers-by to sit and enjoy the view.

The Convent, Portishead.

The Convent, Early 1900s

In 1906, the Sisters of La Sainte Union des Sacres Coeurs purchased Rose Hill, a large house built off West Hill in the 1820s, in order to set up a Catholic school. It was advertised as 'a preparatory boarding school for boys and a boarding school for girls', with day school places as well. The property fell into dereliction in recent years, but redevelopment has commenced.

THE NORE RD PORTISHEAD

Nore Road, Early 1900s

Running adjacent to the coast, Nore Road initially only ran as far as the National Nautical School, but was extended to what became Redcliffe Bay Estate in 1905. Looking back towards Portishead, we can see the golf course with its distinct clubhouse on the left-hand side. The course was designed by Harry Vardon, a six-time British Open winner and a US Open winner, and opened on 17 July 1907. Its 18 holes measured over 5,000 yards long, spread over 82 acres on both sides of Nore Road. A clubhouse was built in 1908, incorporating a disused windmill's tower dating from the mid-nineteenth century. Today, Portishead Golf Course has a 9-hole course and the old clubhouse is home to the Windmill Inn public house and restaurant.

Nautical School Church and Redcliffe Bay Estate, 1920s

The Nautical School church stands on Nore Road by the entrance road to the National Nautical School. Fifteen acres of land for the school and its ancillary buildings were obtained from the Bristol Corporation at the start of the twentieth century, when it became apparent that the 2,289 ton, two-decker training ship *Formidable*, loaned from the Admiralty and moored off Portishead, had reached the end of its working life, and an onshore establishment was needed to replace it. When completed, the school had a boathouse, outdoor swimming pool, playing fields, parade ground, storerooms, a laundry, dormitories, training shops and its own jetty, as well as the impressive church seen here, in its grounds. Note also the newly erected bungalows on the right of the picture.

National Nautical School Chapel, Early 1900s

The foundation stone for the church was laid on 20 May 1911, some seven years after the school itself was built. It was designed by Edward Gabriel and funded in part by the Right Hon. Sir W. H. Wills, who gave £1,350 towards the cost of £6,500 (other members of the Wills family gave £2,000, and the remainder was raised through smaller gifts). The church was dedicated to St Nicholas, the patron saint of sailors and young boys, in a service conducted by the Bishop of Bath and Wells on 14 May 1912. While attendance at communion services was voluntary, other Sunday services were ceremonial parades with a band, choir, servers and readers (which required weekday practice), and were compulsory for all the 350 boys training at the school.

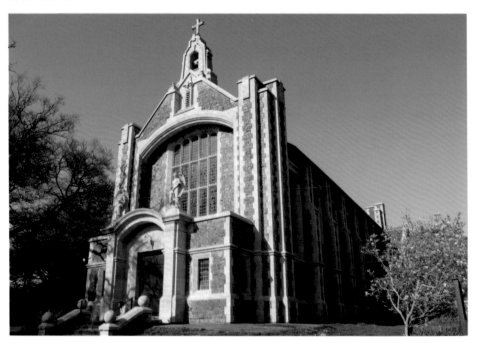

National Nautical Training School, Postcard Dated 6 August 1912

Mr Harry Fedden, a Bristol philanthropist, and Augustine Woodward, were instrumental in setting up the school in October 1869, when they leased the BTS *Formidable* 'to train boys who would otherwise through poverty or parental neglect, or being orphans, be left destitute and homeless, and in danger of being contaminated with vice and crime'. The school subsequently moved onshore at the start of the twentieth century. The school's foundation stone was laid by HRH Princess Henry of Battenberg on 14 July 1904, and the imposing new building, with its 116-metre façade and 27-metre central clock tower, designed by Edward Gabriel, was officially opened on 5 May 1906 by HRH Princess Christian of Schleswig-Holstein. The school, a Grade II listed building, was closed in 1982, and is now a private gated community called Fedden Village.

Black Nore Lighthouse, Early 1900s

Known locally as the 'lighthouse on legs', Black Nore lighthouse was erected by the Trinity House Brethren and began operating in April 1894. As can be seen above, it aided shipping past the rocks of Black Nore Point, a potentially dangerous part of the coastline, something Brunel's steamship *The Great Western* discovered when it ran ashore in the vicinity in March 1873. The lighthouse was also a useful safety beacon for the trainee sailors at the nautical school, who launched their boats from just below it. The inset shows the training ship *Formidable* lying at anchor close to Portishead pier. It housed the nautical school from 1869 to 1906, when it was decommissioned and sold. In total, some 3,500 boys were trained on board, with half of them gaining employment in the Merchant Navy.

40726 Portishead Lighthouse.

Blake Nore Lighthouse, Postcard Dated 12 September 1911

From 1894 to 1979, three generations of the same family, the Ashfords, were the keepers of the lighthouse. Until 1940, the light was gas fuelled, which required the keeper to visit twice daily to light and extinguish the lamp. The gas came from the village mains and a reserve storage tank was installed so that a two-day supply was always available. The keepers were also responsible for winding the clockwork mechanism that turned the optical system. The light was switched to electricity in 1940 and, thirty years later, the clock mechanism was replaced by electrical motors, resulting in the maintenance work being reduced to periodic cleaning of the optical system.

The Beach, Redcliffe Bay, *c.* 1920s

Further to the south of Black Nore lighthouse lies Redcliffe Bay, with its broad, rock-strewn beach. This scene of the beach at high tide shows how popular swimming in the Bristol Channel used to be. On the left-hand side of the postcard above can be seen the balcony of the café and changing cubicles, installed on the beach during the interwar years to cater for the crowds of people keen to enjoy the waters of the estuary.

The Beach, Redcliffe Bay, c. 1920s

Portishead's beaches may lack sand, but they are still fine places for family picnics. However, it is advisable to choose your spot carefully before laying out the picnic hamper – a comparison between the photograph below and the old postcard on the previous page shows how great the tidal range is. Many people in the past have also been caught out by the surprising speed of the rising tide.

The Beach, Redcliffe Bay, 1920s

In the late nineteenth and first part of the twentieth century, there was a positive effort to promote the use of the beaches around Portishead. Further up the coast from Redcliffe Bay, seen here, part of the beach at the attractively named Sheepwash Bay was given over to a ladies-only swimming area in the 1890s. The beach, commonly known as Sugar Loaf Beach, had a diving board, changing rooms and a children's pool (filled twice daily by the rising tide) installed by the Urban District Council in the interwar years.

Redcliffe Bay Beach, 1930s

This crowded scene at Redcliffe Bay shows how successful the council's attempt at promoting Portishead's beaches was. The people seen here would have been a mix of day-trippers from Bristol and the surrounding area, and local residents, including the owners of the new bungalows on Redcliffe Bay Estate. Today, far fewer people are prepared to brave the murky waters, and the majority of holidaymakers opt to enjoy the relative comforts of the newly refurbished open-air swimming pool, below Battery Point, instead.

71

Redcliffe Bay Estate, c. 1930

In the 1920s, a local landowner, Mr Albert Heaven, built a number of bungalows on plots of land in the Redcliffe Bay area. They were initially planned as holiday homes, but, despite lacking modern conveniences such as electricity and running water, they soon became popular as permanent residences. Eventually, proper amenities were installed and Nore Road was even extended to provide better access to what was known as the Redcliffe Bay Estate. Today, modern houses, such as those on Belton Road (which leads down to the Portishead Yacht and Sailing Club), have replaced the old timber and asbestos structures.

from Shirehampton

PILL

Pill Ferry Arriving at Shirehampton, 1950s

The Lamplighters/Pill ferry ran between North Somerset and Shirehampton, crossing the River Avon at its lowest and safest point before it empties out into the Bristol Channel. A ferry operated here from at least the medieval period, but the arrival of the M5 motorway viaduct with a footpath, in 1974, meant that people could now walk across the river and the service became redundant. The slipway on the opposite bank now leads up to the clubhouse of the Portishead Cruising Club, and beyond that The Duke of Cornwall public house and Pump Square. Members of the Shirehampton Sailing Club are seen here launching a vessel.

Paddle Steamer Passing Pill, 1950s

Pill has seen ships of all shapes and sizes pass by on the River Avon. Obviously merchant ships were the most common sight going to and from Bristol Docks (often with the aid of Pill citizens), but other more unusual vessels have also meandered up the Avon Gorge, including paddle steamers carrying day-trippers on excursions up and down the Severn Estuary, and the replica of John Cabot's *Matthew* (*see below*). Built to commemorate the 500th anniversary of Cabot's voyage to Newfoundland in 1497, the *Matthew* is moored in Bristol and takes visitors upstream to the mouth of the Avon (she also goes further afield for events such as the Queen Elizabeth's Diamond Jubilee pageant held on the Thames). The one thing spectators always comment on is her diminutive size.

The Ferry, Pill.

Pill Riverfront, Early 1900s

Navigating the dangerous waters of the Severn Estuary and River Avon required specialist knowledge, and Pill pilots became famous for their skill in steering ships and their cargo to Bristol Docks. Competition for business was fierce, not just with their rivals at Portishead but also among villagers themselves. The larger boat in the creek in the old picture is a Pill Cutter. These 12–15 metre boats were built beside the creek for individual pilots and were famous for their speed and manoeuvrability. They were eventually replaced in 1918, when the pilots grouped together to end competition and bought a steamboat. Some boats are still moored at Pill, but the creek suffers from silting up problems.

Pump Square, Pill, *c.* 1800

This collection of cramped houses, shops and taverns was the lively heart of Pill 200 years ago. Just yards from the riverfront, the square was frequented by the gangs of heavy-drinking Pill pilots and boat haulers, and it is not hard to imagine the noise and smells that must have filled the air. To the left, just by the side of The Duke of Cornwall, is the water pump, which was rented to one George Turner in 1829 for £6 per annum. The building in the centre, Propect House, is still recognizably the same. The inset drawing by George Cumberland shows the street on the right-hand side in 1814.

Victoria Park, Pill, Early 1900s

Once a village green, Victoria Park is now surrounded by housing and partially hidden behind the 1960s shopping plaza. The viaduct was part of the railway line from Bristol to Portishead, which opened in 1863. The railway had a two-fold impact on Pill – a considerable amount of farmland was lost and a number of houses had to be demolished during its construction and, secondly, many of the navvies working on the line met and married local girls, bringing new life to the village. This influx of workers probably added to Pill's reputation as a rowdy place, though the population was devout. There has been a Methodist church in Pill since 1757 (the church on the right here was replaced by a new one in 1972), along with Pill Baptist church, Christ church and the Salvation Army.

The Anchor, Ham Green, *c.* 1930

The Anchor Inn is one of only a handful of hostelries left in the area; in the nineteenth century, there were reputedly twenty-one pubs in Pill, which may help explain its historically unsavoury reputation. The founder of the Methodist Church, John Wesley, recorded in his journal in 1755: 'I rode over to Pill, a place famous from generation to generation, even as Kingswood itself, for stupid, brutal, abandoned wickedness.'

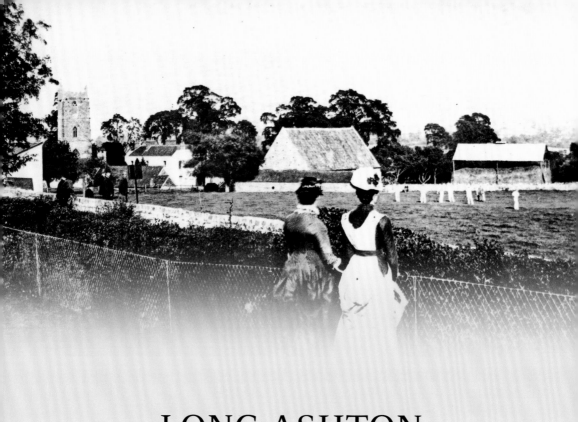

LONG ASHTON

Church Lodge, Long Ashton, Early 1950s

Sat facing the junction of the Long Ashton Road and the Clarken Coombe/Ashton Road, the Church Lodge was the final lodge house built for the Ashton Court Estate. Owned by the wealthy Bristol mercantile Smyth family, from 1545 onwards, Ashton Court was to play an important part in the lives of Long Ashton inhabitants for 400 years, both as an employer and landlord. Heavy death duties in the first part of the twentieth century took their toll and, after Mrs Esme Smyth died in 1946, the estate was sold. In the inset, a group of post office workers are preparing for an outing to the Somerset countryside aboard a Bristol Tramways & Carriage Co. charabanc, around 1920.

The Smyth Arms, 1867

This coaching inn on the Ashton Road was originally a cottage, before being turned into an alehouse in the sixteenth century. By 1739, it had become known as the Coach and Horses, and a sign on the photograph above can just be seen advertising Landau flys for hire. The inn changed its name in the 1860s to the Smyth Arms, in deference to the Ashton Court owners, and is currently undergoing renovation work while under the name The Dovecote.

The Church, Ashton Bristol.

All Saints Church, Early 1900s

The parish church was founded in about 1380 by the Lord of the Manor of Ashton Lyons, Thomas de Lyons, and his family's coat of arms can still be seen above the west window of the church tower. All Saints has undergone a number of alterations over the centuries and was restored in 1871/72. On the right of the modern photograph can be seen the remains of the Church Cross, which was removed from its original spot beside the Angel Inn at the top of Church Lane in the 1880s. All Saints church is a Grade II listed building.

Long Ashton Church, Bristol.

All Saints Church, Long Ashton, Early 1900s

All Saints church has some noteworthy features, including a late medieval rood screen dividing the chancel from the nave and aisles, a Royal Achievement of Arms of Charles II's reign, and the tomb of Sir Richard Choke, a judge of the Court of Common Pleas, who purchased the manor in 1454. In the churchyard there are some interesting graves, including the burial site of members of the family of Robert Southey, Poet Laureate 1814–43. A churchyard trust was set up in 1994 and, as can be seen in the photograph below, the grounds are well maintained.

The Angel Inn, Long Ashton Road, 1869

Located just to the north of the parish church, the Angel Inn is the oldest public house in Long Ashton. Known originally as Church House, it dates back to 1495, when Sir John Choke gave it and some adjacent land to the parish in return for prayers for the souls of his family. By the eighteenth century, it had become known locally as the Angel Inn. Parish meetings and the Court Leet, an ancient court that dealt with minor offences, were held here, and the cellars are said to have once acted as the village lock-up. In the picture above, the Church Cross is still standing outside the inn.

Long Ashton Road, c. 1905

These ramrod-straight children are standing on Long Ashton Road, which was the main route from Bristol to Weston. Their rather uncomfortable pose was to prevent blurred movement in the photograph, as a result of low shutter speed (the lady in the previous Angel Inn image has clearly shifted position during the exposure). It would probably not be a good idea to allow children to pose in the middle of the road today.

Old Post Office, Long Ashton, Early 1900s

This view along Long Ashton Road, back towards Bristol, is a reminder of how relatively quiet the main road was at the turn of the twentieth century. The road itself is rough and uneven, and has the tell-tale sign of horse-drawn traffic marked across it. At the time, travel to Bristol was via the Clifton Suspension Bridge, Bedminster, or the Rownham ferry, which operated from the Bower Ashton area, but access was improved in 1906 with the opening of the Ashton Swing Bridge, which gave a direct route to the city via Hotwells.

Old Post Office, Long Ashton, 1910s

This busy scene outside the post office shows the sub-postmistress, Miss Emily Nurse, who worked here until the 1930s, standing in the doorway of the shop. Her sister is holding the bicycle on the muddy road. As well as the dog on the pavement, another can be seen peering out of the shop window just above the advertisement for Wills's 'Gold Flake' Cigarettes.

Long Ashton Road, Early 1900s

Just a bit further on from the post office is this section of the Long Ashton Road with a raised pavement. At this time, Long Ashton appears remarkably quiet, but the arrival of the automobile was to drastically alter people's lives. By the 1950s, the large numbers of cars and lorries passing through the village had become a serious problem – as many as 1,300 vehicles per hour were driving through at peak times. Eventually, the opening of the Long Ashton bypass on 6 December 1968 eased the problem, but commuter congestion is still a major irritant.

A. J. Poultney's, Long Ashton Road, 1880

Up until the 1930s, house building had been sporadic in Long Ashton. There were a few large properties dating from the eighteenth and nineteenth centuries that belonged to wealthy Bristolian merchants, and some small groups of houses spread along the main road. Here, a residential house is also home to A. J. Poultney, Baker and Corn Factor, and a small post office branch. A corn factor was essential a corn merchant.

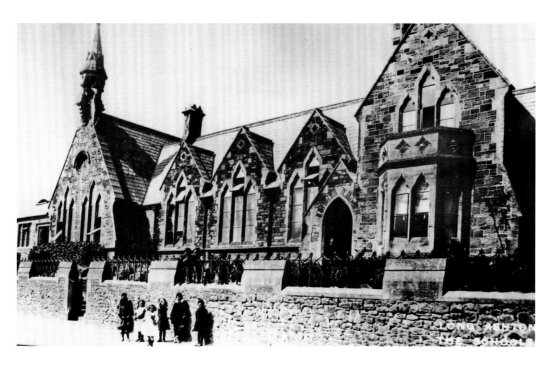

Northleaze VC Primary School, Early 1900s

Over the years, charitable bequests had been made for the education of poor children of the village and, in 1818, a parochial school was built in Church Lane with a £75 grant from the National Society. This was replaced in 1861 by another national school, open to children of all denominations on Long Ashton Road. It was built at a cost of £3,000 on land granted by Sir Greville Smyth. Today it is known as Northleaze VC Primary, and was joined by another primary school in the Birdwell part of Long Ashton in 1967.

The Lady Smyth Almshouses, Long Ashton Road, Early 1900s

Built in 1902, the almshouses were paid for by Dame Emily Smyth, as a way of expressing her gratitude for surviving a raging storm in the Bay of Biscay while returning from holiday in the previous year. Initially, places were first offered to workers at the Ashton Court Estate and close relatives, but these conditions ceased to apply with the estate's demise. The inset shows the original architect's (Edward Gabriel) drawing plans. The almshouses consist of four bedsits and four, one-bedroom units.

Birdwell Shops, Long Ashton Road, 1960s

Like all large villages, Long Ashton has always had a number of small shops and local businesses. These increased in number after the Second World War, partially as a result of the sale of Ashton Court Estate, which opened up the opportunity for new businesses and, partially, through the building development boom of the 1950s and '60s. In total, 1,041 new dwellings were built between 1947 and 1998, and many of the new shops catering for the growing population were located in the Birdwell part of the village.

Birdwell Shops, Lovelinch Gardens, 1960s

As with everywhere in the country, small shops in Long Ashton have been hit hard over the years by changes in customer habits. Traditional general stores fell victim to the irrepressible spread of supermarkets, and many of the old premises are now dental practices, physiotherapy clinics, cafes, takeaway restaurants and hairdressers. Fortunately for local residents there is still a post office.

The Bird-in-Hand, Long Ashton Road, c. 1890

Said to be over 300 years old, the Bird-in-Hand was a particularly popular inn at the end of the nineteenth century, with Bristolians arriving in horse-drawn buses from Redcliffe Street several times a week. The exterior of the Bird-in-Hand has altered very little, save for a security camera on the wall keeping watch on the front door, instead of a rather sleepy looking black Labrador, but the interior and the food on offer is now aimed at the gourmand rather than the ploughman.

THE LAST TRAIN
to Portishead

Acknowledgements

The author would like to express his gratitude to the staff at Portishead Library, the Fredrick Wood Room at Weston-super-Mare Library, Long Ashton Library, Bristol Reference Library, Bristol Record Office, the Gordano Society, the Long Ashton Local History Society, Ruth Poole and the Bristol & Avon Family History Society, Andy Brisley, Matt Westley, RoseMary Musgrave and especially to Gordon and Aili Purdy. Many thanks to all the authors and local historians who have contributed to the knowledge and appreciation of Portishead, Pill and Long Ashton through the years. The following books were of great help: *North Somerset and Bristol* (Yale University Press) by Nikolaus Pevsner, *Around Nailsea, Long Ashton and Yatton* (Alan Sutton Publishing) collected by Michael J. Tozer, *Long Ashton and Leigh Woods* (The History Press), and, in particular, the works by Kenneth Crowhurst: *Images of England: Portishead* (Tempus Publishing Limited), and *Portishead 1900–1920; The Photographs of E. H. Wright, Portishead in Old Picture Postcards* and *Portishead Past and Present* (all published by European Library).

The following are the reference numbers for the images used in this book from the Portishead Library archives – Filing cabinet numbers: 3, 5A, 5C, 7, 8A, 8B, 11, 14, 18, 21, 23, 24A, 25, 26A, 26C, 29, 30, 31C, 31D, 31E, 79E, 79F, 153S, 153T, 153U, 154. Folder numbers: 1, 4, 7, 8, 9, 13, 17, 19, 20, 21, 23, 25, 27, 29, 30, 31, 33, 35, 36, 43, 49, 52, 53, 61, 62, 66, 71, 74, 85, 86, 88, 90, 91, 94, 97, 98, 99, 101, 102, 104, 108, 113, 125, 126, 127, 142.